ON INFANCY AND TODDLERHOOD

An Elementary Textbook

Despairing infant Macque monkey who has been separated from its mother (photo courtesy of Dr. I. Charles Kaufman).

On Infancy and Toddlerhood

An Elementary Textbook

David A. Freedman, M.D.

INTERNATIONAL UNIVERSITIES PRESS, INC.
Madison, Connecticut

INTERNATIONAL UNIVERSITIES PRESS and IUP (& design) ® are registered trademarks of International Universities Press, Inc.

Library of Congress Cataloging-in-Publication Data

Freedman, David A.
    On infancy and toddlerhood : an elementary textbook / David A. Freedman.
        p.   cm.
    Includes bibliographical references (p.   ) and index.
    ISBN 0-8236-3785-9 (hardcover)
    1. Infant psychology.   2. Toddlers—Psychology.
3. Psychoanalysis.   I. Title.
    [DNLM: 1. Personality Development—in infancy & childhood.
2. Child Development.   3. Psychoanalytic Theory.   WS   105.5.P3 F853o
1996]
BF719.F74   1996
155.42'2—dc21
DNLM/DLC
for Library of Congress   96-37168
                                                                             CIP

Manufactured in the United States of America

To
B. D. F.
Without Whom This Work
Could Not Have Been Accomplished

Contents

Acknowledgments

I wish to thank Dr. I. Charles Kaufman for permission to reproduce illustrations from his seminal work on the relation between child-rearing practices and reaction to separation and loss in macaque monkeys.

I owe special thanks to Beryl Freedman, Jean Gates, and Carolyn Stubbs, all of whom contributed immeasurably to the preparation of this manuscript.

Some of the expenses incurred in preparing this volume were defrayed by a grant from the Houston-Galveston Psychoanalytic Institute.

The cartoons by William O'Brian on pages 170 and 171 are reprinted with permission. © 1964, 1992 The New Yorker Magazine, Inc. All Rights Reserved.

Introduction

In the Spring of 1994 the Education Committee of the Houston-Galveston Psychoanalytic Institute voted to establish a curriculum in psychoanalytic psychotherapy. This was to be targeted at practitioners from a number of clinical disciplines, such as psychiatry, psychology, social work, and psychiatric nursing, who wished to enhance the skills they already used in their practices, with a greater understanding of the psychodynamic perspective.

The Curriculum Committee asked me to take responsibility for a ten-session seminar devoted to the epochs of infancy and toddlerhood. I was provided with both a series of topics to be covered and a recommended reading list. The chapter titles in this book follow the original list of topics while the reading list is included as an appendix. Because of the schedule, the required reading had to be limited. The specific book chapters cited in the various volumes were those the members of the class were expected to have read for a specific session. In no case should these required readings be considered to exhaust the usefulness of the work in question.

At the same time the recommended readings seemed to me to be too narrowly focused on those aspects of maturation and development which are most readily available to the observing clinician. This is congruent with the history of psychoanalytic thinking and observational research. Freud, after all, was primarily a clinician. His understanding of infancy and toddlerhood was based on the retrospective inferences he drew from his experience with adults. He was also limited by the paucity of knowledge about the form and function of the nervous system available to him at the point when he gave up the effort to make a neurobiological model of the mind. As a result, Freud had a tendency to adultomorphize; even though he did not subscribe to such egregious hypotheses as Rank's theory of the importance of birth trauma, or Melanie Klein's attribution of cognitive competence to neonates, he did ascribe to infants and toddlers cognitive understandings which, we now know, they do not possess.

I agree with Sulloway (1979) that Freud was, to begin with, a neurobiologist. It also seems clear that when he gave up his efforts to make a neurobiological model for the mind, he also lost interest in the evolving understanding of how the maturationally and developmentally determined changes in the nervous system alter the functional potentialities of the growing child. Progress in the understanding of the anatomy of the nervous system is illustrative.

In appendix A I contrast how Freud envisioned the relation between neurons at the synapse with how this is understood today. The magnitude of the increase in knowledge and understanding, however, goes much beyond the anatomy of the synapse. I am not competent to discuss and, therefore, can only allude to the fact that some forty neurotransmitters have now been identified. How they and the properties of the membranes of nerve cells may turn out to be relevant to the understanding of the mental processes of infancy and toddlerhood, I leave to some future author. One can only wonder how Freud's metapsychology might have been influenced had he known about these findings.

At the same time, it is important to keep in mind that even if he had been interested, much of what is included in the following pages was unknown or very little understood when Freud died in 1939, and some of the most important findings were not published until after his death. Spitz, who introduced the use of natural experiments as a means of testing psychoanalytic hypotheses, did not publish his work on hospitalism until 1945. Erikson's seminal work was done in the 1930s and 1940s. Piaget, who had had a brief flirtation with psychoanalysis, did not begin his systematic study of the emergence of cognitive abilities until the 1920s. It was not until the 1930s that we began to have an understanding of the function of the frontal lobes of the brain. Papez's proposed mechanism for the experience of emotion only appeared in 1937, and Kluver and Bucy's demonstration of the role of the temporal lobes in memory and affective expression was not published until 1939. It was not until 1967 that Yakovlev and LeCours, by providing us with a timetable for the deposition of myelin, made it possible for us to think in terms of the *availability* to infants and toddlers of the tissue wherewithal for the various modalities of thinking and experiencing which we tend to impute even to the youngest of people.

The contributions of these workers as well as many others have changed the way we look at the relation of brain function to psychology in general and, in my opinion, at early development in particular. I have attempted to incorporate some of their findings into a coherent presentation of the two epochs of early life, infancy and toddlerhood. Inevitably, in particular in relation to the impact of cognitive development, I have overstepped the usually accepted age limits for toddlerhood. I think my reasons for doing so will be apparent.

CHAPTER 1

Maturation and Development

> The first age is childhood when the teeth are planted, and this age begins when the child is born and lasts until seven, and in this age that which is born is called an infant. Which is as good as not talking, because in this age it cannot talk well or form its words perfectly, for its teeth are not well arranged or firmly implanted, as Isidore says and Constantine. After infancy comes the second age . . . it is called *pueritia* and is given this name because in this age the person is still like the pupil in the eye, as Isidore says, and this age last till fourteen [quoted by Aries, 1960, p. 21, from *Le Grand Proprietaire de toutes choses*, a thirteenth century Latin compilation].

In a very real sense, this volume could just as well have been called "Maturation and Development" rather than "Infancy and Toddlerhood." I say this because the most characteristic aspect of the infant–toddler experience is the ongoing, twin processes of maturation and development. I refer to these as twin processes but the phrase doesn't, at least for me, quite grasp the degree of intimacy and reciprocity which characterize their interconnection. The two are entirely interdependent. Even though, in very exceptional circumstances, one can identify aspects of the one in the absence of the other, it is clear that for the creation of a functioning, adapted individual the two processes must go hand in hand. The following are the two working definitions used by René Spitz (1965, p. 45), who is to many of us the father of all psychoanalytic investigations of very early growth and development.

1

Spitz (1965) defined maturation as: "The unfolding of phylo-genetically evolved and, therefore, inborn functions of the species which emerge in the course of embryonic development, or are carried forward after birth, or are carried forward as Anlagen and become manifest at later stages in life" (p. 45). *Anlage* may be translated as predestined, later to emerge, gene-determined char-acteristics. An example from very early life would be eye color. During the first weeks of life all infants' eyes, regardless of their ethnicity, tend to be of a nondescript bluish color. Some time during the first two months of life, pigment is deposited in the irises and the eyes take on the shade they will have for the rest of the individual's life. I know of no evidence that this emergence is affected by the environment in which the infant is living. It appears to be a gene-determined potentiality, an Anlage with which the individual is born, and which is expressed some time after extrauterine life begins. Handedness is probably the mani-festation of yet another Anlage. Infants appear to be ambidex-trous, but some time between 4 and 6 years one hand, usually the right, becomes dominant. I say probably because by the time the child is this age the role of environmental influences cannot be ig-nored.

For Spitz, and for us in these chapters, development is the emergence of forms, of function, and of behavior which are the outcome of the exchange between the maturing organism on the one hand and the inner and outer environment on the other. The following somewhat hypothetical example is intended to clar-ify what Spitz meant by "inner" and "outer." Very tall, physically agile individuals have been born in Central Africa since time out of mind. It required a sequence of events in the "outer" environ-ment, beginning with the invention and development of a game originally intended to be played by girls at a YWCA college in Springfield, Massachusetts, for boys and young men blessed with such inborn functional potentialities to develop into individuals with great skill as basketball players. At the same time, not every agile, physically competent, 7-foot-tall man has been able to de-velop an "inner" environment (self-confidence, freedom to be aggressive in a contained, directed way, willingness to be a team player, etc.) which would make it possible for him to compete successfully in the NBA.

It is fairly obvious that we cannot understand how phenomena like great basketball players, great musicians, or even ordinary, everyday people come about by looking at the end product alone. It becomes necessary for us to have some understanding of the underlying processes which were necessary preconditions for the end result to happen. In this volume we will take the position, as psychoanalysts always have, that what we see in an individual today is the *current manifestation* of the continuously ongoing interaction between maturational and developmental processes.

There are four terms which are important to our discussion at this point: epigenesis, critical period, sign specific stimulus, and internal releasing mechanism.

EPIGENESIS

According to the *Oxford Unabridged Dictionary*, the theory of epigenesis has its origins in the field of embryology. It holds that the germ of what will later be an anatomical structure is brought into existence by successive accretions and not merely developed in the process of reproduction. This means that the biochemical equivalents of anatomical and functional potentialities are stored in the egg. Whether and how those potentialities will become manifested in the completed organism will, in very large measure, be determined by the environment in which the egg-embryo is developing. For example, left to itself, various regions of a frog embryo will develop into specific organs and ultimately become a tadpole and then a frog. However, early in its development one can take a snippet of tissue which if left at its original site would have developed into an eye, and move it to the region destined to be the animal's back, whereupon it will develop as a piece of back skin. Later in the frog's development, tissue from the same area, when transplanted, will develop into an eye no matter where it is located. Something has happened to the biochemistry of the region from which the snippet of tissue is taken, such that it is no longer responsive to its new immediate environment. Its essential "eyeness" has been irrevocably established.

CRITICAL PERIOD

There is, in other words, a *critical period* during which the potentiality to be an eye gets organized. During this period, the particular region in the embryo which, under normal circumstances, would have become an eye will, if it is moved, not do so. Once the critical period has passed, it will develop into an eye no matter where it is. Similarly, the processes of psychological maturation and development in the human are also characterized by critical periods. This was first recognized by Freud (1908) and elaborated in a series of papers by his colleague Karl Abraham (1921–1925), who had been an embryologist. They identified a sequence of developmental periods which they designated as oral, anal, phallic, and oedipal. They proposed that all individuals pass through these phases during their growing years. Much of what we will be dealing with in the course of this book will have to do with how this concept of critical periods has been elaborated and its fundamental role in psychodynamic thinking. Although the concept of critical periods continues to be at the center of psychodynamic thinking, we now recognize that Freud and Abraham's characterizations of them, while still very useful and descriptive of aspects of early behavior, are not sufficient. They do not catch the flavor of many of the epigenetic, or staging patterns that we can observe in the maturing and developing infant and toddler. Indeed, there is no one classification that adequately serves the purpose of conceptualizing the stages of early development.

SIGN SPECIFIC STIMULUS

Sign specific stimulus, a term which comes from the field of ethology, refers to environmental stimuli which evoke very specific patterns of behavior. The important thing to remember is that the infant, human or animal, doesn't have to *learn* to respond to these stimuli; the response pattern is *built in*. There are innumerable examples of such built-in patterns. One, to which we will be returning, is the evocation of the smiling response. Spitz (1965) showed that in the 2- to 3-month-old infant this response can be evoked by a full frontal view of the adult's eyes. It can even be evoked more intensely by a pair of big black circles painted on a white balloon. The stimulus is very specific and anyone interested, who has access to an infant in this age range, can check this out. If you look directly at the baby you will elicit a smiling response. Turn your head to show your profile and you will wipe off the smiling response as with a sponge. Put on a pair of black-rimmed harlequin glasses and you will get an even bigger smiling response. Needless to say, when a mother who has not read Spitz sees this response, she is delighted, believes her baby is responding to her, responds in turn to him or her, and thus facilitates the process of bonding. This enhancing of the parenting one's attachment to the infant is, in turn, essential to the whole process of maturation and development. One can characterize the parent's delight as a "beneficent form of adultomorphizing"—of imputing to the infant intentions and understandings which are, in fact, beyond its capacities at the time. Regrettably, not all adultomorphizing is so beneficent. Anyone who has walked the floor night after night with a colicky baby knows about becoming irritated and angry with the baby and being tempted to impute malevolent intentions to it.

The sign specific stimulus is so named because of its ability to evoke an innate releasing mechanism.[1] This releases a coordinated pattern of behavior—a smile, a cry, a suck, or a startle response—which does not have to be learned. The constellation of muscular reactions which makes possible such organized behaviors comes prepackaged. Neonatal "smiles" look so much like the smiles of older people that we are inclined to attribute analogous psychological significance to them. For better or for worse, the attribution is erroneous. What are released by the innate releasing mechanisms are patterns of reaction which will, over time, come to have psychological significance providing the process of growing up is occurring under appropriate circumstances.

---

[1]Lorenz (1971, pp. 135–140) uses this term to refer to the ability of the organism to respond with complex patterns of behavior to quite specific stimuli. Thus, in the neonate, the brushing of the lips with a nipple will induce a neurologically complex pattern of muscular activity. Lorenz (p. 136) takes pains not to confuse this releasing phenomenon with Jungian "archetypes." He points out that fixed patterns, like sucking, require very specific, narrowly defined sign specific stimuli.

Defining **"appropriate circumstances"** poses yet another problem and requires the introduction of yet another pair of terms. It is clear that all infants grow up under vastly different circumstances. There is no one "right" way to rear a child. For any given culture, however, there are some parenting practices which are fairly prevalent. These have been referred to as "average expectable" by the psychoanalyst Heinz Hartmann. D. W. Winnicott, the British pediatrician turned psychoanalyst, used the phrase "good-enough mothering" to refer to the same issue. Neither could write a definitive, unequivocal prescription for exactly what a neonate, infant, or toddler needs. This is the case because the essential ingredients always come imbedded in practices which derive from the idiosyncracies of both the individual parenting one and from the culture in which the infant is being reared. In his pioneering work, Spitz (1945a) observed infants in extremely aberrant circumstances. He compared the early development of infants who had been placed in a foundling home with that of infants born to women in prison who were able to care directly for their babies. Since then, there have been studies of the effects of a variety of unique situations, such as congenital blindness and congenital deafness, which have helped in our understanding of at least some aspects of what must be included if an average expectable environment is to provide good-enough mothering.

When we as psychotherapists work with older people, people with whom we can communicate on a verbal level, it is rarely necessary for us to pay attention to the fact that both our own and our patients' brains are busily at work. Barring the relatively special problems of patients with demonstrable organic disease of the nervous system, we can take the functioning of the brain for granted. Certainly even those of us who are aware of their existence, rarely spend much time contemplating the function of our own synapses. This is a luxury which, I think, we can ill afford when we try to follow the maturation and development of the infant and toddler. Brain maturation and (barring extraordinary circumstances) psychological maturation and development during this period proceed at an "explosive" rate. How important for later life this early period is, is indicated by the aphorism, often attributed to Jesuit educators, "Give me your child until he is seven and you may have him thereafter." In a similar vein, when Charles Darwin was asked what he thought were the most influential years of life, he replied, "without doubt the first three." He went on to explain that at this age the brain is a virgin entity adapted to receive impressions although unable to formulate or memorize these. They nonetheless remain and can affect the whole future life of the child recipient (Bowlby, 1990b).

I placed "explosive" in quotes because, despite its rapid pace, brain maturation is actually very orderly, as is also the process of development in average expectable circumstances. The changes that take place in the tissue substrate of the mind appear to follow a predictable and orderly sequence. Some, but by no means all, of the steps in the sequence have been identified. They are important to us as observers of infants and small children because they are indicators of what, at any given point in its life, the small person is capable both of doing and understanding. The two are very different concepts and I would like here to offer an illustration of the difference. A patient once told me that his mother often boasted that he could tell time when he was 3 years old. Undoubtedly, after she spent long hours inculcating into his head that he should respond to certain positions of the hands on the clock by saying "ten after two" or "quarter before twelve," he was able to do this. As we will discuss later, however, he could not understand the implications of what he was saying. The concept of "time" evolves over a period of years and is only fixed in the child's mind when he reaches middle childhood.

SUMMARY

I will now summarize some of the salient facts about the nervous system, which should be kept in mind as part of the personal filter through which we listen to what our patients, not to mention our own growing children, say and do. Brain maturation and development follows epigenetic principles just as do psychological maturation and development. Indeed, it is probably the case that you can't have one without the other. In addition, since the brain "got there first," it is arguable that the emergence of psychology is dependent on the availability of an adequately functioning brain.

The "finished" brain (i.e., the kind that sits in each of our heads) has a cerebral cortex with something on the order of 100 billion nerve cells. Each of these nerve cells makes anywhere from one thousand to one hundred thousand connections with other nerve cells. The number of possible interconnections which they can have with one another is literally incalculable. It is said to be the most complex structure yet to be found in the natural world. These connections are called *synapses*, a name invented early in this century by the English physiologist Sherrington (1906). Actually the possibility that the brain is made up of separate cells which interconnected at specific points had only begun to be widely considered some fifteen years earlier. Up to then, the prevalent opinion was that the nervous system consisted of a continuous series of tubules whose contents flowed from one to the other. Freud, it turns out, was among the earliest to espouse the separate neuron theory. He called the points of connection between cells "contact barriers." He attempted, and failed, to develop a general psychology based on their functioning. There was not enough known about the physiology of the brain a century ago for him to achieve this goal. Actually, it has only been in the past few years that we have been able to imagine achieving it. Unequivocal demonstration of the existence of synapses did not come about until the invention of the electron microscope in the 1950s. It is at these synapses that messages are transmitted from cell to cell, or, perhaps more accurately, it is through the actions of constellations of synapses belonging to many presynaptic cells on constellations of postsynaptic cells that information gets processed and transmitted. All the drugs used in psychiatry influence such transmissions in one way or another. We can add to the tale of complexity the fact that at the present time something over forty neurotransmitters have been identified. These are chemicals which serve to activate postsynaptic cells. More than one such transmitter may be involved in the activation of any given cell. In the 1940s and 1950s, when I was beginning to learn about the nervous system, we knew of only two neurotransmitters—acetylcholine and epinephrine. (See appendix A for a brief history of the discovery of the synapse and figures which contrast Freud's concept of their structure with what we know today.)

The finished brain of the adult, however, is vastly different from that of the neonate, infant, and toddler. And those of the infant and toddler are also vastly different from one another. When we contemplate the behavior of infants and toddlers, and their interaction with their environments, it behooves us to keep in mind that the actual structures of their brains are being modified both by maturational processes and by the very facts of their interactions with us and the rest of their environment.

We can regard maturational changes as being gene determined via the idiosyncrasies of the deoxyribonucleic acid (DNA) which each of us inherits from our parents. One *probably* inherited characteristic of the brain is the number of nerve cells with which one comes equipped. It is fairly obvious that it would not be very easy to make accurate counts of this order of magnitude on a large sampling of individuals. The number 100 billion which I have already mentioned is an estimate and it is certainly possible that there is variation from person to person. In any event, the absolute number is probably less important than the vast number and the intricate patterns of interconnections they make. There are, however, other inherited characteristics which are more predictable, such as the general functional layout of the brain: occipital lobes as the primary receiver of vision; temporal lobes as the primary receiver of hearing; parietal lobes as the primary receiver of general bodily sensation; the frontal lobes as the area essential for the capacity to experience anticipatory anxiety; the hippocampus and limbic system as areas essential for memory and the experience of emotion and affect, is characteristic, not only for humans but also for all primates. Indeed, the same grand plan seems to hold true for all mammals.

Also, apparently gene-determined and uniformly characteristic of all humans, is the pattern of deposition of myelin. Knowing something about myelin is essential if we are to understand the processes of maturation and development in the small person. Myelin is a fatty substance which surrounds the processes which extend from one nerve cell, or neuron, to others, and insulates them from one another. We refer to these processes as either *dendrites*, which receive messages from other cells, or *axons*, which

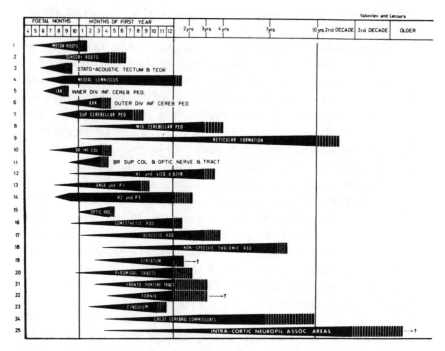

Figure 1.1. Timing of myelin deposition in various CNS tracts. (From Yakovlev and LeCours, 1967. Reprinted with permission of the publisher.)

carry messages forward. Without the protection of their myelin sheaths, neurons cannot transmit messages. They short-circuit just as surely as do bare uninsulated electric wires. We know this from our experience with some diseases which are characterized by the loss of myelin, the best known of which is multiple sclerosis. Anyone who has seen a person suffering from this condition has witnessed how devastating the loss of myelin can be. This is of vital importance in the understanding of maturation and development for two compelling reasons. First, the neurons of the neonatal brain are virtually totally unmyelinated. Second, myelin is deposed in various neuronal pathways according to a gene-determined sequence. Some pathways, and therefore some neuronal functions, become available (come "on line") before others. Figure 1.1, from the work of the neuropathologists Yakovlev and

LeCours (1967) illustrates this sequence. It is, in effect, a time-table for the availability of the designated neuronal paths. The sharp points of the wedges represent the beginning of the process of depositing myelin in the tract in question, and the cross-hatching at the blunt right ends indicates that there is a certain variability with regard to when the process is complete.

There are some rather striking clinical correlates with the Yakovlev and LeCours timetable. For example, bars 11 and 15 represent the deposition of myelin in the visual system. This process is virtually complete when the baby is approximately 6 months old. At this age babies have all the ability to receive visual stimuli that they will ever have. The neural pathway from the eyes to the cerebral cortex is completed, and the baby's cortex is able to register and be modified by visual stimuli. In the late forties and the fifties there was a pandemic of a condition named retrolental fibrous dysplasia which was ultimately traced to the exposure of premature infants and newborn babies who were considered to be at risk, to oxygen-rich environments. This resulted in the development of a fibrous web behind the lenses of the baby's eyes and permanent blindness. Because they did not reach the infant's central nervous system, the baby did not respond to visual stimuli. The "normal" developmental changes, which should have occurred secondary to visual input, did not occur. Because there was nothing in the infant's external appearance to lead one to suspect blindness, the parents of these babies characteristically did not become concerned about them until they were 6 months old. Until then, they tended to attribute their lack of responsiveness to their being "good" babies who slept through the night. The consequences of being denied visual stimulation during this period proved to be devastating. At least 25 percent of the afflicted children present with an autisticlike syndrome. For the most part, the rest are also quite deviant, although some turn out quite well. Some possibilities about why this should be (i.e., why so many congenitally blind children turn out to be deviant while a small proportion turn out to be reasonably well adapted individuals) will be discussed later when we turn to a discussion of the processes of development as opposed to maturation.

These observations about the consequences of congenital blindness are in striking contrast to what is observed in the adventitiously congenitally deaf (i.e., infants for whom there was no

apparent reason to assume that they might have been born deaf).
Bar 3 shows the time of myelinization of the lower "reflex" pathways relevant to hearing. It is apparent that by the time the baby
is born he or she is able to respond to noises in an automatic
way. Bar 17, however, shows the timing of myelin deposition in
the pathways which bring auditory signals to the cerebral cortex
(i.e., which makes them potentially psychologically available).
These neurons are not completely myelinated until the child is
somewhere between 3 and 4 years old (i.e., no longer an infant).
When the child's deafness is identified, he or she is at the upper
end of the toddler stage. There is a striking clinical correlate here
too. Parents of such congenitally deaf children typically find them
bright and engaging as well as somewhat frenetic. Because of all
the other evidence that they are "normal" bright kids, the parents tend to dismiss their not talking with some comments as,
"he is too busy to talk." Not infrequently it is only as the child
approaches 4 years that the parents become concerned and seek
medical help.

Some years ago, on the basis of such clinical observations as
these, I prepared the following chart. This is intended to represent the *relative* importance of the indicated sensory modalities
during the first 36 months of life (Figure 1.2). Because it was
prepared before I knew about Yakovlev and LeCour's work, it
is particularly noteworthy that my observations about vision and
audition coincide so well with their anatomic findings.

The number of nerve cells which each of us has at birth, the
predetermined regional specialization of areas of the brain, of
which I have cited only a few obvious examples, and the timetable
according to which myelin is laid down in various areas of the
brain, are all gene-determined *maturational* phenomena. If not
the phenomena themselves, at least their Anlagen—the potentiality that they will emerge according to a predictable time schedule—are present from birth. Their emergence over time is
correlated with the growing individual going through, or having
gone through, the various stages of somatic development. They
do not, however, account for the individual differences which
make each one of us unique. Some people are born with the
potentiality to be great athletes or great scholars, but unless the
ambience in which a person grows up provides age-appropriate

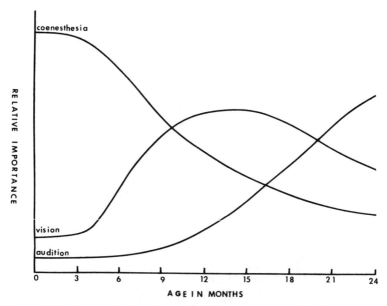

Figure 1.2. Curves indicating relative importance of indicated sensory modalities at given ages.

experience during the various critical periods, the likelihood that the gene-derived potentialities will be realized is extremely remote. From the standpoint of the brain, this is a question of its *development*, the other one of the twin processes which are the subject of this discussion.

In order to clarify the basis for the processes of psychological development, it will be necessary for me to turn once again to some details of the maturation and developmental processes in the nervous system, as well as introduce some details about the anatomy of nerve cells. Thus far I have only mentioned that the cell, or cell body (i.e., neuronal body), has a long myelinated process, called the axon, which goes to other cells. Axons vary in length from a fraction of a millimeter to nearly a meter. In a 6-foot man, the axons of the corticospinal tracts, which extend from the cerebral cortex into the spinal cord, are on the order of three feet in length. Especially as they approach their termination, they branch so that each axon makes connection (synapses) with many postsynaptic cells. This is how "messages" get from a presynaptic

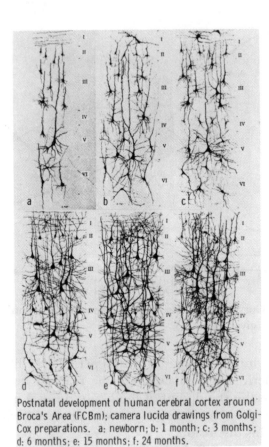

Postnatal development of human cerebral cortex around Broca's Area (FCBm); camera lucida drawings from Golgi-Cox preparations. a: newborn; b: 1 month; c: 3 months; d: 6 months; e: 15 months; f: 24 months.

Figure 1.3. Changes in nerve cell during first two years. Reprinted by permission of the publishers from THE POST NATAL DEVELOPMENT OF THE HUMAN CEREBRAL CORTEX by Jesse LeRoy Conel, Cambridge, Mass.: Harvard University Press, Copyright © 1939 by the President and Fellows of Harvard College; © renewed 1966 by Jesse LeRoy Conel.

cell to a constellation of postsynaptic cells. But how does the message get to the presynaptic cell to begin with? Remember that all nerve cells are in constellations of connections with other cells. In addition to its single axon, each nerve cell is characterized by a plethora of processes, called dendrites, onto which the axons of other cells impinge. The presynaptic axons also impinge on the postsynaptic cell bodies (of course, each presynaptic cell is also a postsynaptic cell for other neurons whose axons make contact with it). The number of presynaptic terminations on a postsynaptic cell body is so great that one neuroanatomist (Lorente de No, 1939) called it the synaptic scale, likening it to the scales on a fish. As I have already mentioned, it is estimated that anywhere from one thousand to one hundred thousand connections are made with other cells on the body and dendrites of each neuron.

Figure 1.3, from the work of Conel (1919–1959) illustrates how dendritic patterns change during the first 24 months of postpartum life while the numbers of cell bodies and axons change little, if at all. The dendrites, however, increase enormously both in number and complexity. When Conel did his work it was believed that the increasing complexity of the dendritic pattern was a result of the maturing process. Virtually no responsible neuroanatomist thought that the maturation of the brain was influenced by the environment—that in addition to gene-determined maturational processes, environmentally derived developmental processes were affecting the growth of the brain. Today we know better. The next figure (Figure 1.4) shows axons from the brains of two Jewel fish, a tropical fish which ordinarily lives in schools. The authors of this study reared some Jewel fish in isolation; that is, without the environmental stimulation which is inherent in being part of a school of fish. The fish reared in isolation have dendrites with dramatically fewer branches and many fewer points at which synaptic exchange can occur.

From our standpoint as psychotherapists, these facts concerning the maturation and development of the nervous system have considerable significance. Even at the microscopic level of neurons the structures of the brain are not static. While some synaptic connections may be gene-determined and, therefore, stable from birth, others certainly are not. Of the latter, some become stabilized during critical periods when sign specific stimuli are effective in evoking releasing mechanisms. The modifications of brain structure induced under such circumstances are most likely to be permanent. A Jewel fish reared in isolation will be a permanent loner, unlikely later in its life to be able to swim with a school. In more advanced organisms, even later in life, the nervous system is more

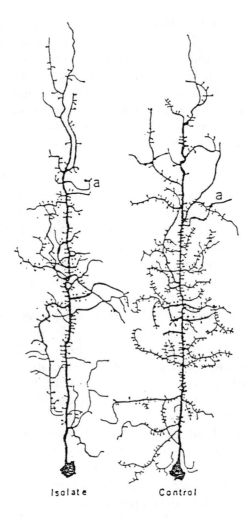

Isolate   Control

Figure 1.4. Comparing axons from a control Jewel fish and one raised in isolation. (Reprinted with permission from R. G. Coss and A. Globus, Spine stems on tectal interneurons in Jewel fish are shortened by social stimulation. *Science*, Volume 200, pp. 787–790. Copyright 1978 American Association for the Advancement of Science.)

malleable. Environmentally induced alterations in patterns of synaptic connection continue to occur. Higher animals are, after all, capable of learning and modifying behavior. This later malleability,

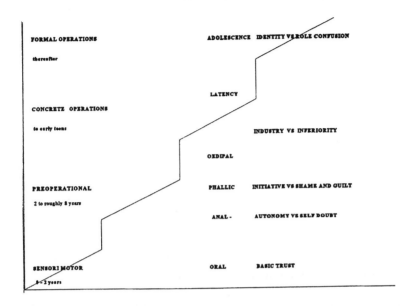

FORMAL OPERATIONS   ADOLESCENCE IDENTITY VS ROLE CONFUSION

thereafter

                                     LATENCY

CONCRETE OPERATIONS

to early teens   INDUSTRY VS INFERIORITY

                                     OEDIPAL

PREOPERATIONAL   PHALLIC   INITIATIVE VS SHAME AND GUILT

2 to roughly 8 years

                                     ANAL -   AUTONOMY VS SELF DOUBT

SENSORI MOTOR   ORAL   BASIC TRUST

0 - 2 years

Figure 1.5. Maturation, a saltatory, gene-driven process. Three perspectives of the process are presented. On the left is Piaget's maturational sequence; in the middle, the libidinal phases; and on the right Erikson's sequence.

which is so important for the adaptation of higher animals like ourselves, nonetheless rests on a foundation of fixed patterns of expectation and reaction which has its origins for all of us in early experience. The result of all of this, from the standpoint of ourselves as clinicians, is that we deal with two very different groups of problems, often in the same person.

Figures 1.5 and 1.6 are intended to present the maturational and developmental processes in pictorial form. Maturation (Figure 1.5) is a saltatory process. A number of neural systems are maturing simultaneously, albeit at very different rates. By the same token, their psychological and behavioral manifestations are also emerging in different contexts. Three of the latter, cognitive, libidinal, and psychosocial, are included in the figure. Development (Figure 1.6), by contrast, is a cumulative process. The interaction of the organism and its environment is ongoing and has

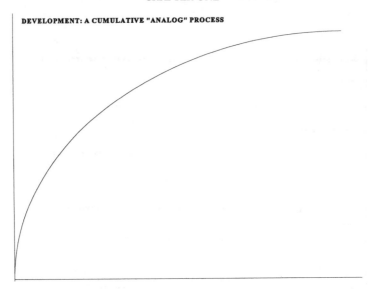

DEVELOPMENT: A CUMULATIVE "ANALOG" PROCESS

Figure 1.6. Development, a cumulative process.

cumulative effects. How a particular environment–organism interaction will affect the maturing and developing individual will depend on (1) the state of maturation and (2) the residua of all
the organism's previous interactions with the environment.

The nervous system with which the human neonate comes
equipped is incomplete and immature. Its postpartum destiny will
be determined by a combination of gene-determined influences
which are derived from the baby's parents and the vicissitudes of
the environment in which he or she is being reared. The pattern
of maturational, gene-determined, changes unfolds according to
a timetable which defines what input from the environment the
maturing organism can register and respond to. If relevant neural
pathways are not yet myelinated, input from the environment
cannot be registered. For any given individual the pattern of maturation is fixed and predetermined. Environmental (developmental) influences by contrast are highly variable. They are
reflected in the brain in the form of alterations in synaptic patterns and, in the functioning individual, in the idiosyncratic characteristics which define him or her.

CHAPTER 2

Earliest Object Relations

The past is a palimpsest, Prior thought. Early memories are always obscured by accumulations of later knowledge [Barker, 1995, p. 55].

The most important thing to remember about the earliest object relations is that they don't exist! The term *object relation* refers to a state of connection or a transaction going on between two individuals, each of whom has a degree of awareness of him- or herself as a separately existing being, as well as of the other as another separately existing being. In all probability, therefore, newborns are incapable of participating in object relations. This is a fact of the beginnings of maturation and development, however, which the proud and adoring parents of newborn infants are not likely to find palatable or even acceptable. Neither is it likely to be supported by other less loving parents, those who neglect or abuse their children. These latter represent the malevolent extreme of a phenomenon which characterizes all parent to child relations—as parents we all adultomorphize. In the average expectable world of good-enough parenting this imputing of great sophistication to the infant tends to be benevolent and have a positive effect. Regrettably this is not always the case. Adultomorphizing can also be malevolent and have devastating long-term effects when, for example, the parent imputes malicious intentions to a colicky baby who is maturationally and developmentally incapable of having such intentions.

19

What we all impute to our small children are understandings, intentions, and motivations which make sense to us as adults. Even if we don't make the assumption explicitly, in our interactions with them we tend to behave as though infants are possessed of a sense of self and of other. We are all guilty of this. It is difficult especially, but not only, at times of stress, to keep in mind that small people come from very different psychological places than do we older folk. The infant does not start out with an awareness of the surrounding world. Indeed, it is arguable that from the standpoint of the infant, the earliest object relations (i.e., the earliest awareness that there is an outside universe by which the infant is surrounded and which is not consistent and predictable in the ways in which it impinges on him or her) emerge out of how the baby's brain is specifically and uniquely modified by the particular experiences to which he or she happens to be exposed. No parent can be exactly the way the infant or child "anticipates" simply because the child "wants" the parent to be a particular way. I put "anticipate" and "want" in quotes because it seems to be the case that "anticipatory behaviors"—such as sucking when placed in the nursing position—will occur long before they are associated with anything like the awareness of self. The subjective experience "I want" is anticipated by behaviors which parents interpret as "He or she wants." Early on this is particularly an issue with regard to the parenting ones. However, it is also relevant to all the unique complexities of experience which are the lot of anyone who is in the process of growing up. I refer to such unpredictable but ubiquitous matters as place in the family, number of siblings, attitudes of parents toward being parents, and on and on. Just as the structure of the brain emerges into its mature form through an epigenetic series of gene-defined maturational events and appropriately timed experiences, which influence the developmental process, so does the capacity to enter into object relations. Indeed, as we will discuss later, as much is also true with regard to the development of the ability to be aware that even inanimate objects have an existence of their own—that is, independent of our interaction with them.

Three implications of this last statement deserve particular emphasis because of their importance to us as therapists when we work clinically with adults as well as children. They are:

1. Old experiences never die. They remain as elements in what we have come, after Freud, to call our unconscious.
2. The internalized effects of new experiences (ultimately modifications of patterns of dendritic connections) are either superimposed or intermingled with the residua of earlier experience.
3. In our later lives we are very likely, in times of stress or high anxiety, to revert to states of feeling and behaving which are reflective of such earlier times. Technically we call this *regression.*

Before going on to a fuller discussion of the emergence of object relations and object relatedness, I would like to clarify the above points by a consideration of the emergence of the smile. The ubiquitous icon, the yellow button with upturned lips, demonstrates that the smile is universally recognized and interpreted as conveying positive affect. It appears to be a simple and straightforward expression and communication of feeling. Yet, in fact, it is by no means so simple. There are four readily identifiable and temporally discrete steps involved in the emergence of the smile whose ultimate significance we all take for granted. They are:

1. The neonatal smile. At birth, or shortly after, infants' facial musculature can take the form of what we, as adults, interpret to be a smile. It is a source of never ending delight to their parents when the infants' perioral muscles assume the "smiling pattern." They have been known to say, usually somewhat ecstatically, "Look! He or she is smiling at me." There is no doubt that the assumption of a smiling constellation on the face of an infant facilitates the bonding process on the part of the parent. His or her behavior, in turn, leads to alterations within the infant which ultimately come to have relevance to the development of object relations. Indeed, in the absence of "appropriate" parental responses, object relations either do not develop or are grievously distorted. This initial smile, however, is actually devoid of psychological content. It is a patterned response to some physiological change in the infant and has nothing to do with what is going on in the world around it.

2. When the infant is somewhere between 2 and 3 months old, the reflex smile emerges. This is the smile I have already mentioned, the one which was studied so closely by Spitz (1965). By this time the smile is no longer simply a reaction to an internal state. It now is induced by specific stimulus constellations (sign specific stimuli) coming from the outside world. But it continues to be reflexive in the sense that the effective stimulus constellation is very specific. It can, as I mentioned earlier, be induced and removed by the simple expedient of turning the face from full forward to profile. It can also be made bigger by making the sign specific stimulus bigger. Harlequin glasses and great big black circles on a white balloon, will induce a bigger smile than will your ordinary, everyday pair of a loving mother's eyes.

3. During the next several weeks, however, maturation and development continue and the baby begins to discriminate between familiar and unfamiliar stimulus constellations. By somewhere in the neighborhood of 6 or 7 months the infant will respond to a familiar constellation with a smile and to an unfamiliar one with evidence of distress. This latter phenomenon we refer to as *stranger anxiety*. It appears to be the case that one of the striking results of changes in child-rearing practices in the past several years has been a change in the conditions which will induce stranger anxiety. In any event, at roughly 6 months the baby is able to check the stimulus constellation, with which he or she is being confronted in the here-and-now, against a databank he or she has been accumulating over time. Presumably this databank exists in the form of idiosyncratic changes in synaptic patterns. Whether he or she smiles or cries in the presence of a new stimulus will be determined, not only by the characteristics of that stimulus, but also by what the databank contains. The smile can now be regarded as recognitory and the infant can be said to have made major progress toward the state of being able to enter into object relations as an active participant.

4. But this is not the end of the matter. Much later, at roughly age 2, the fourth stage of the smile emerges. By this time the toddler can be seen smiling to *himself*. It is possible to determine that he is smiling in response to a memory, to the internalized residua of past experiences. That is, both the stimulus

which induces the smile and the smile itself are entirely internally derived. Neither need have any demonstrable relation to what is going on around the youngster. This is very different from the earlier, also endogenous, "smile" of the neonate. It is a response to a mental event (a memory or a reminiscence) not to a bubble of gas or some other physiologic stimulus.[1]

While we feel confident that the ability to have such an entirely intrapsychic experience is the result of dramatic changes in the infant's pattern of synaptic connections, our certainty is an article of faith rather than a "demonstrated fact." As one neuropsychiatrist is said to have put it, "We know a great deal about the physiology of memory in general, but it will be a long, long time before we are able to define the physiology of any single memory."

We have now left the world of neurology for that of psychology and psychiatry. While we may have occasion to refer to the nervous system from time to time, it will not be possible to think of direct relations between specific intrapsychic content (e.g., thoughts, feelings, associated memories, etc.) and specific neuronal activities in the brain per se. Henceforth we will consider issues of maturation and development, as well as the emergence of object relations, in strictly psychological terms. From this perspective—looking to the unique individual and his or her functioning—rather than the brain inside the person's skull, as the "bottom explanatory line," we can identify several successive phases of maturation and development and, correlated with them, corresponding changes in both the capacity to enter into, and the quality of the infant's object relations. The discussion of the smiling response has already anticipated this. Because one can see essentially the same four phases in the emergence of many phenomena, it may be worthwhile to present them with some examples. There is, however, a caveat which I must include. Everyone who has thought about early human development has recognized that it is divided into defined stages. However, the number of identified stages, the pattern of their emergence from

---

[1] It is of interest that it is at this age too that the child becomes able to recognize his or her reflection in a mirror as just that, rather than being another object "Out there" (Amsterdam, 1972).

one into the next, as well as their defining characteristics have
varied from writer to writer. I will summarize the viewpoints of
those I regard as the most significant in terms of understanding
where we are today. Because their names and ideas are the most
frequently referred to, it will be useful to consider how they relate
to one another (see also Figure 1.5). It will also be important to
keep in mind that my summaries are not entirely "objective." I
have significant prejudices in this area; for example, it is my opinion that far too little attention has been paid to the emergence
of cognitive competence (see chapter 5).

As noted in chapter 1 Freud (1908) and Abraham
(1921–1925) identified four libidinal stages, the oral, anal, phallic
(genital), and oedipal. The names derived from the nature of
what these early investigators were hearing from their patients.
They came to the conclusion, on the basis of the deductions they
made from what their adult patients were saying, that in the
course of their growing up, the maturing and developing individuals' relationships were focused successively, first on each of these
bodily areas and, ultimately, on a search for sexual gratification
from the mothering one in competition with the father. It is important to underscore that the libido theory was not based on
the direct observation of infants and children. It was derived from
the data early psychoanalysts obtained in their clinical work and
then applied retrospectively to infants and children. The thrust
of their work was carried forward by Anna Freud (1951) who,
with her father's blessing, did work with children, Heinz Hartmann (1964), and many others who continued, with some modifications, to work within the framework set by Freud. The libido
model was supplemented by the structural model which conceived of a maturational process proceeding from an "undifferentiated phase," in earliest infancy, to the differentiation of a
tripartite mental structure (i.e., ego, id, and superego). Most early
analysts believed that the id, as manifested in instinctual drives,
is a part of the inherent equipment with which individuals are
endowed at birth. They believed that maturation and development might help to determine how the drives would be expressed,
but that the drives were in some sense inherent. It was always,
moreover, important not to confuse the instinctual drive with the

manner of its expression. An individual intent on murder, for example, could be sweet and loving in external appearance.

Melanie Klein was another early worker who had great influence. It was Klein's special contribution to assert that infants were inherently different from older people and that they experienced the world and their relations to others in a very different way. Regrettably, she also assumed that infants came fully equipped with extremely rich, not to say bizarre fantasy lives, enormous and detailed knowledge of sexual anatomy, and great cognitive skills. Despite all this, her emphasis on direct observation of infants was seminal. The British Object Relations theorists, Guntrip (1961), Fairbairn (1963), and Winnicott (1965) were all influenced by Klein. Aside from Winnicott, who identified and described such extremely important phenomena as the "holding environment," the "transitional object," "good-enough mothering," and the "true self/false self dichotomy," all of which are directly relevant to our day-to-day clinical work, this group seems to me to have had relatively little impact on current thinking (see appendix B).

Of the many nonpsychoanalysts who have studied early childhood development, I will mention only Piaget. The omission of others is not meant to discount the importance of their work. Piaget, however, added a whole new dimension to our understanding of early maturation and development. Not a psychoanalyst, and indeed sometimes very critical of psychoanalysis, his interest was in epistemology, the theory of knowledge. His studies of cognitive development have had an impact not unlike that of Freud. He identified only two major stages during the period in which we are interested. However, he divided his first stage, the sensorimotor period, into six subperiods (Piaget used the word *period* to refer to what we are calling *stages*). I mention him here because his work, which continued into the 1950s, began in the 1920s, about the same time as that of Klein. Unlike her, he made direct and meticulous observations of infants and toddlers, as well as older children (see chapter 5).

Following World War II there began a period of intense interest in early development which continues today. Of the many participants, Spitz (1958), Erikson (1959), and Mahler, Pine, and Bergman (1975) are particularly important to keep in mind. Each

identified a series of stages through which the developing individual passes. Because each approached the study of the child from
a slightly different perspective, the stages they identified were
different. Yet their relation one to the other is, I think, apparent.

First and, in my opinion, foremost among them was René
Spitz. His studies of hospitalism can justifiably be said to have
begun the systematic empirical investigation of the effects of environmental circumstances on early development. Before Spitz little attention was paid to the nature of what transpired between
the infant and the individual(s) carrying out the parenting function. He emphasized the importance of what he referred to as
the "dialogue." Of course, he was aware that to begin with the
dialogue was in the mind of the parenting one. He was, however,
also aware that this *illusion* of a dialogue and the affective climate
this created, were essential if later development were to proceed.

Spitz thought of postpartum, extrauterine life, at least during
the first two years, as a continuation of intrauterine embryologic
processes, as a continuing series of interactions between emerging maturational readiness in one or another area of development, and the availability, from the environment, of "input" to
which the organism, because of its state of readiness, could respond. He likened what we have been referring to as stages, to
what the embryologists, at the time he was writing, called organizers. Organizers, according to Spitz, are the "confluence of several
lines of biologic development at a specific location in the embryonic organism" (Spitz, 1965, p. 117). He cites the example of the
frog's eye, which I used in the first chapter, as evidence of the
operation of an organizer. Before the critical confluence has happened, the destiny of a region of skin depends on its immediate
environment. After the confluence (i.e., the establishment of the
organizer) its destiny is fixed. An eye will be an eye no matter
where it is. Organizers obviously include influences from the environment as well as the physiological and biochemical events going
on inside the baby's skin. Spitz assumes that the infant exists in
an objectless state until the emergence of the first organizer, the
smiling response. In his words, its emergence indicates that
"trends have now been integrated, organized, and will hencefor-
ward operate as a distinct unit within the psychic system" (Spitz,

1965, p. 119).[2] Two additional organizers for Spitz are the emergence of stranger anxiety at roughly 8 months, and the emergence, as he put it, of *No* (a.k.a. the terrible twos). It should be evident that my way of thinking is particularly heavily influenced by Spitz.

Margaret Mahler also described a series of developmental stages which were clearly based on how she understood the relation between child and parent to evolve. From an initial, undifferentiated, symbiotic phase the child "hatches" into a relatively prolonged practicing phase during which the now toddler becomes progressively more able to maintain physical separation from the parent. Mahler assumes this is reflective of his or her evolving ability to maintain a mental representation of the parenting one. In order to maintain such a representation, one must first establish it. It is in itself a product of the infant's earlier experience which is part and parcel of his or her interaction with the average expectable environment. For Mahler, the practicing phase culminates in what she refers to as rapprochement. In order to engage in rapprochement one must, of course, already have established a psychological object (i.e., an internal representation of the parenting one) to which to return. During this period of establishing such internal representations, the child is involved in what Mahler calls the twin processes of separation and individuation. This involves a continuing testing of both the physical and affective limits of tolerable boundaries.

Erikson, whose interest was in psychosocial development, identified three stages during these same years. He classified them as oral-sensory, muscular-anal, and locomotor-genital. He also proposed, and many of us find his ideas extremely useful, that the small person's experiences during each of these stages will affect his later character on a particular continuum. Thus, his or her experience during the oral–sensory period will be reflected in where the older individual will be situated along a continuum which Erikson characterized as basic trust versus mistrust. Experiences during the muscular–anal period will be reflected in where the older individual falls along a continuum which extends from

---

[2]He is referring here to the smile of the 2- to 3-month-old baby responding to an external stimulus, not to the internally initiated "smile" of the neonate.

autonomy to shame and doubt; and, for the locomotor–genital period, the corresponding continuum ranges from initiative to guilt.

Each of these writers dealt with a different aspect of the emergence of the individual's functioning and his developing relation to the world around him. Freud and Abraham were concerned with "libidinal" development. One can characterize this as a sensual investment in aspects of one's own body functioning. As Freud pointed out, it is not the function as such that is of interest to the child. Rather it is the pleasurable stimulation of mucocutaneous junctions[3] that gets his or her attention. The fact that this shifting series of interests occurs in a predictable sequence, suggests that it involves maturational changes in the nervous system. That is, one's anus is presumably present and functioning at least from birth and throughout the "oral" period. It will also continue to function during the phallic–genital period and thereafter. It is only during the relatively brief anal period, however, that it is the focus of particularly intense interest to the child and often, one might add, to parenting ones. To the extent that such an investment involves a search for pleasure or gratification in relation to a given function, the libido theory is also a theory of motivation. Erikson was particularly concerned with "psychosocial" development. Otherwise stated, this has to do with how the environment interacts with the emerging libidinal preoccupations and associated motivated behaviors of the child. Piaget was concerned with "cognitive" development; that is, the emergence of the child's ability to differentiate him- or herself from the surrounding world and to treat the world as existing independently of his or her or, for that matter, anyone else's perception of it.

The description of the four steps which culminate in the emergence of the full-fledged smile, can serve as a model for the succession of maturational and developmental steps which characterize the establishment of a multitude of functions and

---

[3]Those areas, for example mouth, anus, and vaginal orifice where the skin meets mucus membranes, are particularly richly endowed with sensory receptors. The perceived pleasurable sensations which arise from their stimulation is reflected in the zonal libido theory.

relations. In the following paragraphs, I will enumerate the broad general categories I have in mind and provide some illustrations of the vicissitudes one might expect to encounter in the course of the emergence and unfolding of each. I reiterate, these are by no means the only way to view the sequence by which object relations get formed. I, however, find them useful and I offer them on that basis. The illustrative material I present indicates something about how variegated the role of the other element in the object relation dyad, the parenting one, may be. It will be apparent that my "classification" is derivative—it is dependent on all the earlier ones I have mentioned. For me it has the special virtue of emphasizing the extent to which object relations mature and develop out of ongoing but critically timed experience.

AUTOMATIC FUNCTION

The neonate comes equipped with a variety of built-in patterns of muscular activity. It is above all important to recognize that these are not simple reflexes. Smiling, sucking, breathing, moving the eyes, crying, moving the limbs, urinating, defecating are all activities which require the coordinated contraction and relaxation of groups of muscles. Indeed some of the same muscles are used in various combinations for many of these activities; for example, smiling, sucking, and crying all utilize the same perioral muscles. No one teaches the baby how to do these things. Like the wheels on a new car, these skills are part of the initial equipment. Because they are so much like what the parenting one is used to responding to in relation with older people, he or she is inclined to impute the same psychological significance to what the baby does as he or she would anticipate in the older person. He or she will adultomorphize. Some illustrative examples:

A very proud young mother announced to her newborn's grandparents that he was "talking to" her. She was sure that when she cooed at him he responded with coos and gurgles. The equally proud grandfather (this was his first grandchild) decided to record a "conversation" between mother and infant son. Needless to say, once the taperecorder was turned on, the baby neither cooed nor gurgled in response to his mother's vocalizations. She concluded that her then 6-week-old baby didn't feel like "talking right then." Sometime later the grandfather, who had a special interest in early development, found a report on the cooing and gurgling of normal infants, infants of congenitally deaf parents who were growing up in a soundless environment, and a congenitally deaf infant. It turned out that the amount of cooing and gurgling done by each of these three groups of babies was identical until the youngsters were approximately 12 weeks old (Lenneberg, 1967). That is, any vocalization the younger infant might make may have been due to a postnasal drip or an irritation in the throat, it most certainly was not in response to, or a part of, an oral/aural conversation with his mother. The mother's reaction in this case, however, was an instance of a beneficent form of adultomorphizing. Both her enthusiastic interpretation of what he was doing and her reaction to his not responding were consistent with this characterization.

The following is a somewhat more problematic instance of adultomorphizing. A young resident, father of two children born a year apart, would come home after his thirty-six-hour on-call stint and spell his wife in the care of the babies. The younger of the two, who was 10 weeks old at the time, was colicky. About 3:00 A.M. one night, after pacing the floor for hours in his effort to quiet the little boy, he found himself enraged. He held the baby in front of him and at the top of his voice he yelled, "Shut up, shut up." Fortunately he then said to himself, "What the hell am I doing, I know he doesn't *mean* to be doing this." He was sufficiently upset by his reaction that he came for a consultation.

Finally, there are instances of what one can only characterize as totally malevolent adultomorphizing. We read about this in the stories of child batterers. According to Steele and Pollock (1968), the person who batters little people imputes to them adult intentions and motivations. Indeed, they often ascribe to them parentlike intentions to criticize. The term *role reversal* is used to refer to this situation, one in which the distressed parent, in effect, "parentifies" the child and experiences him or her as being unjustly critical and demanding.

FUNCTIONS SWITCHED ON AND OFF BY STIMULI FROM THE ENVIRONMENT

It is not possible to say precisely when the infant begins to respond to environmental stimuli. Certainly one can make the case that the induction of breathing by slapping the buttocks, immediately after birth, is evoking a response from the environment. It also *appears* to be the case that infants' eyes will follow some bright objects from a very early age—perhaps from a few weeks old. There also appears to be some evidence that when he is placed in a situation to which he has been exposed before, the baby will make some movements which *can be interpreted* as anticipatory. For example, an infant placed in the nursing position may turn his or her head toward the breast and nipple. I italicize to indicate (1) my own skepticism about the findings, and (2) my concern about their being overinterpreted, if, indeed, they are valid. There is little reason to believe that the baby is responding to objects "out there" in the same manner as a toddler is responding when he gets excited as he passes an ice cream vendor. The object to which the baby is responding isn't one that carries implications of future good or bad times. It becomes part of a whole, a Gestalt, which includes object, action, and baby. The induction and wiping off of the smiling response described above is an example of this. Two other examples are what are known as the looming response and the visual cliff response (Gibson, 1970). It appears that these are also part of the original "factory installed equipment" with which we were all provided at the time of birth. I cite them because they are instances in which very specific and complex, preprogrammed, unlearned behavioral reactions are seen in infants in response to very specific (sign specific) stimuli. They are, moreover, seen from as early in the life of the infant as he or she can be tested.

We are all familiar with them as adults. When we see a baseball or some other rapidly advancing projectile heading for our faces we all feel anxious and take evasive action; so do neonates. Rather than throw baseballs at them, experimenters use a spot of light which they enlarge rapidly in order to create the illusion that it is approaching the baby's face. The baby responds to the looming light with the same manifestations of anxiety as the adult shows when faced with an oncoming projectile. The visual cliff (Figure 2.1) is somewhat more complicated. We all know about how we feel when we stand at the edge of a precipitous decline. Most of us step back and have trouble looking over the edge. The baby is not different. This was studied in infants by creating a visual illusion of a cliff. A platform is constructed with a plate glass surface. The structure is built so that a uniformly patterned material is stretched under half of the glass surface but is in direct contact with it. Then there is an abrupt decline, not on the glass surface but beneath it. Because of the change in the apparent patterning of the material, the visual stimulus is the same as if one were looking down into a chasm (Figure 2.2). No crawling baby will venture out over that visual "crevice," even though the plate glass surface is uniformly there. When the baby approaches the edge, he or she shows visible evidence of anxiety. Lest we preen ourselves with ideas of the wisdom of the human infant, I must tell you that the looming response was found in a wide variety of animal species in addition to humans. Similarly, the visual cliff response is seen in the infants of all terrestrial mammals tested, but not in birds or fishes which are adapted to live in a three-dimensional world.

Perhaps of more interest to us in dealing with infants is the "inverted bottle response." With development the baby becomes able, indeed eager, to feed itself. It will spontaneously hold onto its bottle, first with the parenting one's assistance and then by itself. If, after the baby is used to holding the bottle and inserting the nipple into its mouth, one inverts the bottle and presents the butt end first, he or she will attempt to put that end into his mouth and will make sucking movements on its edge. Once I described this phenomenon to a group of residents, one of whom had a roughly 6-month-old baby; needless to say she didn't believe me. She went home that night and repeated the experiment. The results, of course, were as I predicted. Her husband, who was observing, said "Well we don't have to worry about getting her into St. John's!"[4] Of course he was wrong. She is now a very bright little girl and a candidate for the best schooling available.

---

[4] St. John's is a highly selective private school in Houston.

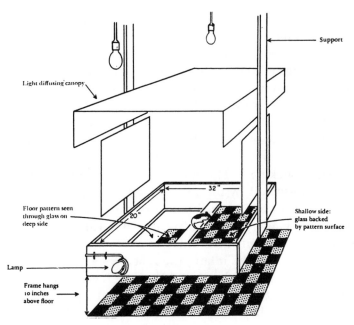

Figure 2.1. Experimental setup for visual cliff (from Gibson, 1970).

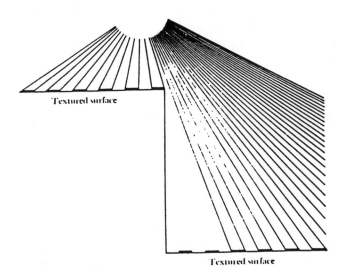

Figure 2.2. Optical illusion created by the visual cliff (from Gibson, 1970).

In all of these instances the infant is responding to the environmental stimulus as a whole. While by some measure (e.g., in the bottle experiment) he or she may be using some beginning, rudimentary, internalized representations (the baby will not respond in the same way to square or other nonfirm, noncylindrical object) his response is to the object as a whole. With regard to the bottle he has not yet developed in his mind some sort of formulation which we might verbalize as, "Aha, this is a bottle of food which I can extract by putting the nipple end in my mouth before I begin sucking." The most we can attribute to him is "cylinder-mouth-suck." By the same token neither the looming nor the visual cliff evokes, on the part of the infant, any understanding of the danger he is confronting. We can prove this by comparing what happens with older more sophisticated people in these situations. For the infant, the reactions are constant and predictable. Those of us who are older, and have gone on past this phase of the maturational and developmental processes, can be instructed about the nature of the experiments. We are able to generate mental structures which include the knowledge that the looming light and the visual cliff are optical illusions. Once we have such structures available, we are much less likely to be intimidated by them. I say this even though, I confess, I still don't like the image of something which appears to be rapidly advancing into my face.

AWARENESS OF AND DIFFERENTIAL RESPONSE TO PROPERTIES OF THE ENVIRONMENT

We can use what I have referred to as the third stage of the smiling response as a model for the emergence of the *ability* to enter into object relations. I emphasize the word *ability* because, as we will discuss further, it does not follow inevitably from the fact that the infant has reached a "certain age" that the ability to discriminate first "familiar" from "strange" and ultimately "self" from "other" will automatically emerge. These skills which, under "average expectable conditions," do emerge successively, are also products of the twin processes of maturation and development.

In the world of good-enough parenting, the child of somewhere between 6 and 7 months will begin to differentiate between the strange and the familiar. He or she will also begin to show evidence of distress when the familiar parenting one leaves him (i.e., what has been called in the past "separation anxiety"). Parenting practices have changed radically since the days when the observations upon which my statements are based were made. It was possible then to assume that babies, at least those who were likely to be observed by people interested in development, were being reared in a nuclear family and by a primary "mothering one." Of course, that was largely a fiction even back then. In contrast to the ubiquity of day care now, however, the model had some plausibility as a prototype when one was thinking about early development. In any event, given age-appropriate input from the environment, the baby will develop internalized "templates" (presumably based on neuronal patterns which have become fixed) against which he or she will check current experiences in the here-and-now. The baby will react to a familiar face, physical presence, or even sound with evidence of pleasure, and will react with evidence of displeasure and anxiety to the unfamiliar. In the presence of a stranger he or she is likely to cling to the parent. If the latter is given to beneficent adultomorphizing, he or she is likely to say the baby is "shy." A less benevolent parent might complain about not knowing what has got into the baby and say something like, "She has becomes so clingy." To reiterate, these evidences of differentiating responses to the familiar as opposed to the strange are never clearly manifest until some time around 6 or 7 months. Maturation must have proceeded sufficiently for the possibility of their occurring to be present. Whether or not they will, in fact, emerge, depends on the ambience in which the baby is growing up, that is, on developmental considerations.

AWARENESS OF ELEMENTS IN THE ENVIRONMENT AS EXISTING INDEPENDENTLY OF ONE'S PERCEPTION OF THEM

Increasingly in the course of the second year of postpartum life, the child becomes able to take for granted that important objects in his or her life exist even when they are not being directly perceived. A stable template is being built up during this period. When it is established it will provide the infant with competencies which go well beyond the recognitory abilities of the 7-month-old. The child can now be said to have evocative capacities as well. The mere attaining of a particular age, and the accompanying maturational changes in the brain, are not sufficient to insure that evocative capacities will emerge. The influence of the ambience in which the child is developing turns out to be equally as important. More specifically, unless the infant and toddler have the opportunity to establish a differentiation between self and nonself, an awareness that he or she exists in a larger "nonself ambience" and in relation to other selves and objects, development will not proceed.

The neonate begins postpartum life equipped with a limited repertoire of coordinated patterns of muscular reaction which can be evoked in response to specific patterns of visceral and environmental stimulation. The available evidence indicates that neither the pattern of movement nor the ability to respond to sensory input is accompanied by a sense of self or an awareness of the existence of other selves. To the contrary both of these hallmarks of human psychology appear to emerge as the result of the continuing interaction of the maturing and developing organism and his or her environment. All observers appear to agree that the maturational changes within the nervous system are staged. With each maturational step new possibilities for modification of the individual as a result of his or her interaction with the environment become possible. These developmental changes have been characterized by a number of authors (e.g., Freud and Abraham, Spitz, Piaget, Erikson, and Mahler, Pine, and Bergman) each of whom has viewed and described the developmental process from a different perspective.

CHAPTER 3

Deprivation Syndromes

> Nature is nowhere accustomed more openly to display her secret mysteries than in cases where she shows traces of her workings apart from the beaten path; nor is there any better way to advance the proper practice of medicine than to give our minds to the discovery of the usual law of Nature by careful investigation of cases of rarer forms of disease. For it has been found, in almost all things that what they contain of useful or applicable nature is hardly perceived unless we are deprived of them or they become deranged in some way [Harvey, 1651].

Harvey was talking about the plight of a researcher in the days before the concept of controlled experiments was prevalent. It is still the plight of those of us who try to understand the processes of maturation and development. The complexities of what is going on within the maturing and developing infant is compounded by the complexities of the environment in which the growing individual is immersed. Additional confounding factors include the prejudices which every observer brings to his or her work and the often many years long period which may have to elapse between events which seem, at the time, to be important in an infant's life experience, and the appearance of psychological sequelae which can plausibly be connected to the events. Harvey felt that the observation of anomalous situations had the potential of getting around some of these problems. I agree. Often such experiments of nature can provide us with the opportunity to follow the effects of what appears to be a single, sharply defined difference between the experience of the individual being observed and that of the "average expectable infant in the average expectable" environment.

Deprivation syndromes are the result of one type of natural experiment. They may be defined as the physiological and the psychological sequelae of the failure of the coordination of the maturational and developmental processes which we take for granted in "average expectable" growing up circumstances. Because states of deprivation can occur at any point in the course of an individual's maturation and development, their clinical manifestations will vary enormously. Sometimes they impact the growing individual in very subtle ways; at other times, the impact is very major, even catastrophic. How a specific instance of deprivation will be manifested in a given individual who is its victim will depend on such "variables" as the age of the individual when it occurred, whether it has affected the individual in a relatively limited or in a global way, whether it involves significant, demonstrable tissue pathology as opposed to or in addition to failure of the environment to provide age-appropriate stimulation. Lack of age-appropriate stimulation will, of course, affect the patterns of synaptic connections.

It is arguable whether the first example I present should be included in a chapter on deprivation which is intended to study their psychological effects. I present it because it illustrates some of the difficulties which complicate the use of natural experiments. Even though it does not involve genetic inheritance, it is illustrative of what is meant by Anlagen. I refer to the long time lapse which may occur between a very specific deprivation and the manifestation of its effects, and to the critical importance of the timing of the deprivation (i.e., when it occurred in relation to the individual's maturational and developmental progress). Ravelli, Stein, and Susser (1976) reported an instance in which the effects of very early deprivation were demonstrated in young adults. They studied a cohort of three hundred thousand 19-year-old men who, as either fetuses or neonates, had been exposed to the Dutch famine of 1944–1945.[1] They were seen when they were

---

[1]During the last six months of World War II the Nazis imposed an embargo on those portions of Holland they still controlled. During this period the average available calories

being inducted into the Dutch armed forces for their required period of military service. If the period of famine coincided with the first half of pregnancy, 19 years later the recruits were significantly more likely to be obese ($p < 0.0005$). On the other hand, if the famine coincided with the last trimester or the first months of postpartum life, the rate of obesity was significantly less ($p < 0.005$). This critically timed perturbation in the environment, to which the maturing fetus or neonate was exposed, yielded significant long-term effects on the somatic development of the individual. Presumably, corresponding problems, relating to what it meant to these individuals to be obese, also developed. Presumably, too, any effort to deal with the psychological implication of obesity which did not take this *immutable constitutional* fact into account was doomed to failure.

We are more likely, in our work, to encounter instances of either sensory or environmental deprivation which have occurred, or are occurring, sometime in the postpartum period. I emphasize sometime because the effect of a given form of deprivation will differ as a function of the point in the maturational and developmental process when it occurs. Having been born deaf, for example, will result in very different long-term effects from those which follow having become deaf as a result of an acute illness, like meningitis, sometime in the course of the first two or three years of life. Similarly, never having had the experience of seeing has a very different impact on the growing individual from that of having had the ability to see and then lost it. Finally, a small person who has been the subject of parental neglect or abuse[2] from birth is a psychologically very different person from a similarly aged individual who, having experienced good-enough parenting, then lost it. It is also the case that such enormous deprivations as those which are seen in association with congenital blindness, congenital deafness, and massive environmental deprivation, differ in their effects, both from one another and from the consequences of more limited deprivations (e.g.,

per person declined from 1200 in November 1944 to 580 in February of 1945. The famine lasted until April of that year.

[2]From the standpoint of their effects on their victims, these are very different experiences. Children who are abused tend to make attachments in later life. Children who are neglected do not.

the results of being deprived of the opportunity to engage in average expectable activities because of physical illness or parental peccadilloes). I will give some examples of all of these possibilities.

DEPRIVATIONS WHICH PRECLUDE THE DEVELOPMENT OF EARLY OBJECT TIES

The systematic study of the effects of early deprivation can be said to have begun with René Spitz's work on hospitalism. During World War II, he observed two groups of infants whose parents were from the same lower socioeconomic class. One group was being reared in foundling homes. They were receiving adequate hygienic and nutritional care. However, the kind of handling and cuddling which is automatically embedded in the experience of the infant who experiences average expectable mothering was not available to them. The second group consisted of the offspring of women in prison who were allowed free access to their babies. The difference between the two groups of babies was striking. The babies in the foundling home presented with what we would now call the failure to thrive syndrome. They were very small for their ages, apathetic and unresponsive. They did not mold to the caretakers as babies usually do. They were also sickly and vulnerable to infections. Indeed, Spitz tells us that in the nineteenth century, when foundling homes were very common, the death rate in such institutions approached 90 percent during the first two postpartum years. By contrast, the babies of the female prisoners, who were receiving reasonably appropriate maternal care, met all the standard developmental milestones. Provence and Lipton (1962) made similar observations and came to similar conclusions in a study of infants being reared in an institution in the state of Connecticut.

Interestingly, Provence and Lipton quote from Salimbene, court chronicler for the twelfth century Holy Roman Emperor Frederick II, who wrote concerning the Emperor:

> [H]e wanted to find out what kind of speech and what manner of speech children would have when they grew up if they spoke to

no one before and so he bade foster mothers and nurses to suckle the children, to bathe and wash them, but in no way to prattle with or to speak to them, for he wanted to learn whether they would speak the Hebrew language, which was the oldest, or Greek, or Latin, or Arabic, or perhaps the language of their parents, of whom they had been born. But he labored in vain, because the children all died. For they could not live without the petting and joyful faces and loving words of their foster mothers. And so the songs are called "swaddling songs" which a woman sings while she is rocking the cradle, to put the child to sleep, and without them a child sleeps badly and has no rest [p. 3].

Kingsley Davis (1940, 1946) described some of the later consequences of massive early deprivation. He had the opportunity to observe a youngster who was kept locked up in an attic from shortly after birth until she was "more than five years." Social isolation had been instituted by her mother when the infant was between 6 and 10 weeks old. The nurse, who kept the child for much of the period prior to her isolation, described her as entirely normal. A note made two years after her discovery reads as follows:

Anna walks about aimlessly, makes periodic rhythmic motions of her hands, and, at intervals, makes guttural sucking noises. She regards her hands as if she had seen them for the first time. It was impossible to hold her attention for more than a few seconds at a time—not because of distractions due to external stimuli but because of her inability to concentrate. She ignored the task in hand to gaze vacantly about the room. Speech is entirely lacking. Numerous unsuccessful attempts have been made with her in the hope of developing initial sounds. I do not believe that her failure is due to negativism or deafness but that she is not sufficiently developed to accept speech at this time . . . [1946, p. 433].

In the ensuing two years, before her death at approximately 8 years of age, this extremely deprived child was able to develop adequate toilet habits and to feed herself with a spoon. She became partially able to dress herself and began to talk. Her speech, however, was estimated to be at a 2-year-old level. By then, she was regarded as congenitally feebleminded.

6 yrs. 7 mos.   42 7/8 ins.   8 yrs. 6 mos.   47 1/2 ins.

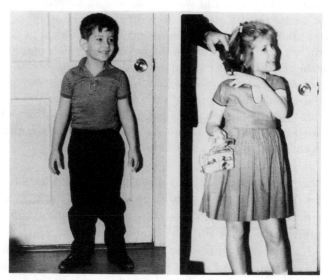

Figure 3.1. Deprived children two years after they were found.

Shortly after I moved to Houston, in 1965, I had the opportunity to observe two youngsters (Figure 3.1) who had been kept in virtually total isolation until they were 4 and 6 years old (Freedman and Brown, 1968). When they were found they were below the third percentile for their ages in both height and weight; they could not speak although they made some inarticulate sounds. They were unable to walk independently. They showed no interest in their surroundings and treated total strangers like myself with the same indifference that they showed to presumably familiar people like the foster parents to whose care they had been removed after they were discovered. When I presented them to a large conference I, who had seen them only once before, went into the waiting room, picked them up, and carried them to the auditorium. Although they were 5 and 7 at the time, they were so small that I could carry both easily. They showed no evidence of distress, maintained their customary vapid demeanor, and made no protest when they were passed from person to person in the room. One couldn't say that they showed no fear for the simple reason that they did not show sufficient awareness of their environments, and I include in this other people, to be able to discriminate potentially dangerous or frightening objects from familiar ones. They appeared not to experience pain in that they would fall, demonstrably hurt themselves, but simply get up and move along. They also appeared not to experience either hunger or satiation in that they never asked for food. When food was presented to them they ate until it was removed. The foster parents who had toyed with keeping them, found their lack of responsiveness so unsettling that they insisted on giving them up after a year. They were moved to the home of a couple who elected to adopt them and to make a "clean break" with their past. They gave them new names. Joe became Paul and Joyce became Dianne, and they responded to the new names as though the old ones had never existed. They never expressed a sense of loss with regard to the foster parents or of strangeness in their new environment.

Over the period I was able to watch them, they remained below the third percentile in height. Figure 3.2 shows the changes in Joey's height and weight during these roughly $3^1/2$ years. Joyce followed a similar course. They developed some capacity to dress and toilet themselves. They would respond to simple commands. For the rest, their speech never got beyond being echolalic. They could not make their wants known verbally, but they were trained to repeat words and phrases. For example, when I had an opportunity to see them, after they had been adopted, their new mother turned to "Dianne" (who used to be Joyce) and asked her: "What do we do at the table?" She replied in a high-pitched monotone, "Don't put your elbows on the table." When mother corrected herself and asked, "What do we say at the table?" Dianne began to recite the Lord's Prayer. At the same time, it was impossible to engage either one in any form of reciprocal behavior like playing a game. I never witnessed either behaving, in relation to another person, as though that person existed as a "separate center of initiative" with whom he or she could interact. Figure 3.3 compares two other youngsters I observed. The boy on the left had experienced similar early environmental deprivation. Standing next to him is an average size little girl who is roughly one third his age. Figure 3.4 is the reproduction of a *Life* magazine cover. The story had to do with three youngsters discovered in an attic where their psychotic mother had kept them from birth until the indicated ages.

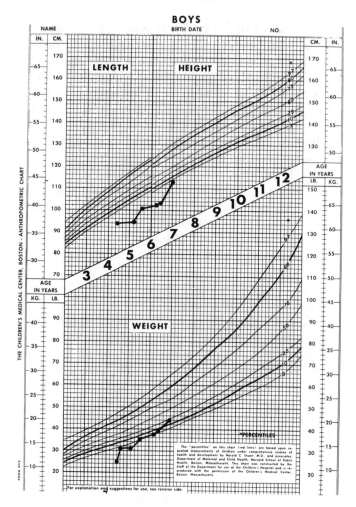

Figure 3.2. Growth chart for Joey.

During the 1940s and 1950s there was a pandemic of congenital blindness. This was largely iatrogenic in origin, secondary to the practice, at the time, of placing premature infants or those otherwise deemed vulnerable, in an oxygen-rich environment. Ultimately it was discovered that the excess of oxygen resulted in the growth of a fibrous membrane behind the lens of the eye. In the meantime we were confronted with a large population of congenitally blind youngsters. A number of observers, including

4 yrs. 8 mos.   I yr. 5 mos

Figure 3.3. Comparing the sizes of a deprived child (L) and one with adequate coenesthetic stimulation.

Parmalee, Cutsforth, and Jackson (1958), and Blank (1957, 1958), Keeler (1958), Burlingham (1961), and Fraiberg and myself (1964) described groups of these children. We all reported essentially the same findings. Approximately 25 percent of the congenitally blind population presented with a syndrome very reminiscent of infantile autism. A provocative implication of this observation lay in the fact that the incidence of autism in the general population is a small fraction of 1 percent. Being born blind, it would appear, greatly increases the vulnerability of the infant to becoming autistic. However, in and of itself it did not cause the syndrome. At the same time, it appeared to be the

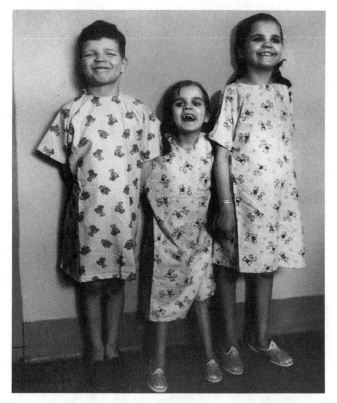

Gordon, 15   Glenda, 13   Constance, 18
3 feet 11   3 feet 4   4 feet 2

Figure 3.4. Children found in an attic in Windsor, Ontario. Joe Clark/
LIFE Magazine © TIME Inc.

case that even those congenitally blind children who ultimately
develop relatively well, do not acquire the first person pronoun
until they are close to 5 years old. Before then they refer to themselves in the third person as do toddlers who are beginning to
acquire language. Mrs. Fraiberg and I entered into our collabora-
tion because we were both asked to evaluate a congenitally blind
boy whom we refer to as Peter. He was the third and totally unex-
pected and unwanted son of a woman close to 40. She had two
teenaged daughters and considered her family complete. Born
prematurely, he was placed in an oxygen-rich environment. When
he first came home, he was considered a "good baby" because

he didn't cry at night. When he was roughly 6 months old, his parents became concerned over his unresponsiveness. The diagnosis of retrolental dysplasia was made at this time. I saw him for a neurological evaluation when he was 7. About a year and a half later Mrs. Fraiberg began to work with him psychologically. When I first examined Peter, I found him to be a "floppy" child. His muscle tone was poor, his gait was awkward, and he was engaged in movements which are so characteristic that they are known as blindisms (Figure 3.5). These consist of the repetitive passing of the hands before the eyes. They often include protrusion of the tongue so that it is touched by the passing hand. It is of interest that one anophthalmic infant I observed did not engage in blindisms. Retrolental fibrous dysplasia permits discrimination of light and dark: This discrimination does not occur with anophthalmic infants, that is, infants who are born literally without eyeballs. On neurologic examination, Peter showed no "hard" neurologic signs such as reflex changes, evidence of loss of sensory functions, other than vision, or asymmetries of movement. He was echolalic. While in my office he kept repeating "Peter not a bad boy, Peter not a bad boy. . . ." At one point, he began to sing nursery rhymes. He sang on key and *while singing* he enunciated the words of the songs clearly. His voice was without expression, however, and he never attempted to communicate verbally with me, or for that matter, anyone else. His mother told Mrs. Fraiberg that he spent hours listening to a record player.

Mrs. Fraiberg's account of her first physical contact with Peter is a vivid description of much of his behavior, of his lack of awareness of himself as a separately existing person or of others. I quote.

> After a while he came close to me and fingered me. Then, without any change of facial expression and without any show of feeling, he began to dig his fingernails into the skin of my arm, very hard, and causing me to wince with pain. From this point on it was nearly impossible to divert Peter from digging his nails into me or alternately pinching me with great intensity. It is impossible to describe this experience. I cannot call it sadistic. It was as if he did not know this was painful to me and I really felt that on the primitive undifferentiated level on which Peter operated he was not

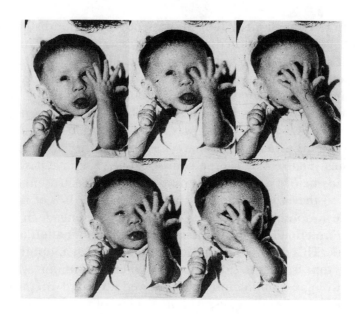

Figure 3.5. Blindisms (frames from a 16mm movie).

able to identify with the feelings of another person. This digging
into me had the quality of trying to get into me, to burrow himself
into me, and the pinching had the quality of just holding onto me
for dear life [pp. 123–124].

Whether Mrs. Fraiberg's speculations about Peter's *motives*
have merit, is an open question. I think it would be more parsimo-
nious to relate them to the blindisms. Both are the sensorimotor
responses of an unstructured brain to a sensory stimulation.

Peter's echolalia, his ability to hear and reproduce words and
other sounds accurately, even though they had no meaning for
him, led to a somewhat amusing and, at the same time, an extremely illuminating episode. At one point his parents, in their
search for help, sent him to an institution in New York City where
there were said to be techniques available to improve his functioning. After several months he was returned home in the same
condition he had been in when he left. Some time later his
mother reported that he was "talking gibberish." After she heard
him, Mrs. Fraiberg told me, "You know Dave, he wasn't talking
gibberish at all. He was talking perfectly clear Yiddish. He was

saying over and over, 'Der Meshugggene shlaft noch nit, der mes-
huggene shlaft noch nit . . .' ('The crazy one isn't sleeping yet.')
We assume that a Yiddish-speaking attendant would pass by his
bed, see him engage in blindisms or other autisticlike movements,
and make this casual observation. His parents are monolingual
in English.

The instances I describe here of massive neglect from earliest
infancy are by no means isolated. Very similar cases have been
described repeatedly over the centuries. Indeed, in the eighteenth century they were so common that the naturalist Linnaeus
included a category *Homo feralis* in his classification of all known
living things. Examples of *Homo feralis* were reported from war-
torn, chaotic countries like eighteenth century Poland after it had
been partitioned. Itard, a student of Pinel, is regarded as one of
the pioneers in the study of mental retardation. He described the
case of Victor, the Wild Boy of Aveyron in early nineteenth century France. Other cases have been described from around the
world. In Houston, we are more likely to see children like the two
I have described. They have suffered massive early environmental
deprivation for other, more readily believed, reasons. Whatever
the antecedent circumstances, whether neonatal institutionaliza-
tion, a psychotic or otherwise malignant parenting one, or, as
happens so frequently with the parents of blind babies, depression and withdrawal because the infant does not provide the parenting ones with age-appropriate sign specific stimuli, the result
is the same. The infant fails to thrive and also fails to establish
those earliest internal representations which are fundamental for
the establishment of all later capacity for object relatedness.

Similar catastrophic consequences do not, however, follow
other forms of neonatal deprivation which may seem to the unini-
tiated observer to be equally as devastating. It would appear, from
the evidence I will present later, that in addition to the modality
of deprivation, the time in the growing up process of one's life
when it occurs is critical. Like the data I have presented up to
now, the material I have to offer about humans is anecdotal. It
is derived from the observation of infants and small children who
have been subjected to extraordinary patterns of experience,
whether because of adventitious circumstance, or because of

some defect in the somatic equipment they had available at critical junctures in the course of maturation and development. There have, however, been confirming observations in primates which also seem to me to support the thesis that patterns of later development are determined by both the timing and the intensity of specific qualities of earlier experience. These have the virtue that it has been possible to follow both experimental and control subjects over periods of years. To paraphrase Ecclesiastes, the evidence seems to me to be consistent with the aphorism, "For all things there is a season, there is a season for coenesthesia, there is a season for seeing, and there is a season for hearing."

SOME SUPPORTING OBSERVATIONS IN LOWER ANIMALS

On a recent visit to the Darwin Research Center in the Galapagos Islands, we were shown a very elderly land tortoise. He weighs something on the order of 500 pounds and he lives in a pen by himself. He is called "Lonesome George." George, the last surviving male member of his species on his native island, was found living alone. All the others had presumably been harvested for food by sailing ships during the nineteenth century. He was brought to the Center in the hope that he would inseminate the few remaining females and reestablish the species. He would not. He now lives in "splendid," but not apparently discontented isolation. Fortunately for the survival of this line of land tortoises, other members of the species had been sent to the San Diego Zoo around the turn of the century. They had lived with one another to the extent that tortoises can. One male, who was lent to the Galapagans, was much more interested in females than George. In the few years he had been "in residence" he has sired forty offspring and presumably, before he is through, will have reestablished the species in his image. I tell this story because it is at least plausible to speculate that George suffered from the tortoise equivalent of environmental deprivation. He did not have the tortoise equivalent of what every infant reared in an average expectable environment automatically gets—coenesthetic stimulation. For him, like for the human who is deprived environmentally, an age-appropriate sign specific stimulus had not been available in time to turn on an innate releasing mechanism which would make later copulation possible. I hasten to add that while the facts about George and the other tortoises are established, the interpretation is, of course, as entirely speculative as Mrs. Fraiberg's interpretation of Peter's behavior. It is, however, consistent with what I have had to say up to now, as well as with what follows.

The term *coenesthesia* was used by Spitz (1945a,b) to refer to the earliest sensory inputs it is presumed the infant can register. It consists of a combination of relatively imprecise and poorly localized stimuli, such as touch, vibration, position, and nonlocalizable hearing and seeing. Over time, and with the progressive maturation and development of the baby's brain, coenesthesia is supplemented and largely, but not entirely, replaced by more discriminating sensory abilities such as those required for the ability to delineate objects with vision, and differentiate among sounds as in language. This more refined mode of sensory experience is referred to as diacritic sensation. Coenesthesia persists, however, as a critical element in such important endeavors as love making. The evidence from the kinds of cases I have already described is consistent with the assumption that the critical lack suffered by those children was in coenesthetic experience. We have some information, from both human and animal studies, about what must be the critical aspects of this modality.

In the 1950s Harry Harlow (1959) attempted to determine experimentally whether "orality" was as important for the making of attachments as psychoanalysts claimed. He defined orality, very narrowly, in terms of the use of the mouth to obtain nutriment. He used macaque monkeys as experimental subjects. This was possible because, from the standpoint of locomotion, these animals are precocial; that is, they are fully mobile from the time of birth and can seek out a nurturing or feeding agency independently. This ability is in striking contrast to the human situation. Human babies must have nurturing and nutrition brought to them. Some degree of coenesthetic experience is, therefore, embedded in those parenting ministrations which are essential if human infants are to survive. Unlike humans, because of their precocial mobility, it is possible for the macaque to separate coenesthetic experience from the feeding situation. Harlow set up what he referred to as a "mother surrogate," a cylinder of wide-meshed carpenters' cloth with a nipple protruding through the meshes. He found that the animals would go to such a "mother" for nutriment. However, if he provided yet another similar cylinder without a nipple, but covered with something soft and furry like terry cloth, the animal would prefer to rest on that. He felt he had demonstrated that orality, as he had defined it, was not all that important.

Subsequent events demonstrated that his definition was much too narrow. The use of the mouth for feeding comes embedded in the whole congeries of coenesthetic experiences. Those of Harlow's experimental animals which grew to chronologic maturity proved to be very strange animals. They could not, for example, relate to other members of their species. The males were never able to copulate successfully. When the females were impregnated, they proved incapable of mothering their offspring. They would literally utterly ignore their existence, even walk on them if they happened to be in their way. John Bowlby is said to have visited Harlow's lab and to have pointed out to him that he had produced "autistic" monkeys. Obviously Harlow's work led to many efforts to clarify what might be the essential ingredient in the nurturing experience which Harlow's animals lacked. One such study, by William Mason (1968), demonstrated that the "Harlow Syndrome" could be averted, if the "mother surrogate" moved unpredictably in three-dimensional space. This not only stimulated the infant through its motion, but also made it necessary that he or she be aware of its presence lest, in its movement, it bang into the infant. Mason's animals were impressively "normal" monkeys when they were seen living in their cages with their mobile surrogate mothers. Later, when they were inserted into a colony of animals which had been reared, like most of their species, with other infants, they proved to be hopelessly incompetent. We will return to this theme of the critical importance of the nature of the environment in which the individual is being reared.

Other studies in even lower animals have defined, even more closely, some of the factors embedded in the parent–infant dyad which are critical for subsequent physiological and, therefore, psychological development. I find the two I will now cite particularly useful because, taken together, they underscore how complex the coenesthetic experience is, and how subtle the critical factors are. In the 1930s, when germ-free animals were first being developed, workers in the field were confronted with a very high mortality rate secondary to megacolon and hydroureter. The problem was ultimately solved by Gustaffson (1948), who observed that periodically during the day, rat mothers spread their pups' hind legs and lick their peronei. He substituted a cotton swab for the mother's tongue. This proved to be equally as effective, and the problems of megacolon and hydroureter were resolved. I'm not sure how many of my psychoanalytic colleagues were aware of Gustaffson. I, personally, found it a gratifying validation of the hypothesis that infantile sexuality was not only a "real" phenomenon, but also critical for survival. Alas, like Harlow, I was, in my enthusiasm, guilty of oversimplification. More recently, Schanberg and Kuhn (1980) have shown that the failure to thrive syndrome in rat pups can be averted by stroking the fur on their backs. He has also shown that this maneuver, one that is automatically and unobtrusively embedded in the caretaking behavior of all mothering rats, results in the elaboration of pituitary growth hormones.

MASSIVE DEPRIVATION WHICH DOES NOT PRECLUDE THE FORMATION OF OBJECT TIES

Marie Mason (1942), who was then Chief of the Speech and Hearing Program at Ohio State University, described a 6-year-old girl who had been born to an unwed aphasic woman. Mother was totally uneducated, illiterate, and was able to communicate with her family only by gestures. From the time the pregnancy was discovered, she, and subsequently the child, were kept in a locked room with drawn shades. Six-and-a-half years later, carrying the child, who could not walk, she made her escape. The little girl was admitted to a children's hospital at the University of Ohio. She spent the first two days in tears.[3] Mason reports that her

---

[3]Neither Mason's report nor her notes, of which I have a copy, make further mention of Isabelle's mother.

overtures were repelled by the "wan-looking, distraught child, whose face bore marks of grief and fear" (p. 296). Isabelle, as Mason called her, had no language. Since she rejected all her efforts to approach her directly, Mason resorted to playing with another girl as Isabelle watched. Ultimately, using this stratagem, she succeeded in making contact with Isabelle. Within a year-and-a-half Isabelle had acquired a vocabulary of between fifteen hundred and two thousand words, could count to a hundred, identify coins, and perform simple arithmetical computations. Mason described her at $8^{1}/_{2}$ as having an excellent sense of humor, as being an inveterate tease, and an imaginative, affectionate, loving youngster. In less than two years, this child had made the transition from a world of silence, fear, and isolation to a reasonable adjustment within the social world of childhood. Mason's report underscores the critical importance of preverbal as well as continuing nonverbal stimulation for the establishment of an awareness of "self" as well as its corollaries—the awareness of and the motivation to interact with other selves. Unlike the children I have described earlier, Isabelle was isolated *with* her mother. While we know nothing beyond what I have stated about the latter, it is apparent that she provided Isabelle with an adequate opportunity to make an attachment to her. The fact that the child could grieve and mourn her mother's absence indicates that she had made an attachment to her mother and preserved an internal representation of her.

A not uncommon clinical problem, which bears much similarity to the story of Isabelle, is that of the congenitally deaf. The plight of people growing up with this affliction also provides us with an excellent illustration of how the preconceptions of the best intentioned caretakers can have devastating consequences for the growing individual. For many decades there was a controversy raging between two schools of thought about how to educate the deaf. The "oralists" believed that deaf individuals should be forced to communicate with speech. The "signers" pointed out that the deaf individual cannot hear speech, and that typically, any speech he or she might produce was barely, if at all, understandable. They argued that by demanding that the deaf use speech, the oralists were shutting them off from the possibility of communicating. The issue hung on the failure of the oralists to distinguish between speech and language. The story of Peter, the congenitally blind child I have already described, is illustrative of the distinction. He could speak very clealy, he had excellent hearing and speech, but he had no language. He was echolalic. The words he pronounced had no meaning for him. He used neither his voice nor any other modality, such as gesture, for the purpose of communicating. Peter's experience, during the period when coenesthetic stimulation is critical, had not been such as to facilitate his ability to differentiate his self from the world around him. Never having established himself as an entity existing separately from those around him, he had no occasion to communicate.

The situation for the congenitally deaf child is radically different. During that same epoch in early infancy when Peter's caretakers were getting no reenforcement from him, the caretakers of congenitally deaf children are continually being rewarded by their bright-eyed, responsive infants. The sign specific stimulus of bright eyes, which appear to fixate on and follow objects, sets in motion parental innate releasing mechanisms which induce age-appropriate parenting behavior. As a consequence the congenitally deaf child, during the early phases of his development, seems quite "normal." Indeed, if there is no external circumstance to lead the parents to suspect that hearing may be impaired, the diagnosis of congenital deafness may not be made until the fourth year, the age when the neural pathways involved in hearing become fully myelinated. Up to then, the deaf child seems so responsive, bright-eyed, and typical of his or her age, that parents are likely to dismiss the failure of speech ("He's too busy to talk"). Those who have read or seen *Children of a Lesser God* know that Sign Language is full and very rich. Metaphor, double entendres, and jokes are as characteristic of the American Sign Language for the Deaf as they are of English or any other language which uses oral speech as its medium of communication. The adaptive and affective problems of the congenitally deaf come later in development. They are related to the problem of communicating in a world in which the oral–aural connection is the prevalent one. By then, the deaf child has differentiated a self from others, and has also, based on gratifying early coenesthetic experience, come to expect communicative interchange with others. At some point, however, as oral language becomes more important, the child will be excluded. Because of the inability to

engage in communications made by voice, the child is often referred to as dumb. This is a most regrettable double entendre.
Peter, and other congenitally blind children, who were not stimulated during the coenesthetic period of their maturation and development, are, indeed intellectually dumb. They cannot
understand, they are unaware, and by any measure of intelligence
they are dumb. Given the opportunity to communicate, the congenitally deaf child shows no evidence of an analogous intellectual deficit.

Groce's (1980) report is particularly impressive in its documentation of the validity of the premises (1) that congenital deafness does not pose a significant interference to those early
processes of attachment and internalization out of which the differentiation of self and the establishment of object relations
emerge; and (2) that given access to an appropriate communications system, the congenitally deaf person (in contrast to the congenitally blind) is able to make adaptations to life which closely
follow the patterns of the normally hearing. Groce studied the
indigenous population of Martha's Vineyard. For roughly 250
years after they settled there in the 1640s, the descendants of the
approximately thirty original families made up the vast majority
of the inhabitants. Under these conditions a recessive gene for
congenital deafness, which apparently was brought with them
from England, became manifest in an extraordinarily high percentage of the islanders. By the latter part of the nineteenth century, the incidence of this affliction on the island was one in 155,
and in one remote village it was one in 25. At the same time, it
was estimated that for the nation as a whole the rate was one in
2730. The Vineyarders saw nothing unusual about this state of
affairs and apparently assumed that all communities had similarly
large deaf populations. Groce learned about the prevalence of
deafness almost incidentally from a passing reference by an elderly islander from whom she was obtaining an oral history. She
was able to obtain the genealogical charts which had been prepared in the 1880s by Alexander Graham Bell, but never published. These confirmed what she was hearing from her
informants. She also learned that the state of being deaf had not
been regarded as a significant disability by the islanders. To the
question, "How were the deaf able to communicate with you

when they could not speak?" one informant replied, "Oh, there was no problem at all. You see, everyone spoke sign language." The deaf, Groce found, were fully participant in all work and play situations. Even at town meetings, "a hearing person would stand at the side of the hall and cue the deaf in sign to let them know what vote was coming up next" (p. 14).

This is not to say that the state of being deaf does not carry its own burdens with it. However, rather than being the result of the absence of internalized representation and expectations, the difficulties follow from the failure of such representations and expectations to be fulfilled. As the congenitally deaf child gets older and communication through the oral–aural medium becomes more important, he or she becomes more isolated. Typically, the parents of the congenitally blind child become "turned off" by his or her failure to respond as visually competent infants do. The parents of the congenitally deaf child are confronted with an analogous but a different problem. Mutual attachments have already been made between them and their children well before the deafness is identified. The child has been engaging in reciprocating relations and has shown every evidence of being intellectually competent. Affective attachments have been established. The problem for the loving parent has become one of fostering adaptation in an individual in whom the process of psychic structure formation has been proceeding but who turns out to be suffering from a specific interfering incapacity, one which has become relevant at a specific point in development. Two other widely known instances of sensory deprivation which occurred, after a period of good-enough parenting, seem to me to be consistent with what I have described. Rather than being secondary to problems inherent in the child, in these cases vicissitudes in the environment resulted in loss of already established sensory functions.

Helen Keller, whose picture I can remember seeing in the newspapers when I was younger, had accomplished the extraordinary feat of graduating from Radcliffe College and being a published author despite the fact that she was both blind and deaf. She lost both her sight and her hearing after a bout of meningitis when she was approximately 19 months old. Up to then she was a healthy, exuberant youngster, a member of a close-knit, loving, and fortunately affluent family. The 1951 edition of the *Encyclopedia Britannica* had this to say about her:

> When she was about six years old, her parents appealed to Dr. Alexander Graham Bell[4] for counsel regarding her education. As a result Miss Anne Mansfield Sullivan (later Mrs. John Macy) came on March 2, 1887 to instruct the child. Miss Sullivan, then 20 years old, formerly blind but partially cured of blindness, was a graduate of the Perkins Institution for the Blind at Boston, Massachusetts. She imparted the gift of language to her pupil. Under Miss Sullivan's constant teaching and with instruction at the Horace Mann School for the Deaf, Boston, and the Wright-Humason Oral School, New York, Miss Keller not only learned to read, write and talk, but became exceptionally proficient in the ordinary educational curriculum. In 1900 she entered Radcliffe college, and graduated cum laude in 1904.
>
> Miss Sullivan, whose ability as a teacher was almost as marvelous as the talent of her pupil, was a devoted companion until her death in 1936. The case of Helen Keller is the most extraordinary ever known in the education of blind deaf-mutes, her acquirements including several languages and her general culture being exceptionally wide. She wrote *The Story of My Life* (1902) and a number of other books. She toured Europe and Japan in 1946 and 1948 on behalf of the handicapped [p. 315].

The story of Ms. Keller, and her teacher Ms. Sullivan, was the subject of a play, *The Miracle Worker*, which was first produced in 1959. It is of particular interest in the present context because of the many similarities between her and Fraiberg's and my patient Peter's background. Both were the children of upper-class Southern families. She from Tuscaloosa, Alabama, and he from New Orleans, Louisiana. Both families had abundant financial resources and were equally willing to spend what was necessary to deal with their child's problem. Ms. Sullivan succeeded with Helen, Mrs. Fraiberg did not with Peter. I suggest that the former's success was made possible by the presence of internalized residua of the 19 months of loving care and connectedness that Ms. Keller had experienced before the meningitis struck her

---

[4]Bell, who invented the telephone and created the Bell telephone system, was married to a deaf woman. He did much to improve the lot and further the education of the deaf.

down. Peter had no such established matrix with which Mrs. Fraiberg could work. By the time I saw him, that is many months before Mrs. Fraiberg was consulted, the critical period had passed.

Kaspar Hauser (von Feuerbach, 1832) was yet another historical figure who had suffered a protracted period of isolation after several years of good-enough parental care. His story, which is quite romantic, bears mentioning here both because it is well documented and is another instance in which remarkable developmental progress was made by an individual who, like Isabelle and Helen Keller, seemed beyond help when he was first seen. Hauser is assumed to have been the legitimate heir to the Duchy of Baden-Baden. During the turbulent times of the late Napoleonic era he was kidnapped and placed in the care of a peasant woman with whom he remained until he was 3.

Subsequently he was incarcerated in a dungeon in which he remained until he was approximately 17. His jailer only approached him from the rear and fed him silently. Insofar as we know, he saw and spoke to no one during his period of incarceration. The following passage, which comes from the report of von Feuerbach (1832), speaks to the effects of such sensory deprivation on the ability of the brain to organize and integrate new experiences, as well as to the powerful residual effects of earlier experience (i.e., Hauser's life experience between birth and age 3) even after nearly two decades of isolation. Feuerbach and Hauser are describing an event which took place shortly after the latter appeared in Nurenberg.

> I directed Kaspar to look out of the window, pointing to the wide and extensive prospect of a beautiful landscape, that presented itself to us in all the glory of summer; and I asked him whether what he saw was not very beautiful. He obeyed, but he instantly drew back, with visible horror, exclaiming, "Ugly, ugly" and then pointing to the white wall of his chamber, he said, "There are not ugly." To my question, "Why was it ugly?" no other reply was made but "Ugly, ugly." And thus nothing remained, for the present, for me to do, but to take care to preserve this circumstance in my memory, and to expect its explanation at the time when Kaspar should be better able to express what he meant to say. That his turning away from the window and pointing at the wall could not be sufficiently accounted for by the painful impression made upon

his optic nerve by the light, appeared to me to be evident. For his countenance at this time did not so much express pain as horror and dismay. Besides he stood at some distance from the window, by the side of it, so that although he could see the prospect pointed at, yet, in looking at it, he could not be exposed to the impression made by the rays of light entering directly through the window. When Kaspar, afterwards, in 1831, spent some weeks with me, at my own house, where I had continual opportunities of observing him accurately, and of completing and correcting the results of former observations, I took an opportunity of conversing with him respecting this occurrence. I asked him whether he remembered my visit to him at the tower; and whether he could particularly recollect the circumstance, that I had asked him how he liked the prospect from his window, and that he had repeatedly exclaimed, "Ugly, ugly" . . . I then asked him, why had he done so? and what had then appeared to him? To which he replied, "Yes, indeed, what I then saw was very ugly. For when I looked at the window it always appeared to me as if a window-shutter had been placed close before my eyes, upon which a wall-painter had spattered the contents of his different brushes, filled with white, blue, green, yellow, and red paint, all mixed together. *Single things, as I now see things, I could not at that time recognize and distinguish from each other.* It was shocking to look at, and besides, it made me feel anxious and uneasy, because it appeared to me as if my window had been closed up with this parti-colored shutter, in order to prevent me from looking out into the open air. That what I then saw were fields, hills, and houses; that many things which at that time appeared to me much larger, were, in fact, much smaller, while many other things that appeared smaller, were, in reality, larger than other things, is a fact of which I was afterwards convinced by the experience gained during my walks; at length I no longer saw anything more of the shutter." To other questions, he replied, that in the beginning he could not distinguish between what was really round or triangular, and what was only painted round or triangular. The men and horses represented on sheets of pictures appeared to him precisely as the men and horses that were carved in wood; the first as round as the latter, or these as flat as those. But he said, that, in the packing and unpacking of his things, he soon felt a difference; and that afterwards it had seldom happened to him to mistake the one for the other [pp. 322–323].

Hauser's ability to acquire usable vision, like his ability to acquire communicative speech, stands in striking contrast to the findings of von Senden (1932). This author searched out and reviewed all the cases of congenital cataracts which had been operated on and reported in the medical literature up to the time he wrote. Because the surgical techniques of the day did not permit early intervention, the children were usually of latency age or older when the "gift of sight" was bestowed upon them. I use quotes because it was most frequently the case that these individuals were never able to integrate visual stimuli. Even though their eyes were optically competent, they could not recognize familiar objects by sight. They would have to resort to other sensory modalities such as touch and sound. To the extent that they could use vision, their ability to do so rarely got beyond the stage Kaspar Hauser was in when he recoiled from the window. Analogous, but in no way as limiting, deficits are seen in the congenitally deaf and hard of hearing. Their speech, to the extent that they can use oral speech, is distinctive. Never having heard the sounds they make, they reproduce them, as it were, by rote. Thus a 40-year-old, very hard-of-hearing lecturer at a major university must take regular speech lessons in order to insure that she will be understood by her students.

Adequate and appropriately timed experience in the coenesthetic, visual, and auditory modes is necessary but not sufficient to insure the establishment of psychic structures. In the next chapter we will consider how these evolve, given an average expectable experience in these modalities.

CHAPTER 4

Psychic Structuralization/ Mental Representation

I have distinguished three stages in this development and have called them:

1. The preobjectal or objectless stage.
2. The stage of the precursor of the object.
3. The stage of the libidinal object proper [Spitz, 1965, p. 16].

Common sense tells us that our psyches are structured. We all know about our consciences as well as, at least something, about the impulses our consciences must work so hard to contain. Each of us who has had adequate and timely experience in the coenesthetic mode also has some sense of his or her personal identity, whether we call it an "I," an "ego," or a "self." Commonsensical enough but, in the late nineteenth century world of medicine, not obviously relevant to the clinical problems with which Freud and others were attempting to grapple. No one, including Freud, thought in terms of psychic structure. In order to clarify how and why the idea of partitioning the mind into a number of separate entities became important, and why it still remains a major topic in psychoanalytic psychology, it will be helpful to make a short historical digression.

A condition called hysteria was a major frustrating problem for the neurologists of the late nineteenth century.[1] DSM-IV does not include this diagnosis (APA, 1994). The various signs and symptoms, which were subsumed under it, are now distributed among a number of entities, such as Dissociative Disorder, Hypochondriasis, and Factitious Disorder. Before DSM-III (APA, 1980), it had been recognized in one guise or another since ancient times, and it was often considered to be a problem which afflicted only females. Indeed, the very name is derived from the Greek word for uterus. The etiology was taken to be related to abnormalities associated with that organ. During the Middle Ages it was not uncommonly believed that hysterical episodes were caused by the womb wandering through the body! Freud brought down much criticism on himself in the early 1890s by reporting the cases of several men, who he claimed were hysterical, to the Vienna Neurological Society (Jones, 1953, pp. 263–264).

In late Victorian times, physicians were known to try to avoid getting involved with hysterical patients much as we, today, are not enthusiastic about taking on seriously borderline individuals. Until the great French neurologist Charcot became interested in it, the whole subject of hysteria was considered to be slightly disreputable. He maintained, however, that it was an important illness and should be studied and treated like any other disease. Because Charcot was the leading neurologist of his day, and he had already identified and demonstrated the neuropathology of a number of diseases (e.g., Amyotrophic Lateral Sclerosis and Multiple Sclerosis), hysteria, as a clinical problem, took on a new respectability. He himself undertook the care of a ward of hysterical women at the Salpétrière Hospital in Paris. His approach was that to be expected of a great clinical neurologist. He observed his patients and carefully described their symptoms. These were dramatic. Many women would fall into trances and experience seizurelike episodes. This presentation came to be known as

---

[1] In the late nineteenth century, there were no psychiatrists or psychologists. There were neurologists who treated what we would regard as the less ill psychiatric patients, and alienists who worked with the more chronically ill, hospitalized individuals. The discipline of psychology, originally taught in philosophy departments, was developed during the 1860s and 1870s as an adjunct to physiology. Sensation and perception were the problems most frequently investigated.

grand hysteria. Charcot also described strange patterns of muscular paralysis as well as areas of anesthesia or hypersensitivity over various parts of their bodies. They were particularly perplexing because the alterations did not follow the already well-established patterns of sensory and motor nerve distribution. Instead, they followed patterns which reflected the patient's functional experience with the body part in question. A loss of sensation in the hand, for example, would be glovelike rather than follow the distribution of the radial, median, or ulnar nerves. One could say they follow a pattern consistent with the way the patient imagined the hand to function—a mental representation based on the way he or she used it. Charcot believed that ultimately specific changes would be found in the nervous systems of hysterics. They would be analogous to those he had described in many other neurologic diseases and would have similar explanatory value. For him, hysteria was a disease which afflicted its victims in precisely the way other illnesses affected their victims. He took it for granted that in due course it would be shown to be caused by some external agent acting on the nervous system (Jones, 1953, pp. 263–264; Sulloway, 1979, pp. 61–65).

Early in his career Freud won a fellowship which enabled him to spend six months working with Charcot, and he later translated a volume of Charcot's lectures into German. He also visited the French clinician and well-known hypnotist Liebault, and was greatly influenced by him. While he was with Liebault, Freud witnessed hypnotic trances and, perhaps more importantly, posthypnotic suggestions. Liebault would give a hypnotized person the command to do something inappropriate (like putting a chair on a table) when he or she woke up. The subject was also directed not to remember having received the command. When aroused, he or she would feel impelled to do as directed. When the behavior was challenged, he or she would say "I just felt like doing it."

Upon his return to Vienna and the practice of neurology, Freud continued to view the psychological disturbances for which he was consulted through the lens of his experience with these men. He felt that the etiologic explanation for the psychopathology he was seeing lay in past traumatic experiences of which the patient was unaware. He assumed that, just as Liebault's patients were responding to posthypnotic suggestions of which they had no conscious awareness, so could his patients' symptoms be caused by forgotten or repressed trauma in their pasts. He was supported in this conviction by his elder colleague Joseph Breuer, who described to him the case of a young woman, Anna O. Like Charcot's patients, she had many bizarre symptoms—atypical seizures, paralyses of muscle groups, inability, for an extended period of time, to talk in her native German, and a multitude of others. Breuer found that he could, at least temporarily, alleviate her symptoms with hypnosis. If, under hypnosis, she could recall and relive the emotional circumstances under which a given symptom began, it would disappear. It appeared that the task of the therapist was to bring traumatic events back into consciousness, help the patient relive them, and thus achieve a mental and emotional catharsis. Breuer and Freud's earliest technical efforts were, indeed, referred to as the cathartic method (Breuer and Freud, 1893–1895).

Implicit in this approach is, of course, the first approximation of a theory of psychic structure. If something could be in an individual's mind, influence his or her behavior, and still remain outside of awareness, then obviously there must be a part of the mind which is unconscious. Later Freud differentiated between unconscious content which was entirely inaccessible to the patient,[2] and preconscious content. The latter was simply out of awareness at a particular moment. The former content, however, required an active repressing agent. To this agent he gave the name *censor*. Its job was to keep repressed material repressed, that is, out of consciousness. There were then two components necessary for repression to occur. The first was a "line in the mental sand" which, in effect said, "thou shalt not pass" to unwelcome memories. The second was the censor which, having a discretionary or judgmental function, could "decide" whether a given unconscious content should be allowed to become conscious. The hypothesis of the censor gave rise to a new problem. If it were to be effective, it had to know all about what was unconscious and why it had been banished from consciousness. At the

---

[2] I say patient because at this time Freud viewed what he was observing in his practice as manifestations of pathology. The idea that unconscious processes characterize all of us evolved out of these observations.

same time, if it knew all this and had the power and responsibility to judge what might be allowed into consciousness, it was difficult to conceive how it could itself be unconscious. We will return to this problem and Freud's solution of it. For the moment it suffices for us to recognize that this model, dubbed the *topographic model*, constituted Freud's first effort to conceptualize how the psyche might be organized. It consisted of several identifiable interacting elements. Some, such as the "regions" conscious, preconscious, and unconscious, could be visualized as layered one upon the next, hence the name topographic. Others, like repression and the censor, were, by the nature of their functions, much more dynamic. Their operation assumed some sort of work, the expenditure of kinetic energy.

The topographic model seemed, at first, to work well. Repressed memories were recovered and patients achieved at least temporary relief. It also fit well with the approach of medicine not only back then, but even today. We still like to believe, as did Charcot, that if we can once identify a pathological process we have a handle on treating it and curing the patient. Indeed, for some people, and for some forms of dysfunction, this approach is certainly optimal. The patient can be, and often is, viewed as the carrier of an illness rather than as an element in the problem. One could characterize the physician–patient relation in this situation as experience distant. The physician can treat a disease while remaining at a remove from all other aspects of the patient. It doesn't much matter, for example, who has pneumococcal pneumonia. Properly selected antibiotics will cure the illness whoever the sick person may be. In the middle 1890s Freud's approach to the neuroses was much along this line. He felt that the conditions he was seeing could be traced back to a variety of specific traumatic events. Almost invariably, in his experience, these traumas related to long forgotten or repressed sexual experiences. Once these were identified and the affect bound up in maintaining their repression was released by catharsis, the patient would be cured of the affliction. At some point, however, Freud had an epiphany. No doubt this had something to do with the therapeutic failures we assume he must have been experiencing. In any event, he seems to have come to the conclusion that if all

the lurid accounts of sexual abuse and exploitation he was eliciting were historically accurate, Sodom and Gommorah combined
could not have held a candle to Vienna. In many instances, he
became convinced that the childhood sexual traumas being reported to him were the products of his patients' imaginations.

Contrary to some people's allegations, this did not lead
Freud to doubt that the sexual abuse and exploitation of children
takes place. It did, however, lead him to the conclusion that the
fact that a patient "remembered" such experiences, did not always mean that the memory was historically accurate. Memories
of traumatic events, he seems to have concluded, could indeed
be historically accurate; however, they could also be partially accurate, distorted, or entirely false. One could not assume that the
retrospective accounts of adolescents and adults reliably reflected
the actualities of their early experience. Indeed, as we will see
later, it is virtually impossible to recall an event without one's
recollection being tainted both by one's emotional and cognitive
state at the time of the experience, and by subsequent events
which may color one's memory. For Freud, the possibility that
past history could be worked over and modified, that is, the possibility of retrospective fantasy and falsification, implied a motivational force operating from within the individual. In effect he was
led to ask why someone would concoct such stories. At the very
least, he had to conclude that in addition to reactive forces such
as those which could explain a response to trauma, one had to
reckon with the operation of proactive forces. He had to take
into account the possible role of sources of motivation, such as
wishes and fantasies, which arose entirely from within the individual. He now postulated that these, together with infantile trauma,
the vicissitudes of early life, and contemporaneous external
events, determined his patients' clinical presentations.

Considerations such as these contributed to the continuing
modification and evolution of Freud's way of conceptualizing the
mind. The anomalous position of the censor between the unconscious and conscious (or preconscious), together with the evidence of many unconscious ideas and intentions which had no
manifest connection with traumatic experience, led him to introduce the structural model. According to this model, the structures
of the mind are delineated along functional lines, into ego, id,

and superego. These are the names which have been given to the structures by English translators who preferred Latin to the vernacular used by Freud. He himself used the German equivalents. The structures would seem a lot less arcane and mysterious if we were talking about the I, the it, and the over-I. While the terms *conscious, preconscious,* and *unconscious* continue to be as important as they ever were as characterizations of the current status of particular mental contents, they are no longer reified as regions of the mind.

According to the structural model the wellsprings of all psychological activity lies in the id. It is from the id that all the energy, all the motivation, and, therefore, all goal-directed behavior ultimately derives. The two other structures are often thought of as having differentiated out of the primordial id. The ego evolves in order to regulate the relation between the impulses of the id and the exigencies of the world "out there." That is, the individual is not likely to survive very long if his or her behavior doesn't take into account the possibility of adverse consequences. Freud, in his early efforts to picture the relation of id and ego, used the metaphor of a horse and rider. He pointed out that a relatively weak rider has the capability of channeling the energies of a relatively powerful horse. The ego has an analogous ability to modulate id impulses so that their overt manifestations are compatible with the exigencies of external reality. Freud also recognized yet another "reality" which we designate in English the superego. The superego includes moral and ethical constraints which most people impose upon themselves, even in the absence of the imperatives of external reality. It is also the site of the ego ideal, those moral and ethical ideals which we strive to achieve in our lives. It is evident that the superego reflects the norms of the familial and cultural ambience in which the individual grew up. This model of the mind has considerable organizing power. One can often conceptualize the clinical problems one sees, in terms of the interaction of id, ego, superego, and the exigencies imposed by the external world into which the individual is attempting to adapt. Problems arise, however, when one asks, "Where did these structures come from?" Because of this question I say "organizing power" rather than "explanatory power."

The performed functions are unequivocal, the structures which are said to perform them are entirely hypothetical.

For Freud, the generators of the forces within the id were the instincts. He regarded them as the demand made upon the mind by virtue of its connection with the body.[3] They had the four defining characteristics: source, aim, object, and energy. The source lay in the physiology of the individual. For example, gonadal hormones were the source of the sexual instinct. He proposed that the aim was to relieve the tension produced by the pressure of the feelings induced by the source. Unfortunately, according to his account, this could never be fully accomplished because there is no escape from visceral (as opposed to external, somatic) stimulation. The object was that upon which, or in conjunction with which, the attempts to relieve the exigency of the aim was made. Finally, all this obviously required an expenditure of energy. He distinguished between the unavoidable imperatives of instinctual demands, which came from within the body, and the greater flexibility of possible responses to external stimuli. The former are experienced as needs; one has no option but to respond to them. He also postulated that the "task" of the nervous system is to rid itself of stimulation so as to achieve a state of total quiescence. This is rendered impossible because there is no escaping from the instincts. Human psychological development, he felt, is in effect the result of the nervous system's effort to fulfill the impossible task imposed on it by the unremitting and inescapable pressure of the instincts.

There are several aspects of this picture which require critical assessment. In my opinion it has led to conceptual dead ends which for many years arrested the progress of psychoanalytic thinking, especially in such areas as the emergence of psychic structures[4] and the formation of mental representations. While the worst of that "paralysis" may be over, it has not gone away.

---

[3]In *Instincts and Their Vicissitudes* (1915) Freud wrote, "an 'instinct' appears to us as a concept on the frontier between the mental and the somatic, as the psychical representative of the stimuli originating within the organism and reaching the mind, as a measure made upon the mind for work in consequence of its connection with the body" (pp. 121–122).

[4]I am referring here to the idiosyncratic fixed patterns of thinking, feeling, and acting which characterize all people.

The implicit significance of the terms Freud used and, paradoxically, their continued usefulness in formulating many adult patients' here-and-now problems, affects our thinking about how psychic structures get formed and how mental representations are created. There is also a tendency to apply such terms as *ego* and *superego* to infants and toddlers as though those structures were present from the beginning rather than being the result of extended maturational and developmental processes. To the extent that such attributions are made, they also must interfere with how we assess and attempt to treat the problems we see in children.

Freud, like most scientists of his day, believed in teleology. He believed that goals and purposes are implicit in all physiological and psychological activity. In addition, he never made use of the concept of homeostasis—of a dynamic equilibrium between a multitude of forces which, when they are in balance, might give a superficial observer the illusion of stability and quiescence. That is, an observer would not be aware that this superficial appearance of stability is being maintained by a continuing balancing of the underlying forces. For Freud the state of quiescence which the psyche "sought to achieve" would literally be quiescence. From the perspective of the late twentieth century, two aspects of this hypothesis[5] are particularly problematic. In the first place, Freud's assumption that goal and purpose are inherent in biological processes led him to several successive classifications of instincts. Each of these was based on the premise that within the individual there exist inborn a priori motivational forces. These he defined in contrasting pairs. He began with sexual and self-preservative forces, then went on to sexual and aggressive, and finally, to life and death. Second, he assumed that instincts or, as I would prefer to call them, motivational forces, are elements in the original equipment with which the infant comes into the world. Presumably, because the problems with which he was dealing were so frequently related to sexuality, Freud tended to use the word *libido* to designate instinctual energy. He did, however, also talk about aggression as an instinctual force. It will not be necessary for us

---

[5]Freud's conceptualization in this area can be traced to the German physiologist Fechner who had enunciated the "Constancy Principle" a generation before Freud.

to discuss the relation between the two. That he was never entirely satisfied with this formulation is evident from the fact that he changed his classification of instincts several times over the years. The four defining characteristics, the assumption that one is born with instincts, and the teleological point of view, however, remained unchanged.

It is, I think, clear that both the definition and the classifications of instincts were couched in very general terms. From the standpoint of the practicing therapist they were experience distant. That is, one might be very familiar with an aggressive person or a loving person but, short of using drugs which suppress feelings, one cannot separate either quality from the context in which patients present themselves. Neither was it possible to make a judgment of the adaptive value of either loving or aggressivity except in such a context. In addition, because the instincts themselves were always conceived of as occurring in contrasting pairs and were so broadly defined, it was possible to apply them to all the vagaries of human behavior. Any thought, feeling, or action could, albeit with some mental gyrations, be conceptualized as representing some mixture of sex and aggression. In my opinion, from a practical, clinical standpoint the instinct theory has not proved very helpful. Other difficulties followed from Freud's definition. Because it included both an object, and an aim, it implied some intrapsychic representation of the outside world. Objects have to be both significant to the individual, and acceptable within the context in which he or she lives. They must coincide with mental representations which already exist in his or her mind. One had to either assume that neonates were born with some sensibility of the outside, or reassess the value of the structural model.

Like its predecessor, the topographic model, it turned out to have some value in characterizing aspects of what we see, especially in adults and older children. It is less valuable in helping us understand the processes by which mental representations get established. These, it would appear, must have their beginnings before mental structures can be identified. Indeed, the evidence suggests that the more or less cohesive constellations of psychic processes which we might identify as structures result from the ongoing process of making internalizations and their subsequent "metabolism" into mental representations.

The following episode from Itard's (1801) account of Victor, the Wild Boy of Aveyron, is illustrative. Beginning in 1797 Victor was observed periodically, running naked in the woods, by the inhabitants of the village of Lacaune in South Central France. In 1800 he was captured and ultimately placed under the care of J. M. G. Itard, a student of Pinel. Victor was estimated to be about 11 when he was found; inevitably, he ultimately became pubescent. The following episode describes how he experienced,[6] or rather responded to, the gene-determined maturational changes in his body's physiology. These changes occurred despite the fact that he did not have the benefit of the developmental experience we take for granted as part and parcel of the growing up years. Itard tells us that the "somatic evidence" of puberty was unequivocal. Victor's behavior in response to his bodily changes, however, cannot be reconciled with Freud's criteria for instinctual behavior. He became increasingly restless and agitated. Tragically, even when he was given the opportunity to respond to the obvious physiological imperatives by an available, ready, and willing female, he showed no evidence of understanding what to do. He paced around her and touched her,[7] but he was incapable of translating his state of physiological arousal into aim and goal-directed behavior. The somatic source of the instinct was there, as was the evidence of a sufficiency of "energy." Victor, however, lacked mental representations which could provide him with either an intrapsychic aim or a meaningful object representation. Itard comments that concern that he also lacked the potentiality for "superego" function, led him to refrain from instructing Victor with regard to the relevant behavior. As he put it, he could very easily have seen to the education of his young "savage" in the mechanical details of sex. He refrained from doing so because he was "afraid to make known to our savage a need which he would have sought to satisfy as publicly as he did his other wants and which would have led him to acts of revolting indecency."

---

[6]We can know nothing about Victor's ability to have subjective experiences, those which could take the form of "I want" or "I feel" etc.

[7]Presumably he was responding to pheromones, about which Itard could know nothing.

Victor, he points out, remained essentially selfish. He could not think of another person as existing in his own right—what Kohut would refer to many years later as a "separate center of initiative." He was, therefore, incapable of commiserating with other people's sufferings or of being concerned with their feelings and interests. He also had not made the kinds of internalizations which, in the average expectable growing up situation, result in a superego.

Victor's story is, of course, entirely consistent with the accounts we have already reviewed concerning the long-term consequences of very early environmental deprivation. In addition to not having established the precursors of a superego, he had not been exposed to other relevant age-appropriate qualities of experience. Without these precursors, it was not possible for him to establish such mental representations as that of an appropriate object upon which, or in connection with which, he could resolve the physiologically defined aim which followed from his pubescent state.

How and when the processes of internalization, psychic structure formation, and the creation of mental representations get underway is less clear than the fact that they do. We know the brain undergoes maturational and developmental changes but we don't know, with any precision, how these changes get translated into either the cognitive or affective aspects of psychic functioning. We do have some data about timing, however, from a variety of clinical observations which give us some sense of when, in the course of his or her early life, an infant provides evidence of differentiating strange from familiar and evidence of a reaction to object loss. In this regard we have already discussed the smiling response and stranger anxiety. These phenomena indicate that by 7 months, the infant has established a template in his or her brain against which new stimuli in the form of persons can be checked. Its application results in a discriminating response.

The observations of Schaffer and Callender (1959) indicate that by 7 months the infant has developed something more. In a study of infants who were hospitalized during their first year, they found two distinct syndromes related to the infants' ages. One occurred in youngsters who were less than 28 weeks and the other in those of 29 weeks or more. The older youngsters were fretful.

They cried and displayed increased mobility and markedly decreased interest in both their human and nonhuman environment. The younger group, on the other hand, accepted the new environment without protest. When the infants were returned home, members of the younger group would, for periods ranging from twenty to thirty minutes up to no more than four days, display an unusual interest in their environment. They would scan their surroundings as though totally absorbed by them but they would not focus on any particular feature. The preoccupation was so intense that it was impossible for their mothers to distract them with toys or make contact with them. The infants of 29 weeks and older, on the other hand, were markedly overdependent on their mothers. They would refuse to be put down, cried when they were left alone, and showed fear in the presence of strangers, and occasionally, in the presence of such familiar people as fathers and siblings. It is also impressive that the mean period of upset after returning home was less than three days in the younger and more than fifteen in the older group.

How to interpret observations such as these? I will attempt to put the problem in the most general, least adultomorphic terms. That the older infants had behavioral reactions which suggest to adults a feeling of "something missing" seems clear. Equally clear is the evidence that they associated what was missing with the individual who was the principal mothering one. There was behavioral evidence of a feeling of loss, of some kind of internal representation of the mothering one, and an intensification of attachment behavior when reunion occurred. To what extent does all of this indicate that the infant is experiencing the mothering one as a separate person with whom he or she interrelates? If one considers his or her affective behavior alone, the answer would seem obvious. The infant is responding like an individual who has experienced first loss and then restitution. But what can a 7-month-old infant know, in a cognitive sense, about the existence of another person? Does the evidence of an affective reaction in such a situation suffice for us to be able to impute awareness of the existence of one's self and of other selves to the infant? I leave these questions hanging until we have reviewed the contributions of Jean Piaget.

CHAPTER 5

Piaget's Cognitive Development

> More importantly, really revolutionary change in the whole
> field of education and human relations seems to be a direct
> consequence of a deeper understanding of Piaget's theory.
> Who dares to guess how our primary education would change
> if teachers really took seriously Piaget's proposition that knowl-
> edge is an operation that constructs its objects? [Furth, 1969,
> p. 7].

Freud was a physician who dealt with the clinical problems presented to him by "sick" people. Piaget was a zoologist who became interested in the process by which individuals differentiate
themselves from the world around them and acquire knowledge
about it. Freud was concerned with the alleviation of the symptoms with which his patients presented and which he found to
be related to their affective states. Piaget, for reasons we don't
know, deliberately eschewed all consideration of the role of emotion in his studies of epistemology and cognition. Freud obtained
the raw data he used for the constructing of his theory of the
mind from the reminiscences of his patients. Piaget obtained the
data, from which he constructed his theory of the emergence of
intelligence and the acquisition of knowledge, from the direct
observation of infants and children. He also invented ad hoc experiments, on the scene, in order to clarify the significance of

what he was observing at the moment. Many of these experiments have become standardized and are now used in the evaluation of children's functioning. Freud's work sprang from his effort to understand the symptoms with which his patients were presenting. Piaget took his subjects' "wellness" for granted and sought to learn how the ability to "know" came about. Freud was a psychopathologist, a student of mental illnesses, who developed a theory of the mind out of his clinical experiences. Piaget was an epistemologist who studied the processes by which knowing becomes possible. They worked with separate but complementary aspects of mental functioning. One could say that Freud was concerned with what people felt and why they felt it, whereas Piaget was interested in what people knew and how they came to know it. A contemporary understanding of human psychology requires familiarity with the work of both men.

Like all other workers in the field of human development, Piaget differentiates a series of stages or periods through which maturing and developing individuals pass. These are identified by qualitative changes in the intellectual functioning of the growing individual. The following précis of the four main stages Piaget described will be elaborated on later in the chapter.

1. *Sensorimotor.* During this period the infant gradually becomes aware that there is a world of objects which exist independently of his or her direct perception of them. This is finally accomplished when the child is between 18 months and 2 years.
2. *Preoperational.* During this period the child continues to experience both personal relations and natural phenomena as though they exist only as they are relevant to the child (e.g., the sun sets because it is time to go to bed). With gradual modification, that is, increasing awareness of him- or herself as only one among many "centers of initiative," this period extends from roughly 2 to roughly 8 years.
3. *Concrete Operations.* During this period the youngster can think about and operate on specific concrete systems which he or she perceives as having an existence and integrity which is entirely independent of him or her. A boy might, for instance, become curious about and learn how to manipulate an automobile engine or a radio. He would be able to think of either's

functioning without considering his wishes and desires relevant. This period extends from roughly 8 years to the beginning of adolescence.

4. *Formal Operations.* During this period the individual develops the capacity to think abstractly. Rather than requiring a concrete problem, like a malfunctioning engine, to cogitate about, he or she can think about general principles like energy or the nature of religion and morality, etc.

Piaget found that the ages varied at which individuals passed from stage to stage. Variation could be secondary to either innate (constitutional) or environmental factors. He also pointed out that not all people achieved the capacity for formal operations. We can add, on the basis of the observation of environmentally deprived children, that not all people appear even to achieve the capacity for concrete operations. The sequence in which the stages emerge, however, is invariant. Everyone begins his or her cognitive life in the sensorimotor period and all individuals who have good-enough mothering pass through the preoperational phase. Infancy and toddlerhood encompass the whole of the former and a large proportion of the latter. We will focus our further discussion of Piaget on these two stages. Piaget considered what we think of as intellectual functioning as the continuation of the adaptive aspect of all biological functioning. What we refer to when we use the word *intelligence,* he regarded as a more complex elaboration of the processes by which any organism adapts to the world around it. He traces the maturational and developmental processes out of which this complexity derives.

At the outset of the sensorimotor stage the individual possesses only the harbingers of intelligence. He or she responds automatically to stimuli coming from either the outside world or his or her own metabolism. The responses have no psychological significance for the responding neonate. Nonetheless, even at this time the responses are not simple reflexes. As we have already discussed, infants come into the world equipped with "factory installed" patterns of neuromuscular activity. Piaget referred to such functional units (e.g., smiling, grasping, crying) as schemas. These are the fundamental units of the neonate's neuromuscular equipment. Schemas, not reflexes, can be evoked by either internal processes or by events in the environment. Because they look like motivated behaviors which, in later life, have communicative significance, schemas often evoke responses on the part of the human environment which would be appropriate for motivated behaviors. Both when they are invoked in response to stimuli from the environment and when they are initiated from within the infant, the schemas, therefore, lead to secondary consequences. Changes are induced in both the infant's patterns of neuronal connections and in the relation of caretakers to him or her. You slap a newborn infant's buttocks and you evoke a crying schema which, in turn, evokes soothing behavior from the available mothering one. Some physiological change in the infant is manifested by a "smile," and this also evokes a response by the mothering one. In each instance the response of the environment affects the conditions, both within the infant and the environment, which will evoke the schema thereafter. The properties of an evocative stimulus will also lead to an adaptive modification of the original schema. Sucking movements have to change if they are to accommodate to such different objects as nipples, fists, or thumbs. The interactions of schemas with environmental stimuli lead both to modifications of the conditions which will evoke them and to modification of the schemas themselves. In psychodynamic terms we can say that the harbingers of mental representations emerge out of the interaction between the infant and the environment. Piaget would say we are witnessing the operation of the functional invariants, organization and adaptation.

Although, like psychoanalysts, Piaget assumes the infant is, to begin with, unaware of the world around him, he does not use such terms as *primary narcissism* or *infantile omnipotence*. For him, I believe, both would have undesirable metaphorical implications. They reflect our adultomorphic thinking. The term *primary narcissism* clearly suggests that the infant has a capacity for self-love, and therefore has in some sense already differentiated a sense of self. Similarly, the term *infantile omnipotence* could be understood to imply a degree of selfobject differentiation which permits the infant to have some sort of sense of power (i.e., the ability to affect another object). Piaget assumes only that the infant is born with specific gene-determined patterns of coordinated muscular activity and sensory responsivity. A sense of power can only emerge out of the evolving awareness of the results of actions. To the best of my knowledge he did not address directly the relation between the stages of cognitive development and the alterations in the structure of the brain which result from its maturation and development. It may, however, be worthwhile to refer in particular to the illustration from Conel (p. 14) in the course of following the cognitive changes which occur during the first 18 to 24 months of postpartum life.

Neither does Piaget address the question of motivation which plays so large a role in the work both of psychoanalysis and dynamically oriented psychotherapists. Rather than assume that we are born with intrinsic drives, he takes the position that the infant's brain is, to begin with, organized in such a way that the inevitable result of its interacting with the environment is the establishment of cognitive structures, modifications of the intrinsic schemas with which he or she came equipped. This begins a never ending process of modifications or, in Piaget's terminology, adaptations in the infant's mental processes. These will continue throughout life, as surely as the individual and his or her environment continue to interact. On the other hand, as the examples of environmental deprivation indicate, in the absence of age-appropriate input, cognitive structures do not get formed. It should also be noted that Piaget paid little attention to the *idiosyncratic* properties of each individual's structures. Those properties which reflect the unique circumstances under which each individual matures and develops were not of immediate concern to him.

Adaptation, the modification of what we will now refer to increasingly as cognitive structures rather than schemas, involves the two coordinated processes of assimilation and accommodation. One can use the metaphor of the ingestion and metabolism of food to clarify what Piaget has in mind. One takes in (assimilates) nutriment. This involves not only ingestion, but also the modification of the food so that it can be metabolized. As the nutriment is assimilated and metabolized, the organism accommodates to the products of the process; that is, it is modified by the results of the metabolic process. So stated, this is a very active process, one in which the organism modifies the nutriment in order to assimilate it, and the newly metabolized products modify the "host."

Piaget considered adaptation to be the result of the ongoing processes of assimilation and accommodation, which he called functional invariants. They are the processes by which all intellectual and cognitive development proceeds and, as already stated, they continue throughout life. Because the products of new assimilations and accommodations are always added to, as well as modified by what is "already there," complexities of the process obviously increase enormously as the organ of mind matures and develops. For example, the behavioral manifestations of assimilation seem, to begin with, to be mere repetitions of an already performed piece of behavior—a "reproductive" assimilation. With time, as was mentioned earlier, assimilation to the schema or structure becomes "generalized." The sucking process becomes competent to be applied to a great variety of objects. Ultimately, two or more schemas can "reciprocate" or coordinate. The infant, for example, can combine looking at an object with touching it. As the child grows older and the results of earlier adaptations make for more complex structures, these processes become more difficult to follow. Things are simpler in the early years when, to paraphrase Darwin, the mind is still virginal. Piaget carried out the studies we will now review concerning the sensorimotor period on his own three infants. They have been repeated, and validated, countless times since.

THE SENSORIMOTOR PERIOD

The sensorimotor period is further subdivided into six successive stages. Piaget followed the emergence of such intellectual–adaptive functions as the capacity to imitate, the capacity to engage in play, the concept of an object, the concept of space, the concept of causality, and the concept of time through this period. His studies with regard to the emergence of the concept of an object are illustrative both of his methods and the kinds of discoveries he made.

During stage 1 (0–1 month) and 2 (1–4 months) the infant does not appear to conceive of objects other than as sensations.

He or she is incapable of differentiating between the sensory experience and the agent (i.e., the physical stimulus "out there") which created the sensation. The only evidence he could find that the infant of this age was developing awareness was its tendency to continue to look in the direction from which a visual stimulus had come, after it disappeared.

During stage 3 (4–8 months) the infant begins to engage in behaviors which have the effect of making "interesting sights" last. He or she appears to extrapolate from a here-and-now perception in such a way as to maintain or recapture sensorimotor connection with it. The object, however, remains an integral part of the child's actions in maintaining this connection. An observation Piaget made on the behavior of his 7-month-old daughter is illustrative:

> Jacqueline tries to grasp a celluloid duck on top of her quilt. She almost catches it, shakes herself, and the duck slides down beside her. It falls very close to her hand but behind a fold in the sheet. Jacqueline's eyes have followed the movement. She has even followed it with her outstretched hand. But as soon as the duck has disappeared—nothing more! It does not occur to her to search behind the fold of the sheet, which would be very easy to do (she twists it mechanically without searching at all) . . . I then take the duck from its hiding-place and place it near her hand three times. All three times she tries to grasp it, but when she is about to touch it I replace it very obviously under the sheet. Jacqueline immediately withdraws her hand then gives up. The second and third times I make her grasp the duck through the sheet and she shakes it for a brief moment but it does not occur to her to raise the cloth [Piaget, 1954, pp. 36–37].

This represents the outer limits of the infant's cognitive ability, at this stage. It defines his or her ability to be aware of and interact with objects which exist, for us adults, in what we as adults perceive as the world around the baby.

During stage 4 (8–12 months) the baby becomes able to coordinate more and more complex schemas and to apply them to the world around him or her. Unlike Jacqueline at 7 months, the stage 4 child, for instance, begins to search for objects which have slipped out of sight or are deliberately hidden. That the object is

still experienced as tied to the baby's activity is demonstrated by
the fact that he or she will only search for it where it was last
experienced, in relation to his or her activity. Thus, when, at this
age, Piaget took away something with which Jacqueline was playing and hid it under a pillow, she would brush the pillow aside
and retrieve it. If, however, after hiding it under the pillow, he
removed it, as she watched, and hid it again under a diaper, she
still looked for it only under the pillow! For the 8- to-12-month-
old, the object, it would appear, is not yet a separately existing
entity on which he or she acts. It still remains part of the act itself.
Again to quote Piaget:

> At 10 mos. 18 days Jacqueline is sitting on a mattress without any-
> thing to distract her . . . I take her parrot from her hands and hide
> it twice in succession under the mattress on her left, in A. Both
> times Jacqueline looks for the object and grabs it. Then I take it
> from her hands and move it very slowly before her eyes to the
> corresponding place on the right, under the mattress at B. Jacque-
> line watches this movement very attentively, but the moment the
> parrot disappears at B she turns to her left and looks where it was,
> at A.

> During the next four attempts I hide the parrot in B every time
> without first having placed it in A. Every time Jacqueline watches
> me attentively. Nevertheless, each time she immediately tries to
> rediscover the object in A [Piaget, 1954, p. 2].

Jacqueline, it should be emphasized, was not a retarded or
otherwise defective infant. What we are observing is the limited
ability of any 10-month-old to separate an object, as a solid entity
with three-dimensional properties of its own, from the conditions
under which he or she has last had contact with it.

During stage 5 (12–18 months) the child begins to treat objects as though they are "things" in their own right. He or she
begins to search for an object at the place where it was last seen,
rather than where he or she first lost contact with it. However,
even at this time, if the object's "journey to its hiding place" is
not directly observed, the child fails to find it. If one, for example,
moves an object under the child's scrutiny from one, to a second,
and then a third hiding place, at stage 5 he or she will immediately

go to the third place and retrieve the object. If, however, one transports the object in a closed fist and places it behind a screen, the child will search the fist assiduously, but never think to look behind the screen. This maneuver is, of course, a game many of us have played with our infants. It is dependent on the fact that during this period the child has not completely separated the object from the actions involved in his or her direct perception of it. In the form of a game this also becomes part of the positive affective ambience between parent and child, an aspect of early maturation and development to which Piaget paid scant attention.

During stage 6 (18 months and beyond) the child's evolving ability to conceive of objects as separate, independently existing entities, has progressed to the point where even their invisible displacement poses no problem. He or she can leave a toy in one place before going to bed and, not finding it there the next day, look for it and find it elsewhere. He or she has achieved the capacity to conceptualize the permanent independent existence of objects. They now exist, for him or her, on their own and not as extensions of him- or herself. Yet another example from the "Adventures of Jacqueline" is illustrative:

I. At 19 months and 20 days Jacqueline watches me when I put a coin in my hand and then put my hand under a coverlet. I withdraw my hand closed; Jacqueline opens it, then searches under the coverlet until she finds the object. I take the coin back at once, put it in my hand and then slip my closed hand under a cushion on the other side (on her left rather than her right); Jacqueline immediately searches for the object under the cushion. I repeat the experiment by hiding the coin under a jacket; Jacqueline finds it without hesitation.

II. I complicate the test as follows. I place the coin in my hand, then my hand under the cushion. I bring it forth closed and immediately hide it under the coverlet. Finally, I withdraw it and hold it out closed to Jacqueline. Jacqueline then pushes my hand aside without opening it (she guesses there is nothing in it, which is new) she looks under the cushion then under the coverlet where she finds the object [Piaget, 1954, p. 79].

Jacqueline has now begun to give evidence of making use of past experience. In Piaget's terms she is using *representational thought.* Her behavior is guided, not only by her immediate sensory experience, but also by the application to that experience of the memories of past experience. She has now entered into the preoperational phase of her development.

This very brief review of Piaget's studies of the sensorimotor period obviously do not do him justice. The illustrations I have drawn from the development of the concept of objects could be complemented by similar data from all the other areas, such as play or time, which are enumerated above. One consideration, however, which Piaget seems to have ignored and which is of critical importance to us, is the affective climate in which his observations were made. His subjects were his own children. His "experiments" could also be viewed as play. In the course of carrying them out he was also nurturing an affective bond between himself and the child and, thus insuring that in later life the child would have the capacity to enter into other affective bonds, to make attachments, and to experience conflict. He apparently did not think any of these considerations relevant to what he was investigating. From the observations of environmentally deprived children which were discussed earlier, we are inclined to think differently. Gouin-Decarie (1965) addressed this problem, and distinguished between *objects,* which is what Piaget was interested in, and *objectal relations,* a term she devised to designate the kind of affective ties with which we, as therapists, work. Piaget, with whom she corresponded, agreed that such a distinction was necessary.

THE PREOPERATIONAL PERIOD

The preoperational period extends from roughly age 2 to roughly age 9. It encompasses the entire anal, phallic, and oedipal phases of libidinal development. Alternatively, it can also be viewed as encompassing the Eriksonian phases in which the critical adaptations of the child are first along the continuum from autonomy to self-doubt, and then the continuum he refers to as initiative versus shame and guilt. In Mahler, Pine and Bergman's (1975) frame of reference the child will have passed through the symbiotic and either be well into, or have also passed through, the practicing subphase of the process of separation and individuation. In the paragraphs which follow, we will consider what the changes are in the growing individual's cognitive competence during this period. How is he or she experiencing the surrounding world—their parents as people, the relation between objects, matters such as time and space, numbers and arithmetic, relative ages—as he or she passes through these years? We will also consider how the dissonances between the child's and the adult's understanding—the cognitive dissonance—which must inevitably characterize their interaction must also affect the growing individual's affective development. The following anecdotes, not from Piaget, are intended to capture the flavor of the preoperational period.

A three-year-old boy stood at his mother's knee while she was nursing his baby brother. He asked, "When I grow down to be little like Sethie are you going to do that for me too?"

A five-year-old boy was taken with his kindergarten class to the Natural History Museum where he was shown a dinosaur skeleton and told about the fate of the dinosaurs. That night he announced to his parents that he intended to bathe every day from then on. He explained that he didn't want to be ex*stink* like the dinosaurs!

Mrs. Selma Fraiberg (1951) described a 7-year-old boy who came to his appointment in an unusually high state of distress. He told her that he was going to "get" a new baby and, in order for this to happen, his father was going to have his penis cut open because it was as big as a marble. He knew this from a book he showed her at their next meeting. It was a volume which his very concerned parents were using to teach him about the facts of life. In it there was a picture of a single spermatozoon, as it might appear under a microscope. As portrayed in the book, it was certainly as big as a marble.

All these children's use of words was age appropriate. Superficially, they appeared to be conveying the same meaning, when using a given word or sentence as would an adult. However, it is clear from the anecdotes that nothing could be farther from the truth. Not only their use of words, but also their whole experience of themselves vis-à-vis the world was radically different from what seems so patently obvious to grown-up people. It did not occur to the parents of Mrs. Fraiberg's patient, or the teacher of the little boy who worried about becoming "exstink," that the youngsters' understanding of what they were being told, was very different from what had been intended.

There are, according to Piaget, several distinctive characteristics of preoperational thought. While, like Jacqueline at 19 months, the child at this time can make use of the representational residua of past experience, his or her ability to do so is limited by very definite developmentally related constraints.

1. He or she is *egocentric* with respect to the representations used. Thus, the child knows, from past experience that he or she goes to bed when it is dark. The child concludes from this that the sun goes down and it gets dark because it is time for him to go to bed. One somewhat unscrupulous baby-sitter I knew, would draw all the curtains and then say to her preoperational charges, "Look its dark, you have to go to bed." They would dutifully comply.

2. The child *centers* on a particular aspect of his or her immediate experience to the exclusion of all other considerations. The child can understand a contemporary event only from the perspective of his or her own past experience. Thus, when a 3-year-old was confronted with a baby, who was well known to him in one context, but was now in a different place and dressed in a different costume, he assumed he was seeing a different baby.

3. He or she lacks "cognitive *equilibrium*"; that is, the child has no internally consistent stable cognitive organization which can be used to help him or her make sense out of a new experience. The child lives on a moment to moment basis which does not permit relating what is happening now to what has happened only a few moments before.

Although he or she is capable of using representations in specific here-and-now situations, the preoperational child is still oriented toward neuromuscular action and immediate results. In matters pertaining to morality and justice, for example, the preoperational child makes no distinction between the intent of one's action and the result. Piaget would pose the following hypothetical situation to children in the 5-year-old age group:

Johnnie was helping his mother clear the table. He was carrying three dishes to the kitchen when he tripped and fell. All the dishes were broken. Peter was running through the house after his mother told him to stop. He bumped into the table and knocked off a dish which fell down and broke. Who was naughtier? When one is five, the answer is obvious. The person who broke the most dishes is clearly the worse culprit [Piaget, 1932, pp. 120–121].

Phenomena which adults would regard as personal or insubstantial (e.g., dreams, thoughts, moral obligations, etc) are treated by the preoperational child as though they were as substantial as are objects in the environment.

4. Irreversibility, the inability of the preoperational child to reason backward even after having observed directly the process which led to a particular result, is one of the more striking and dramatic characteristics of the preoperational phase. Piaget's well-known demonstration of the child's inability to conceive of volume as a constant is an example of this. The child is confronted with two containers, one tall and slender, and the other shorter and wider. A third container is also filled with water and emptied into the taller cylinder. It is then refilled and emptied into the shorter, wider cylinder. This is all done under the child's direct inspection. Nonetheless, he or she will maintain that the tall slender cylinder has more water in it. If one of the cylinders is emptied, and the water from the other is poured into it, the child insists that the quantity of water has changed. He or she will insist that this is the case, even when the water is poured back and forth. Because the child cannot reverse in his or her mind from the here-and-now conditions to those which existed just a moment before, he or she is bound to judge from the here-and-now appearance of the container. During the preoperational period it appears

to be axiomatic that taller is more and shorter is less. Although the child is operating at a new, qualitatively more developed level, it should be apparent that the difficulties he or she is experiencing are very reminiscent of the problem Jacqueline was having, at a little more than 10 months, when she couldn't follow the multiple displacements of her toy which her father was carrying out as she watched.

His studies of the emergence of the ability to enter into a "social contract," and of the concept of "age" are typical of Piaget's approach to the understanding of the preoperational child. It is important, again, to keep in mind that these studies did not take into account the affective state of the child. What Piaget appears to have established is that there is a consistent pattern in the manner in which the child's ways of thinking about, and of experiencing, the way the world unfolds. To reiterate, he did not concern himself with how the specific manifestations of cognitive development are affected by the idiosyncratic experiences of a given child.

To study the ability to enter into a social contract, Piaget investigated how preoperational boys went about playing marbles. He found that their approach to the game goes through the following four distinct phases.

1. A phase of purely motor and individual character in which the child handles the marbles, at times in a quasi-ritualized way, but does so purely as an individual, without regard for the other "players."
2. A second, still egocentric phase during which the child appears to be imitating the examples of others, but still plays by himself or side by side with playfellows. The concepts of winning and losing, like the concept of mutually agreed upon rules for playing, has not yet become available to him.
3. The third phase involves the possibility of cooperation with other players, and emerges when the child is somewhere between 7 and 8 years old. Because children at this age are concerned with winning, they begin to concern themselves with the problems of consensus and mutual control. However, when children of this age, who are classmates in school and

play together every day, are quesioned individually about the rules, they give very different, often contradictory accounts! An example of third stage thinking follows:

Baun (6¹/₂) begins by making a square and puts down 3 marbles, adding: *"Sometimes you put 4, or 3, or 2.—Or 5?—No, not 5, but sometimes 6 or 8.—*Who begins when you play with the boys?*—Sometimes me, sometimes the other one.*—Isn't there a dodge for knowing who is to begin?*—No.*—Do you know what a coche (starting line) is?*—Rather!"* But the sequel shows that he knows nothing about the *coche* and thinks of this word as designating another game. "And which of us will begin?*—You.*—Why?*—I want to see how you do it."* We play for a while and I ask who has won: *"The one who has hit a mib (marble) well, he has won.—*Well! who has won? *I have, and then you."* I then arrange things so as to take 4 while he takes none. "Who has won?*—I have, and then you."* We begin again. He takes 2, I none. "Who has won?*—I have.*—And I?*—You've lost"* [Piaget, 1932, p. 128].

4. The fourth stage, in which rules are codified, does not begin until the child is between 11 and 12. The rules are now generally acknowledged and are known beyond a given child's immediate ambience. He (marbles are now largely a boy's game) can go from one neighborhood to another and engage in the game with strangers. Because there is such general, mutually shared agreement, a degree of flexibility is also introduced in the way rules are applied. Within the general convention, a given group of youngsters can modify the "condition" under which the game will be played. The following is a summary of Piaget's discussion of the rules with a boy in this age group. Ross at 11 is on the cusp between the third and fourth stages.

Ross (11;1) *"First everyone puts two marbles on the square. You can make the square bigger when there are more playing."* Ross knows the method of the *coche* for knowing who is to begin. He allows both *roulette* and *piquette* (two marble games with different rules). He also allows what is not only contrary to all established usages but also to the sense of the words, a way of playing which he calls *femme-poussette* which consists in carrying one's hand along with the marble as one throws it (push stroke in billiards). Now this is always forbidden, and the very word that Ross has deformed says so—*fan poussette* (pushing forbidden). According to Ross, you play from the place you have reached with the last shot, and when you have won a marble you have the right to another shot straightaway. To change your place you must say *du mien*. *"If a stone gets in our way, you say 'coup-passe' and have another shot. If it slips* (if the marble slips out of your hand) *you say 'lache'* (gone). *If you don't say that, you can't have another turn. It's the rule!"* . . . Finally, Ross knows of a rather peculiar custom . . . *"If you stay in the square you can be hit and then he picks up the marbles* (= If your shooter stays inside the square and is touched by your opponent's shooter, he is entitled to all the marbles in the square). *He* (the opponent) *can have two shots* (to try and hit the shooter in question) *and if he misses the first he can take* (at the second shot) *the shooter from anywhere* (though of course only from the outside of the square) *and make the marbles go out* (= *take them*)." This rule has generally only been described to us by children of the fourth stage, but the rest of Ross's interrogatory is typically third stage [Piaget, 1932, pp. 36–37].

From the standpoint of the psychodynamically oriented psychotherapist, it is noteworthy that Ross (age 11) makes a clear allusion to the female genital—*femme-pousse*. Piaget, however, explains that what he "really" meant was *fan-poussette*, ignoring whatever significance the parapraxis might have had. From the standpoint of his interest in cognition, this apparently seemed to him irrelevant.

To us as adults, the concept of *relative* ages seems very obvious, so much so that it was not until the 1930s that the fact that it is not a given for the preoperational child was noted. The Belgian psychologist Decroly (1970) observed that his daughters, aged 4 and 6, tended to confuse age and height. Investigating further, he posed the following questions to several groups of children under the age of 7: (1) How old were you last year? (2) How old will you be next year? (3) How old were you when you were born? Seventy-five percent of his subjects under age 7 failed to answer the first two questions correctly, and the third question eluded even older children who failed to grasp the relation between age and order of birth. His subjects would give such replies as, "I can't remember how old I was when I was born. It was much too long ago" (Clare, age 4), or "I can't remember . . . Oh yes, I was two months old" (Jacqueline, age 5.6).

Piaget detected in these observations a constraint in the children's thinking analogous to the one he had already demonstrated with regard to their concept of physical time. For the preoperational child, velocity is determined by the "time of arrival." If, for example, you have two toy cars moving from A to B and one (a) takes a direct route, whereas the other (b) takes a circuitous route which is much longer than (a)'s, (a) will be judged to go faster, even though (b) arrived at the destination barely after (a). The fact that (b) had to move two or three times the distance as (a) during the same time period, has no relevance to the preoperational child. With regard to age, Piaget found a similar discontinuity. In his words, "One thing that in particular strikes one directly, namely the static and almost discontinuous character of the child's idea of age. To him, aging is not perpetual and continuous but rather a process of change tending toward certain states: time ceases to flow when these states are attained" (1969, p. 202). Piaget was able to distinguish three stages in the development of the child's conception of age. During the first stage age is independent of the order of birth and age differences are thought to be modified with time as a hetereogeneous flux. During the second stage the child believes that, though age differences are not maintained throughout life, age depends on the order of birth, or alternatively that age differences are maintained but do not depend on the order of births. In the third stage, duration and succession are finally coordinated and their relation is henceforth preserved. Some examples of the child's thinking during the first two stages will clarify. The child's responses to Piaget's interrogatories are presented in italics.

Stage 1:

Rom (4;6) does not know her birthday. She has a small sister called Erica. How old is she? *Don't know.* Is she a baby? *No, she can walk.* Who is the older of you two? *Me.* Why? *Because I'm the bigger one.* Who will be older when she starts to go to school? *Don't know.* When you are grown up will one of you be older than the other? *Yes.* Which one? *Don't know.* Is your mother older than you? *Yes.* Is your granny older than your mother? *No.* Are they the same age? *I think so.* Isn't she older than your mother? *Oh, No.* Does your granny grow older every year? *She stays the same.* And your mother? *She stays the same as well.* And you? *No, I get older.* And your little sister? *Yes* [Piaget, 1969, p. 202].

Pti (4;9) How old are you? *4 and ¹/₂.* Is it a long time since your birthday? *It hasn't been yet, it will be in June.* How old will you be? *8 years.* Come, come! *No, 5 years.* Have you any brothers or sisters? *I have a big brother. He goes to school in Sceron.* [the big school]. Were you born before or after him? *Before.* So who is older? *My brother, because he is bigger.* When he was small, how many years older was he than you? *two years.* And now? *four years.* Can the difference change? *No. . . . Yes. If I eat a lot of soup I shall grow bigger than him.* How can one tell which one is older? *The one who is bigger.* Who is older, your father or grandfather? *They're both the same age.* Why? *Because they are as big as each other.*

Pierre and Paul are two brothers. Pierre was born before Paul. Can you tell who is the elder? *It's Pierre.* But look, Pierre is the smaller of the two. *Then Paul is the older; the older is the one who dies first* [Piaget, 1969, p. 203].

There follows an intermediate stage during which the child will be able to grasp the concept either of succession or of duration. Because the presence of one or the other aberration is so predictable, Piaget refers to them as type 1 and type 2. The following examples are illustrative:

Type 1

Pilk (4;11) (precocious) has an older sister: Are you the same age? *No, because we weren't born at the same time.* Who was born first? *She was.* Will you be the same age as her one day or will the two of you never be the same age? *Soon I shall be bigger than her, because men are bigger than women. Then I shall be older* [Piaget, 1969, p. 207].

Vet (7;10): *I have a little sister, Liliane, and a 9-month-old brother, Florian.* Are you the same age? *No. First of all there's my brother; then my sister, then me, then Mama and then Papa.* Who was born first? *Me, then my sister and then my brother.* When you are old, will Florian still be younger than you? *No, not always.* Does your father grow older every year? *No, he remains the same.* And you? *Me, I keep growing bigger.* When people are grown-up, do they get older? *People grow bigger and then for a long time they remain the same, and then quite suddenly they become old* [Piaget, 1969, p. 206].

Type 2

Dour (7;5) How old are you? *$7^1/_2$.* Have you any brothers or sisters? *No.* Any friends? *Yes, Gerald.* Is he older or younger than you? *A little older, he's 12 years old.* How much older is he than you? *5 years.* Was he born before or after you? *I don't know.* But think about it. Haven't you just told me his age? Was he born before or after you? *He didn't tell me.* But is there no way of finding out whether he was born before or after you? *I could ask him.* But couldn't you tell without asking him? *No.* When Gerald will be a father, will he be older or younger than you? *Older.* By how much? *Five years.* Are you getting old as fast as each other? *Yes.* When you will be an old man, what will he be? *A grandfather.* Will he be the same age as you? *No, I'll be five years less.* And when you are very old, will there still be the same difference? *Yes, always* ... [Piaget, 1969, p. 209].

The type 1 children grasp the relation between age and birth order at the moment when they are being interrogated, but they cannot comprehend that this relation is forever. Conversely, the type 2 child grasps the notion that age differences are forever, but cannot comprehend that they are a consequence of the time of birth. It is only in the third stage that these two reciprocal aspects of age, and their obvious correlation in the cognitive world of adults, are brought together.

For us, as therapists, whether of children or of adults, it seems clear that an appreciation of the difference between the child's cognitive state and that of the adult is critical. When we observe and listen to a child we must keep in mind that the words we share may have very little in common, other than their sound, for youngster and adult. When we work with adults, we must keep in mind that the childhood experiences which they regard as critical, may be very different from what an adult witness to the event may remember. An illustration for which I thank Dr. Melanie Illich (personal communication): A man in his late thirties remembers, as a toddler, having thrown a dish of cereal at his grandmother. This led her to stalk out of the house, never to

return. After he reported this event to Dr. Illich, he was reminisc-
ing about it with his mother. She responded by saying, "Oh no,
that's not what happened at all. I (mother) got into an argument
with her and the cereal got spilt. She got up and left the table
and the house. You were only an observer." Such false memories
are rooted in both the cognitive and affective distortions which
go with the preoperational period. We have always given consideration to the affective aspect. Now we must also keep in mind the
youngster's cognitive limitations.

CHAPTER 6

Gender Identity Formation

Apr. 9, 1935

Dear Mrs. . . .

I gather from your letter that your son is a homosexual. I am most impressed by the fact that you do not mention this term yourself in your information about him. May I question you, why you avoid it? Homosexuality is assuredly no advantage, but it is nothing to be ashamed of, no vice, no degradation, it cannot be classified as an illness; we consider it to be a variation of the sexual function produced by a certain arrest of sexual development. Many highly respectable men of ancient and modern times have been homosexuals, several of the greatest men among them (Plato, Michelangelo, Leonardo da Vinci, etc). It is a great injustice to persecute homosexuality as a crime, and cruelty too. If you don't believe me, read the books of Havelock Ellis.

By asking me if I can help, you mean, I suppose, if I can abolish homosexuality and make normal heterosexuality take its place. The answer is, in a general way, we cannot promise to achieve it. In a certain number of cases we succeed in developing the blighted germs of heterosexual tendencies which are present in every homosexual, in the majority of cases it is no more possible. The result of treatment cannot be predicted.

What analysis can do for your son runs in a different line. If he is unhappy, neurotic, torn by conflicts, inhibited in his social life, analysis may bring him harmony, peace of mind, full efficiency, whether he remains a homosexual or gets changed . . . Freud [Jones, 1957, pp. 195–196].

For fairly obvious reasons, which have to do with the affective baggage we all carry into a discussion of sexuality, this is probably the most difficult aspect of maturation and development to present and discuss. In this chapter we will talk about gender (which is most frequently, but not necessarily, a straightforward matter to be determined by physical inspection); core gender (which we tend to assume is in one-to-one relation to gender, but isn't); and sexual object choice (which does not have a direct and uncomplicated relation to either). We will review (1) what Freud and other early psychoanalysts had to say about these matters; (2) what has been learned about gender determination from embryological studies in animals and the natural experiments which result from aberrations in the prenatal experience of humans; and (3) the findings and conclusions of workers like Stoller (1968, 1988) and Money (1988). They studied individuals for whom, on anatomic, endocrinologic, or psychosocial grounds, the relations between gender, assigned gender, and gender identity were outside the range of the average and expectable. We will also review some anthropological observations which describe a very different process of gender identity formation from those with which we are familiar.

I begin with a review of what has been in the past and continues, for many people, to be the most widely used theory of the development of masculinity and femininity. In reading what follows, it is important to keep in mind that these theories were born out of clinical experience with adults. Inferences were drawn and generalizations were made on the basis of this material. These latter were then applied retrospectively to infants and children. Second, as the above quoted letter by Freud so eloquently reflects, the theories were developed during a period in Western European history when "deviant" forms of sexual behavior were, to put it mildly, frowned upon. Often they were met with active persecution. At the behest of a "court of honor," Tchaikovsky, for example, is said to have literally been forced to commit suicide. The court had been convened to consider the implications of his alleged relation with a male member of the Russian imperial family. The pressures were explicit and direct. This is what one did under such circumstances (Arnold, 1983, p. 1808). A significant consequence of the social stigma was the limiting effect it had on the kinds of people with homoerotic propensities who were likely to consult therapists. In the 1950s one could, on the basis of what one heard from homoerotic patients, think about homosexuality as an entity which included, in addition to the sexual object choice, other fairly predictable psychological characteristics. As a therapist, one simply didn't see many people whom one couldn't, given some allowance for individual differences, fit into the stereotype. I did not know then, as I do now, about individuals living in a many decades long monogamous homosexual relation. I had not yet learned that it was possible for homoerotic individuals to have affective and relationship problems indistinguishable from those experienced by "straight" people.

Then the closet doors opened! We were confronted with having to recognize that it was frequently the symptoms and character traits, which we had regarded as incidental to homosexuality, that brought people to therapy. Most frequently our, or at least my, patients didn't seem to be interested in changing their sexual orientation. We also had to recognize that among those who chose same-sexed love objects, were many solid, successful, contributing citizens. They were no more conflicted about their sexual lives than were their heterosexual counterparts. More often than not, their adaptive problems had to do with the need to conceal, the having to live a lie, rather than the fact that they preferred a homoerotic love object.

The late Robert Stoller, on whose work this chapter depends heavily, describes the circumstances under which he came to question what was then, and for some people still is, the prevailing psychoanalytic view of homosexuality. He was asked by a colleague to evaluate a "transsexual woman" (biological female who considered herself a man). What happened next is best put in his words. "Shortly before the appointment hour, I was approaching stupor at a committee meeting in a conference room with a glass wall that allowed us to see people pass. A man walked by; I scarcely noticed him. A moment later a secretary announced my 11 o'clock patient. And to my astonishment the patient was not what I expected—a woman who acted masculine and, in the process, was a bit too much, grimly and pathetically, discarding her femininity. Instead it was a man [the very one he had seen walk by], an unremarkable, natural appearing—an ordinary man" (Stoller, 1988, p. 4). An eight-year follow-up, until the patient's death, did not change that impression. Stoller later learned that years before he had had a mastectomy and panhysterectomy and was taking male hormones. The "maleness" his interviewee manifested had been present from earliest childhood, was in no way dramatic or overstated, and was taken for granted in the social circles in which he moved. What perplexed Stoller most—and apparently inspired his lifelong interest in problems of gender—was the absence of evidence of intrapsychic conflict. This, according to the conventional psychoanalytic theory of the time, was not possible. The summary of the then conventional theory which follows is adapted from Stoller (1988).

At least among psychoanalysts, until well into the twentieth century, the most widely prevalent and the conventional assumption was that maleness and masculinity are the primary and the more natural states. It was held that both males and females consider femininity less valuable. However, it was also understood that neither maleness nor femaleness is ever unambiguous. Each gender is invaded by characteristics of the other. This innate "bisexuality," which Freud had recognized and described many years before, was generally acknowledged, and it was assumed that it had significant implications for later development. Bisexuality notwithstanding, in the net boys come off better than girls. Their genitals are visible and more readily available for, among other things, erotic experience. While possession of the genital is not without its dangers, in that it is there to be lost, its presence gives the male a considerable advantage over the female. She starts out deprived.[1] Another, presumably advantageous, circumstance for the boy is that, because his first love relation is with his mother, he starts out heterosexual. In Stoller's words, "As was true with his genitals, it is only with a threat, not with primary absence, that

---

[1]The following vignette from my own practice is illustrative of the kind of data that supported this view: A young woman arrived at her session in a rage. She had come home to find her husband masturbating. She was angered, not about what he was doing, but because seeing him masturbating reminded her of the advantages of being a man, and her inherent inferiority as a woman. I said something about social conventions to which she replied with vehemence, "Fuck the conventions, its the goddam prick I am talking about."

he must struggle. He is endowed with a biologically guaranteed, postnatally conflictless core gender identity'' (p. 14).

Despite these initial advantages, in time the little boy will be more or less threatened. Ironically enough, the threats and dangers will reflect the fact that he is masculine and heterosexual. These highly desirable facts of his biology have the perilous consequence that he has sexual desires for his mother. In this regard, his father poses a considerable problem. The more he desires his mother, the more his father interposes himself, threatening him with castration, of denying him those very parts—his genitals—that are central to the fulfillment of his interests and his wishes. Freud apparently discovered this adaptive dilemma, one which he felt confronts all boys, in himself. This came about during the self-analysis he conducted after his father's death. He named the dilemma the Oedipus complex, after the mythological Greek tragic hero who unwittingly murdered his father and, without knowing who she was, married his mother.

Castration anxiety is exacerbated when the sight of penisless female bodies makes the possibility of loss all too real. This "vision" blocks what would otherwise be an uneventful progress to masculinity and heterosexuality. In the face of this terrifying reality,'' the boy must exert extreme caution as he works his way through the oedipal relation. Good-enough parents will help him in this effort in two ways. First he is helped to displace his desire for his mother onto other females. As Freud saw it, to accomplish this displacement the little boy had to defer sexual gratification. Hence the occurrence of a latency period in middle childhood, a period in which the boy seems to have no sexual interest.[2] Second, his father will add to his role as a rival, that of a model. He becomes someone with whom the boy can identify and whom he can emulate in his strivings to assume the role of a man. If the castration threat is too severe, perversions or neuroses result. Under "average expectable" conditions, however, the outcome is

---

[2]The following episode is illustrative. A colleague conducted a sex education class with a group of fifth graders. He reported they had no difficulty understanding his description of the various phases of cell division. However, the concept of coitus, of a cylinder and a piston, was beyond them. Finally one boy said, "Do you mean a guy has to do that to make a baby?" To which the answer was "yes." This led to a pause and the questioner went on to say, "But J's sister is going to have a baby, and she isn't married." The teacher commented that such things happen. To this the 11-year-old expostulated, "But why would a guy want to do that if he didn't have to?!"

"genital primacy," of which heterosexuality and masculinity are essential ingredients.

As Freud saw it, the little girl is in trouble from the beginning. Her genitals are inferior and she begins with a homosexual object choice. In contrast to the little boy, whose problem is to preserve his masculinity against threats from the outside world, the little girl must struggle to achieve femininity. Being deprived of a penis, she is filled with envy (cf. the earlier footnote). If the envy is too great, she will attempt to get a penis either in fantasy, or by developing masculine qualities which will substitute for a penis. There are other possibilities. She might accept defeat and become fixed in a lifelong state of passive masochistic hopelessness. Alternatively she might come to regard her clitoris as a phallus, however inadequate, focus her genital erotism on it, deny the feminine reproductiveness of her vagina and uterus, and be left with a strong masculine tinge.

Her ability to overcome her penis envy and give up regarding her clitoris as a substitute, will determine whether she can "turn towards femininity." If she is successful, she can look to her father as a new love object. She can now turn to heterosexuality and the wish to have a baby. She can now or, better said, does now enter into an oedipal relation, one in which she is competing for her father with her mother. Freud felt that girls very rarely achieve this (i.e., give up their maternal [homosexual] attachment and turn to their fathers and heterosexuality). In contrast to boys, who almost always do, girls, according to him, relatively rarely engage in oedipal conflict. Girls must, nonetheless, forsake their fathers (by postponing genital maturity) and achieve femininity by identifying with their mothers. Femininity, for Freud, is a secondary defensive state which is acquired relatively late in development. It is more the product of renunciation of hope than the anticipation of pleasurable experiences.

This, in brief, is a summary of Freud's, and with some variations, most psychoanalysts' view of sexual development when, sometime in the early 1950s, Stoller saw that man through the window. The theory offers an explanatory context for many of the phenomena we do, in fact, see and deal with. Penis envy, castration anxiety, and a dropping off of overt interest in sexuality in the prepubescent boy do, indeed, happen. No one today questions that ambivalence characterizes parent–child relations. Neither is one likely to be taken aback by a discussion of relations with opposite sexed parents such as has been outlined here. Similarly, rivalry with the parent of the same sex, as an important aspect of the parent–child relations, is taken for granted. These phenomena were certainly recognized before Freud. However, it is the case that they were never taken seriously as relevant to problems of psychopathology. His was the first effort to provide an explanatory context not only for what he learned directly from his patients' declarative statements but also for what he was able to deduce from their free associations. To reiterate, this was a theory based on clinical observation, a post hoc theory. With hindsight, bolstered by a host of new information about early development and what goes into the establishment, in each individual, of a "core gender," we can now see many of its inadequacies.

In the first place, it assumes that the determination of sexual choice must be born out of conflict. There is no place in this theory for the possibility that one might turn out to be homoerotic on the basis of nonconflictual experience, that the conflict such as individual experiences could be between what he or she regards as personally "natural" and the strictures of society. In addition, without specifying an age, it assumes a concern with gender in the very small person that may or may not exist. Third, it assumes the universality of a familial situation during growing up which permits the specific type of complex relations between parents and children that Freud postulated. It also leaves out of account how gene-derived anomalies, aberrant influences such as prenatal exposure to drugs, and idiosyncratic environmental influences might (1) affect the determination of the anatomy of the genitals; or (2) result in such paradoxes as the occurrence of the external genitalia of one sex in an individual with the gonads of the other; and (3) how the infant's early environment might affect the process of establishing his or her core gender identity. The notion that such considerations might be of relevance would have seemed far fetched as recently as forty years ago. Equally far fetched was the now generally accepted fact of mammalian biology that femininity, not masculinity, is primary.

THE SEXUAL DIFFERENTIATION OF THE BRAIN

"Ontogenetically the brain is female and, regardless of genetic sex, would remain so if not exposed to gonadal hormones at a critical stage in its development" (Gorski, 1978, p. 155). According to Gorski, the direct expression of the XX or of the XY chromosomal patterns stops at the level of the gonad. The subsequent development of the brain along sexually dimorphic lines is dependent on the influence of gonadal hormones on the brain. Unless it is exposed to gonadal hormones during a critical period, it remains female regardless of genetic sex. It would, of course, have been impossible to establish such facts by the study of humans. Gorski's studies were carried out in rats. From the investigator's standpoint, they have the convenient gestational characteristic that the differentiation of their reproductive systems occurs before birth, that of their brains after birth. One can, therefore, modulate the brain without directly affecting the genitalia. Under such circumstances any change in genital function which might occur will be secondary to what has happened in the brain. To reiterate, it would be impossible to carry out similar studies in humans. However, the observations of Stoller (1968, 1988) and Money (1988) certainly become more comprehensible against the background of the material I will now review. According to Gorski, there is a critical period[3] (probably in the perinatal period) during which gonadal hormones can determine whether the brain will take on feminine or masculine characteristics (sexual dimorphism). He has shown, moreover, that there are specific histologic changes in a hypothalamic nucleus (called INAH3) which consistently differentiate males from females. Once brain gender determination has been made, it is the brain, not the gonads, which determine gender specific behavior. Estrus, for example, is dependent on the presence of hypothalamic centers in the female which produce a gonadotrophic releasing factor. This, in turn, activates the pituitary which then goes on to produce gonadotrophic hormone. Once the critical period has

---

[3]This is entirely analogous to the critical periods we have already discussed in relation to psychological development.

passed, it appears the brain maintains the gender characteristics it acquired during that period.

These sexually dimorphic characteristics, moreover, are not limited to areas which have a direct relation to the brain's role in regulating reproductive function. Benes, Turtle, Khan, and Farol (1994) reviewed the myelin deposition studies described in the first chapter (see also Figure 1.1). To Yakovlev and LeCours' (1967) original group they added enough new cases to bring their total to 164 psychiatrically normal individuals from birth to 76 years. They found that female subjects showed a significantly greater degree of myelin staining than did male subjects during the interval of ages 6 to 29 years. After 29 years there were no differences in the sizes of the areas of myelinization. The increased staining is particularly noticeable in the subicular area, which is an important projection pathway for the limbic[4] system of the brain. The authors comment, "it is theoretically possible that this finding could be related, perhaps indirectly, to the greater degree of maturity noted in young female subjects. It is pertinent in the discussion to note that boys have a much higher incidence than girls of various types of childhood psychopathology, including Tourette's syndrome, attention deficit disorder, encopresis and enuresis, autism and night terrors" (p. 483). They wonder whether the delays in brain ontogeny in boys as compared to girls may have something to do with the boys' greater vulnerability to these forms of psychopathology.

NATURE-NURTURE

The fact of sexual dimorphism, coupled with the circumscribed role played by the endocrine system in regulating gender specific functions, has to be taken into account when one is confronted with an individual who presents with sexually "deviant" behavior. I put "deviant" in quotes because there does not seem to be a generally accepted consensus as to what expressions of sexuality

---

[4]The limbic system is an interconnected network of neural structures deep within the brain. Functioning as a "system," it is believed to regulate both the experiencing and expression of emotion.

are to be defined as deviant.[5] A priori, there is no way to be certain what aspects of an individual's sexual practices are (1) the result of specific gene-determined characteristics of the brain; (2) the result of particular qualities of experience during a critical period of early development; or (3) a clinical manifestation of identity and relationship disturbances in later life, after the brain's gender has been established. Some examples will help to clarify. Money has described, and illustrated, a gonadal male (46XY) who, because of androgen insensitivity, developed perfectly normal, even voluptuous secondary female sexual characteristics (Figure 6.1). "Her" true gender was only discovered when, as an adolescent, she failed to menstruate. So far as she was concerned she was, and is, a female. She lives the life of a female who, regrettably, lacks pubic hair, is sterile, and must adopt children. While unusual, this case is certainly not unique, nor is its converse, a genetic female (46XX) who because of analogous, but opposite, difficulties develops a fully masculinized body, albeit with an empty scrotum. In all such instances the individual assumes and acts the role dictated by his or her secondary sexual characteristics. The "she male" (46XX) gives every evidence of a masculinized brain. They are regarded by themselves and those around them as average expectable members of their apparent gender. In addition to these instances, in which there is a total discrepancy between manifest gender and gonadal gender, there are many more occasions in which the genitalia are incomplete, and even ambiguous. Money refers to these individuals as intersexed. It becomes the function of the pediatric surgeon, in effect, to assign gender to such individuals. Once the cosmetic surgery is done and the assignment is made, the individual grows up as a member of that gender.

All of this, on the face of it, appears to be a powerful argument for the preeminence of nurture in the determination of gender identity. Clearly, how one feels about one's gender is not directly related either to one's chromosomal pattern or to the actual structure of the gonads. Yet there is contradictory evidence.

---

[5]The question has been raised whether pedophilia is not deviant. According to our culture it certainly is. However, according to the norms of at least two ancient cultures (Greek and Roman) we admire greatly, it was not.

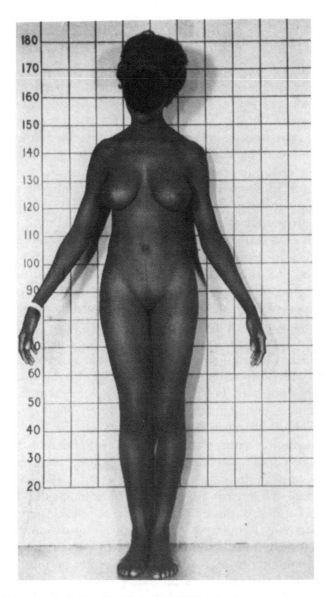

Figure 6.1. An individual with male (XY) chromosomal pattern who was also androgen insensitive. (From *Gay, Straight and In-Between* by J. Money, Oxford University Press, Inc., 1988. Reprinted with permission of the publisher.)

LeVay and Haner (1994) found statistical evidence that the hypo-thalamic nucleus (INAH3) which Gorski had shown to be larger in males than females, is not as large in homosexual men as it is in heterosexual men. Their subjects were victims of acquired immunodeficiency syndrome (AIDS) from the San Francisco area. Flaws have been pointed out in this study by Byne (1994) who takes exception to LeVay and Haner's findings and conclu-sions on several grounds. Beyond the fact that it was drawn from the San Francisco homosexual community, we know nothing about their sample. Was the fact of a homosexual object choice the sole criterion by which their population was selected? Was it, for example, uniform in terms of other personality characteristics in addition to the preference for a homosexual sexual partner? Were the hypothalami they studied all from the brains of effemi-nate men or did they include samples from individuals, who, in their appearance and most of their activities, were quintessentially masculine, but who preferred other males as sexual partners? I have in mind men like the actor Rock Hudson, the conductor and composer Leonard Bernstein, and Richard the Lion Hearted, King of England, and members of the Greek army that defeated the Persians at Marathon. Did they include specimens from bisex-ual men, that is, men who are comfortable in expressing their sexuality with both males and females? It is probably the case that the core genders of LeVay and Haner's subjects derived from circumstances similar to those Stoller (1968, 1988) described in the individuals he classified as transsexual.

It was Stoller's observation that men who fall into this group, whose core gender is female, who have a deep, abiding, and un-shakable conviction that they are females trapped in a male body, have a predictable early life history. He assumed that for all in-fants, boys and girls, there is an early stage of development during which the baby is merged with mother. This assumption is, of course, consistent with all the material we have reviewed concern-ing development during the oral–sensorimotor period. Only after months, he proposed, does mother become a clearly separate object. Stoller felt that this early fused (in Mahler's terms, symbi-otic) state lays the groundwork for an infant's sense of femininity. To quote him, "This sets the girl firmly on the path of femininity in adulthood but puts the boy in danger of building into his core gender identity a sense of oneness with mother (a sense of femaleness). Depending on how, and at what pace, a mother allows her son to separate, this phase of merging with her will leave residual effects that may be expressed as disturbances in masculinity" (1988, p. 16). While he places the emphasis on the necessity for little boys, if they are to become functioning adult males, to give up their relation with mother rather than on rivalry with their father, the problem he poses amounts to an anticipation, in infancy and toddlerhood, of the oedipal problem.

Stoller observed that a male whom he would classify as a primary transsexual (i.e., a male who has been feminine from the first year of life) has had an "excessively intimate, blissful, skin-to-skin closeness with his mother" (1988, p. 16). This intimacy is not intruded upon by the father who, from Stoller's observations, plays no significant role in the rearing of the child. Typically he is remote, passive, isolated, and uninvolved. Indeed, it was Stoller's opinion that he, the father, had been unconsciously selected by mother because these qualities were present. Except to emphasize his unavailability to the boy, this characterization of the father may not always hold true. That is, there are other reasons why a father might be absent and mother be left in circumstances which facilitate the maintenance of an excessively close, intimate relation with her adored son. I, for example, have worked with a man whose father was in the military during World War II. My patient was born after father left to go overseas. Father and son first met when the boy was nearly 4. When he arrived on the scene, he was experienced by the child as an unwelcome intruder. During the intervening years mother had a relation with him such as Stoller describes.

Stoller believed that these transsexual boys are the product of a multigenerational process which began with their mothers' own sad and hopeless girlhood. The mothers' histories have been consistently that of having been rejected by their mothers because they were female. For such a mother, he felt, this baby who is perceived as ideal—beautiful, cuddly and responsive—"becomes the beautiful phallus for which she has yearned since her own sad hopeless childhood" (p. 30). Again, to quote Stoller (1988), "There is nothing complex about this motivation: when she holds the baby she feels marvelous; when he is out of reach she feels less so; and if he were out of sight, she would be anxious" (p. 30). At the same time, mother does not interfere with her son's progress in other spheres. As he matures and develops, and such ego functions as sitting, walking, and talking emerge, they are encouraged. Indeed mother acts to foster the development of intelligence and creativity—especially artistic sensitivity. She insists only that all this development be within her sight and reach. This pattern of a "blissful relation" is certainly not unusual during the first year of life. Indeed, we have only to recall the destiny of the environmentally deprived child to be convinced that in considerable measure, it is absolutely essential if the early phases of maturation and development are to proceed. However, in these cases it continues unremittingly for years. Stoller found it still to be active when the child, aged 4 or 5, was brought to him. "By this age," he says, "the boys act and look like beautiful girls, but *their mothers refuse to recognize this*, they consciously cannot understand why everyone mistakes their child for a girl" (p. 31; emphasis added).

SEVERING (OR AT LEAST LOOSENING) THE BOND

One can regard the transsexual male, as described by Stoller, and the female counterpart which he also describes, as representing extremes along continua which run from identification with, and uncomplicated acceptance of, one's manifest gender, to its vehement rejection.[6] If one is at peace with his or her genitalia and gender role, there is no problem. It was Stoller's contention that his patients' insistence on regarding themselves as females derived from the intensity of the bond that was established with their mothers in earliest infancy, and maintained throughout early childhood. He came to regard this condition as the most extreme manifestations of what he referred to as the gender dysphoria syndrome. Unsettled questions about this syndrome include: (1) To what extent do such states reflect inherited

---

[6]I use the term *manifest gender* in order to include individuals like Money's (1988) transsexuals whose external genitalia and their own concept of their gender are diametrically opposed.

differences in brain structure? (2) Are the manifestations of brain tissue changes which, having occurred as the result of very early postnatal experience, for all practical purposes, fixed and immutable? (3) Are life-style patterns mutable, if the individual is interested and motivated, to change? In any given clinical instance, it is not possible to decide among these three possibilities. Stoller, with increasing experience, became increasingly skeptical about the efficacy of sex change procedures. He felt that most people who present themselves for these procedures suffered from serious personality disorders which affected their lives in many spheres. These were not usually ameliorated by the surgery. The surgical sex change program at Johns Hopkins, which had been in the forefront in the 1960s, had been discontinued some eight years before Stoller wrote to this effect. Today, the only academically based programs in this area are at Stanford and the University of Minnesota.

There is a natural experiment, described by Herdt (1981) and by Lidz and Lidz (1977), which seems to me to shed considerable light on these problems. It indicates that even after a very intense and prolonged mother–son symbiosis, it is possible to break the bond and create, by the defining characteristics of the culture in question, a strong masculine identity. The price the individuals in question, and their culture in general, must pay for this outcome is, by our Western standards, inordinate. For the people in question, however, what I will now describe is natural and normal, the way things always have been and always should be. My highly condensed account is based on Stoller (1988).

The Sambians are an isolated tribal people numbering some 2300 warrior-hunters and horticulturists who inhabit an extremely rugged mountainous region of Eastern New Guinea. They are one of a number of similar groups in the area. As we consider the account which follows, it will be important to keep reminding ourselves that we have no reason to assume that the structure of the brains of these people is inherently different from that of other humans. A Sambian who, as a neonate was removed to, and reared in a Western culture, would, I suggest, find this story as weird and unreal as do we. Their brains are "normal" and the, for us, extraordinary route by which their boys achieve masculine gender identity is, for them, natural and normal. What we would regard as its consequences with regard to how they feel about and relate to females, is for them also natural and normal. Any Sambian male knows perfectly well that "this is the way women are." "Sambian society," Stoller writes, "functions primarily to perpetuate the warriorhood of its men, all of whom are expected to become fierce fighters capable of killing. . . . it allows for no alternatives to the masculine gender role model of the fierce fighter. . . . with one (noted) exception, adult sexual inversion does not exist" (p. 186). All adult Sambian men are heterosexual.

They live surrounded on all sides by enemy groups who, just as they do, raid and kill. They are, therefore, trained to be unendingly alert, aggressive, and suspicious. Because they possess only stone age weapons—bows, arrows, and clubs—they cannot mitigate their vulnerability, as more advanced societies do, with more efficient tools. Because they must depend on their own superior strength, they must be both physically and emotionally powerful. "Theirs is a living example—though an anachronism—of a particularly harnessed maleness, a primordial masculinity" (Stoller, 1988, p. 185). How, Stoller asks, is it created? What do Sambians know, subliminally, that has enabled them to evolve a culture, a family unit, and a form of ritualized male gender identity that has reproduced itself and succeeded over untold generations? The informants from whom the following account was taken were all men; as the story unfolds, it will become apparent why females were simply not available to be interviewed by the male field anthropologists.

Courtship is unknown in this culture. Except in instances when a female is abducted from another village, all marriages are prearranged and, uniformly, they are between strangers. Each married couple, and their children, lives in a separate house. At the same time misogyny is institutionalized. Men belong to a secret male cult, and women are uniformly disparaged as polluting, depleting inferior beings whom men must distrust all their lives. The adult male Sambian must, then, reconcile two complex, conflict laden forces. The first is the importance of the family unit which remains a "given" despite the strain of the male–female polarity. The second is the steadfast concern of the men with their "masculinity." In this regard women are perceived as posing a continuing threat. They are inherently dangerous because of their menstrual and vaginal fluids. It is, therefore, necessary to strictly regulate all contact between the sexes. Eating, drinking, sitting, talking, spitting, looking, and particularly sexual intercourse are all ritualized and inhibited in ways which serve to maintain distance between the sexes. The strictures are more rather than less stringent between married couples. During the three years he lived among the Sambians, Herdt never once observed a man and woman purposely touch one another, not even hold hands, either publicly or in the privacy of their own hut. The hamlet itself, he reported, is a maze of tabooed spaces: paths are either "male" or "female"; many areas are off-limits to one or the other sex. Even the interiors of the houses are split up into "male" and "female" spaces. "All this is to reduce the chances that a woman's lethal body, body fluids, or other products, smells, and glances, will be absorbed into a man's food, water, possessions, or insides" (Herdt, 1981, cited in Stoller, 1988, p. 186).

Add to the above the abiding conviction "that women deplete men of their strength and, eventually even of life itself—emptying them, through sexual intercourse, of their male substance, semen" (Stoller, 1988, p. 186). Semen, for men, is the stuff of their existence, the sole origin of their vitality, and the origin of their male anatomy. Yet it is also needed by women to strengthen themselves so that they can produce babies and provide milk. Boys cannot become men without a steady supply of exogenous semen. It is believed that the male body cannot manufacture it. At the same time women also want semen and their needs and demands are incessant and endless. They are, moreover, not the less exciting for that reason. Women are impregnated, babies are born, and infants and toddlers are reared.

Postpartum taboos prohibit all sexual activity between the couple until the child is weaned sometime in its second year. With weaning, the situation changes: "until then the father's presence, physical and psychological, is shadowy" (Stoller, 1988, p. 187). For the first 9 months the Sambian infant is considered an appendage of the mother. Somewhere between ages 2 and 3, after the child is weaned, the situation changes and the father becomes a presence in his son's life. Unlike the fathers of Stoller's transsexuals, he is now a strong, manly, even dangerous presence—someone worth emulating. For approximately his first 3 years, however,

the little boy has ready access to the breast. He is in skin-to-skin
contact with his mother, eats with her, is carried by her, and sleeps
naked with her. After weaning there is a progressive increase in
the permissible physical distance between mother and son. The
primacy of the little boy's contact with her continues, however,
until he is between 7 and 10.

It is then the first initiation ceremony is held, and with this
an abrupt and permanent change in the child's world comes
about. From the time he is abruptly awakened in the middle of
the night and taken to the secret place were the ceremony takes
place, he must never again see his mother. The several rites are
intended to rid him of his inherent female essence and to instill
him with masculinity. The former is associated with blood. It follows, therefore, that the little boy is made to bleed both from his
nose, and by undercutting his penis. Ridding him of femininity
is, however, not sufficient. He must also be provided with male
essence. To accomplish this he must fellate the older boys, those
who are now in puberty. When the initiate achieves puberty, he
too will become a supplier of semen and be fellated by the new
initiates. Later, with adolescence and marriage, all homosexual
activity ceases.

Some, not many, reliable conclusions can be drawn from this
brief and highly personal review of the problems associated with
the emergence of gender, the establishment of gender identity,
and, as well, the determinations of sexual object choice. As a
review, it is admittedly limited and could be accused of being
parochial. For example, it gives short shrift to the problems associated with the establishment of female gender identity. This is all
the more ironic because the case which set Stoller on the path
of investigating these problems was that of an erstwhile female
who had become convincingly male. Perhaps the most persuasive
case I can make for my "homocentric" tilt is that Stoller, despite
his inspiring epiphany, devoted most of his attention to problems
associated with masculine identity. It appears to be the case that
men have much more problem with establishing themselves as
males than do women as females. The brain is, to begin with,
female, and the condition of masculinity is an "add on" which
occurs sometime around the time of birth but, in humans, well

after gonadally defined gender is established. Whether the hypo-thalamuses of some of the individuals who make homosexual ob-ject choices are different from those of strictly heterosexual men is an open question. In my opinion the evidence is not convinc-ing. Even if it were to turn out to be true for some passive, yielding males who also make homosexual object choices (what we might refer to as "she-males"), it passes plausibility to assume that mas-culine icons like Julius Caesar, or the Greek soldiers who fought the Persians at Thermopile were possessed of brains which pro-moted what we tend to think of as "gay" characteristics.[7] I add these men to those Freud mentioned in his letter and those I enumerated earlier. There is, I suggest, no convincing evidence that the predilection for having sex with a person of one's own gender demands the presence of a genetically determined differ-ent kind of brain.

The evidence, on the other hand, that such a predilection may be the result of very early, even preverbal experiences is, I think, very persuasive. More than the evidence from the transsex-uals' histories, which is certainly impressive, it is the story of the Sambians which seems to me to make a convincing case. These boys, having had essentially the same early experience as the transsexual of Western society, are forced into a way of living which involves both acting the part of a female for other males while, at the same time, being imbued with all the virtues of ag-gressive masculinity as well as fear and suspicion of women. When they emerge into puberty they give up the "degraded" (my term) feminine role and become aggressive men. They are now fellated on demand by the new generation of novitiates. The pull of their infantile experience, however, does not go away. An elaborate system of rituals and beliefs serve to keep women at arms' length, to prevent their seductive enervating influence from taking over men. This concern, the fear that unless they are eternally watchful they will be rendered impotent and helpless by their women, may exist in exaggerated form among the Sambians but is, by no means, limited to them. We can certainly see it in operation in our culture, and it is certainly an issue in all male–female relations. I

---

[7]A recent cartoon in the *New Yorker* has two couples discussing the Clinton policy on gays in the military. The caption read, "When you think of it, the Persian wars might have gone the other way if the Greeks kept Gays out of their military."

close with an anecdote which suggests that, quite aside from the male's yearning to return to the blissful state he once knew with mother, he is at risk because the female, too, may seek to achieve mastery, to have a sense of efficacy in her relation to the opposite sex. The mother of a 12-year-old, who had been reared to "dumb up," reprimanded her daughter for having been too harsh in putting down a male contemporary. The daughter replied, "When we grow up he is going to be bigger than I am, stronger than I am, and able to run faster than I can. But I am going to be smarter than he is." In effect she acknowledged that if she is to achieve her personally defined goals, it will not be on the basis of using brute strength and overt aggressivity after the fashion of successful Sambian men.

CHAPTER 7

Infant Observation

M. Taine's very interesting account of the mental development of an infant . . . , has lead me to look over a diary which I kept thirty seven years ago with respect to one of my own infants [C. Darwin, 1877].

If you ring a bright shiny bell in the presence of a 4- to 5-month old infant, the baby will turn his or her head to the source of the sound, fixate it, and then reach out to grasp it. About twenty years ago (Freedman, Fox-Kalenda, Margileth, and Miller, 1969), however, I established that if you place a screen between baby and ringing bell, you can go on ringing it forever; the baby, having turned toward the sound and not seen the bright moving object which was making it, will not attempt to seek it out and retrieve it. It will not be until the infant is approximately 10 to 11 months old that he or she will use the sound itself as an indicator of the existence of a sound-making object, and be motivated to push the screen aside, and retrieve the bell. I was able to savor the originality of my discovery only very briefly before I discovered that Piaget had made the same observation some fifty years earlier. Then I discovered that Charles Darwin had reported the same phenomenon in 1877. Actually he had made his finding in the late 1830s in the course of watching the development of his firstborn son. To the best of my knowledge the serious systematic observation of the maturation and development of infants began with the diary Darwin kept during that child's infancy.

For both Darwin and Piaget my "discovery" was an almost incidental observation, one worth recording but not particularly noteworthy. For me, however, the finding had more immediate significance. It came out of my effort to explain a perplexing observation Selma Fraiberg and I had made (1964) some years earlier. Tracy, a congenitally blind baby, was being reared in a rich and stimulating environment. She appeared to us to be developing well despite her total blindness, the result of ophthalmia neonatorum. She was responsive to her mother and could distinguish her from Mrs. Fraiberg both by differences she apparently detected in the ways the two women held her and, we thought, by the differences in the sounds of their voices. Yet, she did not respond to a sound-making object, with which she was familiar, and which she appeared to enjoy very much once it was in her hand. From our experience as parents, who had observed their own comparably aged sighted children, it seemed obvious that they had recognized the ringing sound as coming from the bell and, therefore, been motivated to reach out and grasp it. My "discovery" proved that we were wrong. If anything, Tracy was a little ahead of the average sighted baby in this regard. I found that until they are 10 to 11 months old, sighted infants also would not seek out a hidden sound-making object, no matter how much prior experience they had with it. For the younger child the ringing bell did not suggest that there was a something "out there" making the ringing sound. Like a piece of sonar equipment the younger infants would orient their heads to the sound. As noted, if there wasn't a visually attractive object to be seen, the baby would quickly lose interest. That this should be the case is consistent with both the Yakovlev and LeCours (1967) timetable for the myelinization of the auditory system (see Figure 1.1), and Piaget's timetable for the development of the concept of an object which continues to exist after it was last seen. It also should serve as yet another reminder that in studying the maturation and development of the infant's psyche, it is important not to assume that the behavior we see is generated by a central psychic structure, completely equipped with a repertoire of mental representations, like the ones we adults like to think characterize us.

Darwin made a number of other observations which have immediate relevance to how we view infants and children, and to how careful we should be in our extrapolations concerning the long-term significance of what we see. He noted, for example, the differences in the patterns of maturation and development of this oldest son and of his 14-month younger sister. He was struck by how relatively precocious she was. He wrote, "Although this infant thus began to use his hands at an early period, he showed no special aptitude in this respect, for when he was 2 years and 4 months old, he held pencils, pens, and other objects far less neatly and efficiently than did his sister who was then only 14 months old, and who showed great inherent aptitude in handling anything" (p. 405). He also observed a striking difference in temperament as between these two infants.

> When eleven months old, if a wrong plaything was given him, he would push it away and beat it; I presume that the beating was an instinctive sign of anger, like the snapping of the jaws by a young crocodile just out of the egg, and not that he imagined he could hurt the plaything. When two years and three months old, he became a great adept at throwing books or sticks, &c., at anyone who offended him; and so it was with some of my other sons. On the other hand, I could never see a trace of such aptitude in my infant daughters; and *this makes me think that a tendency to throw objects is inherited by boys*" [p. 405].

Elsewhere, in a letter to a friend, Darwin expressed himself further on the subject of small boys as opposed to girls. He wrote, "I congratulate and condole with you on your tenth child; but please to observe when I have a tenth, send only condolences to me. We have now seven children, all well, thank God, as well as their mother; of these seven, five are boys; and my father used to say that it was certain that a boy gave as much trouble as three girls; so that *bona fide* we have seventeen children. It makes me sick whenever I think of professions; all seem hopelessly bad, and as yet I cannot see a ray of light" (letter to W. D. Fox, March 7, 1852). In order to forestall any suggestion about attention deficit disorder, I hasten to add that, without benefit of amphetamines, all of Darwin's sons were successful in later life. This eldest child, as well as at least one of his brothers, grew up to be a distinguished scientist in his own right, and a member of the Royal Society.[2]

---

[2]Sexual dimorphism, the fact that there are significant *gender related anatomical* differences between boys' and girls' brains, was not to be discovered for a hundred or so years.

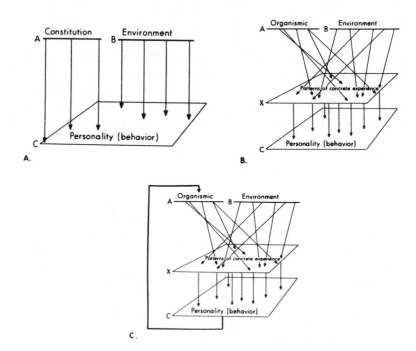

Figure 7.1. Models of relation between inherited and environmental influences in the growing up individual (after Escalona).

The accompanying figure based on the work of Escalona (1965) is intended to give some sense of how the conceptual approach to infant observation has varied over the years. These conceptual models of what may be happening in the brains of infants are important to keep in mind. Conclusions, reached from their application, serve as the basis for making recommendations about how to rear infants and children. In the next several paragraphs I will discuss how such models influenced our understanding of the processes of maturation and development.

In the meantime the frenetic, obstreperous behavior of little boys was (and still is) all too often taken to be evidence of a definable illness variously called minimal brain disease, minimal brain dysfunction, and in more recent years, attention deficit disorder. This is a phenomenologically defined syndrome for which no underlying brain pathology has ever been found. When it is diagnosed the youngster is often treated with such drugs as dexedrine or ritalin.

Many very influential workers, for example, believed that personality and behavior result from the simple addition of the influences of the constitutional givens with which each individual comes equipped, and the effects of the environment (Figure 7.1A). The work of J. B. Watson, the founder of the Behaviorist school of psychology, epitomizes this rather simplistic view. It is arguable that it has no place here. Yet, it had enormous influence in the past and can still be detected in many people's approach to parenting. A book he published in 1928, *Psychological Care of Infant and Child*, was enormously successful. The U.S. Department of Agriculture issued a manual on infant and child care based on Watson's work. To it we owe such ubiquitous practices of the past as strict scheduling of feeding and sleeping, as well as very stringent limitations on the expressing of affection to, or playing with infants and toddlers. One of Watson's adherents, B. F. Skinner, went so far as to construct an air conditioned box in which his own babies could be reared, free from all contaminating parental interference. But I will let Watson speak for himself: "I (have) brought out the fact that all we have to start with in building a human being is a lively squirming bit of flesh, capable of making a few simple responses such as movements of the hands and arms and fingers and toes, crying and smiling, making certain sounds with its throat. I (have said) that parents take this raw material and begin to fashion it in ways to suit themselves. This means that parents, whether they know it or not, start intensive training of the child at birth" (p. 45).

Watson goes on to aver that, "it is especially easy to shape the emotional life at this early age." He draws the "simple" analogy to the fabricator of metal who, "takes his heated mass, places it upon the anvil and begins to shape it according to patterns of his own. Sometimes he uses a heavy hammer, sometimes a light one; sometimes he strikes the yielding mass a mighty blow, sometimes he gives it just a touch. *So inevitably do we begin at birth to shape the emotional life of our children*" (pp. 46–47; emphasis added). He was persuaded that heredity plays a very small part in the determination of behavior. While he regarded fear, rage, and love as driving forces in behavior, he felt their proper use had to be learned. In one experiment he set about teaching a 9-month-old boy how to be afraid of a white rabbit. When the "experiment" began the infant had seemed curious but unafraid. To create fear he positioned himself behind the infant and struck a steel bar with a hammer whenever the rabbit was close to the child. The following is Watson's description of an experiment which is intended to demonstrate that all fears are home made.

> I have my assistant take his old playmate, the rabbit, out of its pasteboard box and hand it to him. He starts to reach for it. But just as his hands touch it I bang the steel bar behind his head. He whimpers and cries and shows fear. Then I wait awhile. I give him his blocks to play with. He quiets down and soon becomes busy with them. Again my assistant shows him the rabbit. This time he reacts to it quite slowly. He doesn't plunge his hands out as quickly and eagerly as before. Finally he does touch it gingerly. Again I strike the steel bar behind his head. Again I get a pronounced fear response. Then I let him quiet down. He plays with his blocks. Again the assistant brings in the rabbit. This time something new develops. No longer do I have to rap the steel bar behind his head to bring out fear. He shows fear at the sight of the rabbit. He makes the same reaction to it that he makes to the sound of the steel bar. He begins to cry and turn away the moment he sees it [pp. 52–53].

It has been said, perhaps apocryphally, that Watson, who did this work while at Johns Hopkins University, had been impressed by Freud's writings on the Oedipus complex. He came to the conclusion that its development was the result of excessive maternal attention. Because so much psychopathology seemed to follow from its presence, he concluded that it had to be prevented from developing, at whatever cost. The obvious preventative was to limit opportunities for interaction between mother and child. It was with this goal in mind that he recommended strict scheduling of feeding and bedtimes. Propped bottles were calculated to reduce physical contact between mother and infant, as well as to discourage any temptation on her part to cuddle and play with her baby. The following paragraph reflects his views on how mothers of somewhat older youngsters should treat their children.

> There is a sensible way of treating children. Treat them as though they were young adults. Dress them, bathe them with care and

circumspection. Let your behavior always be objective and kindly firm. Never hug and kiss them, never let them sit in your lap. If you must, kiss them once on the forehead when they say good night. Shake hands with them in the morning. Give them a pat on the head if they have made an extraordinarily good job of a difficult task. Try it out. In a week's time you will find how easy it is to be perfectly objective with your child and at the same time kindly. You will be utterly ashamed of the mawkish, sentimental way you have been handling it [p. 81].

Watson's recommendations in all these matters were supported by "scientific" laboratory experiments on both lower animals and human infants, of which teaching Albert to be afraid of the rabbit is an example. Both his experiments and the recommendations which followed from them, were based on what was known at that time as the Stimulus-Response (SR) model. The brain, he held, is a black box. Since the "scientific" psychological observer cannot know what is going on in the "box," its functioning, he felt, is irrelevant. To speculate about what may be going on in the brain is wasteful and unscientific. All that matters is that stimuli go in and responses come out. Using techniques like those I quote above, one could shape a particular piece of behavior and that was what mattered. Although, with the passage of time, these positions have softened, behaviorism is still with us. Therapists who specialize in behavior modification are applying Watsonian principles to this very day.

The actress Mariette Hartley, who starred in such works as *M*A*S*H, Ride the High Country,* and *Peyton Place,* is his granddaughter. In her autobiography, *Breaking the Silence* (1990), she describes the experience of growing up, the daughter of Watson's daughter and under the still pervasive influence of his behaviorist approach.

Rather than the direct additive relation to constitutional and environmental factors which, Watson postulated, results in behavior and personality, Escalona suggested the existence of an intervening variable (Figure 7.1B), which she called patterns of concrete experience. Escalona, a psychoanalytically trained psychologist, was attempting to account for the occurrence of infantile autism in populations other than the one from which the original cases were identified. Kanner (1949), when he described the syndrome, characterized the parents of his patients as cold, rigid, meticulous and perfectionistic people. Later observers found that this description did not always fit. The congenitally blind, whom we have already discussed, are very vulnerable to developing an autisticlike syndrome, yet the vast majority of their parents do not share the characteristics Kanner specified. The pattern of concrete experience is the intermix of the organismic state of the individual and environmental input which is being processed, in the infant's brain, at any given moment. I have added (Figure 7.1C) a feedback loop to indicate that the "organismic state," at any given instant, includes the residua of his or her experience up to that instant.

Escalona's model is deceptive in its apparent simplicity. The patterns of concrete experience which determine personality and behavior are, in fact, highly complex. Very quickly they acquire idiosyncratic characteristics for each individual. Thus Tracy, the totally blind infant I mentioned earlier, had by 4 months developed a coenesthetic representation of her mother which resulted in a different quality of response to her from the response she had to Mrs. Fraiberg. I have chosen my words very carefully: It is tempting to say she "knew" her mother. Certainly that would not be the case if one meant by "knowing," the ability to be aware of her mother as a separate object, a complex human being in her own right. Nonetheless, it was clear that she had, at 4 to 5 months, differentiated out a sensory constellation (now an organismic factor) which served to make it possible for her to distinguish between, and react differently to, the familiar way her mother held her and what was for us, as the observers, the indistinguishable technique of Mrs. Fraiberg. At what point the accumulation of such abilities to differentiate become fused into the concept of the existence of another person who is "known" in the sense that older people "know" one another remains an open question. This observation, however, lends credence to Stoller's hypothesis concerning the role of very early mother–infant interactions in the etiology of the transsexual syndrome.

I. Charles Kaufman's (1975) studies of the development of attachment in two related species of macaque monkeys have provided considerable insight into how patterns of concrete experience, once established, become part of the individual's

Figure 7.2. "Social life" among the pigtail monkeys (from I. C. Kaufman, 1975).

organismic state, and thereafter influence his or her personality and behavior. Over a period of several generations he studied colonies of pigtail and bonnet monkeys. Although closely related, these species are characterized by very different social structures and infant rearing practices. The pigtails live isolated and separate lives (Figure 7.2). Each individual has a separate sitting and resting place which is not intruded upon by other members of the colony. When a baby is born, mother is fiercely protective and will not allow it to be touched by any other member of the colony, neither will she allow the infant to move outside her immediate vicinity. This very close relation continues until she has another infant. The older sibling is, then, abruptly pushed into the background and lives on the periphery of mother's orbit until becoming a mother in her own right and repeating the sequence. (I do not know what happens to the male offspring at this point, beyond the obvious evidence that they are able to participate in procreation.) The pattern of attachment relations (concrete experience) for the pigtail monkey begins, then, as an extremely tight bonding to mother which continues until the child is replaced by a new infant. When she, in turn, becomes a mother, she repeats the pattern.

Bonnet monkeys (Figure 7.3) live in as different a cultural context as one can imagine. They are as gregarious as the pigtails

Figure 7.3. "Social life" among the bonnet monkeys (from I. C. Kaufman, 1975).

are isolated. Rather than each individual having its own designated place and avoiding physical contact with others, the bonnets pile all over one another and seem to glory in touching. In addition to their own babies, mothers will tend to any infant in the colony which happens to be at large. Although they do appear to distinguish them from the others, they are not particularly protective of their own babies. All the adult members of the colony are free to "parent" all the available "infants and toddlers."

Kaufman performed the experiment of removing a mother of each species from her colony and, therefore, from her baby. The results were predictable and dramatic. The pigtail baby went through the gamut of response to loss with which we are familiar in humans who experience separation from, or loss of, persons to whom they are attached. Intense agitation (Figure 7.4) was followed by withdrawal and depression (Figure 7.5) and then by a "resigned" continuing state of apathy and depression. Other members of the pigtail community simply ignored the infant or, if it attempted to approach another adult, it would be driven off. When the mother was returned to the colony, there was an intense reunion and the intensity of their physical attachment, if anything, increased—that is, until the mother produced another infant whereupon the older sibling was relegated to the periphery. The bonnet baby, by contrast, reacted to the absence of mother almost casually and moved on to another adult for whatever

Figure 7.4. Acute reaction of pigtail infant to loss of mother (from I. C. Kaufman, 1975).

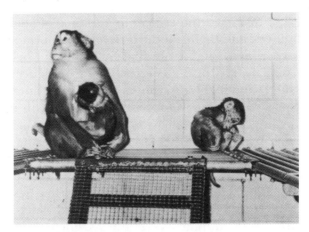

Figure 7.5. Forlorn, grieving abandoned infant. Adult simply ignores it (from I. C. Kaufman, 1975).

ministrations were required. Whereas the pigtail adults had threatened the deserted infants and driven them off, the bonnet adults welcomed them. Reunion between the bonnet baby and its returning mother was correspondingly casual. Figure 7.6 shows a chronically depressed pigtail monkey, one who has passed through both the acute, agitated, and despairing stages, and is now in the stage of chronic depression.

Figure 7.6. A depressed pigtail infant uttering the distress signal "coo" (from I. C. Kaufman, 1975).

Earlier we discussed the critical importance of adequate experience in the coenesthetic mode[3] if development is to proceed. With this experiment, and those that follow, it will become evident that some aspects of the coenesthetic experience are both extremely subtle and highly discriminating. They define from very early on a particular infant–mother relation. This, in turn, may have lifelong effects on the behavior and personality of the growing individual. Thus, during the period when coenesthesia is critical, both the pigtail and the bonnet monkey infants were adequately supplied by their mothering ones. Neither developed the kind of maternal deprivation syndrome Harlow described in the animals he reared on mother surrogates and which has been described frequently in humans. Yet the specific patterns of concrete experience, in the context of which their respective infantile environments provided this all-important mode of experience, were very different one from the other. Their respective reactions to separation from their mothers were correspondingly divergent. The opportunity to observe systematically, and over time, analogous differences in human child rearing practices are virtually

---

[3]"Particularly during the first six months of life, and, to a certain extent even later, the perceptual system, the sensorium of the infant is in a state of transition. It shifts gradually from what I have called coenesthetic reception toward diacritic perception. Unlike that of the diacritic organization, the operation of the coenesthetic organization is not localized—it is extensive" (Spitz, 1965, p. 134).

nonexistent. We know, however, that idiosyncrasies, whether they are related to unique individual experience, or are culturally determined, characterize the maternal contribution to every mother–infant dyad. Winnicott's term, *good-enough mothering*, is appropriately vague. It is, for example, arguable that both the pigtail and bonnet monkey infants had good-enough mothering. Each was able to fit into the context of his or her own "culture" and carry on its traditional way of relating to fellow members of the colony and style of parenting. The human observations to which I will now turn are presented with the intention of emphasizing (1) that a wide variety of environmental and somatic vicissitudes are compatible with the establishment of personalities which fall within a "normal" range, and (2) that the subtlety of the origins of some long-lasting sequelae of very early experience is such as to defy our retrospective efforts to connect the early experience to what we see in later life. Patterns of behavior and personality which derive from very early interactions with the environment, become part of the constitutional givens of the older child and the adult.

At least eight individuals, born with congenital esophageal atresia, have been followed, over extended periods of time, by psychoanalytically oriented students of development. Monica was the first to be studied and was under observation by Drs. George Engel and Franz Eichman the longest—into her adulthood (Panel, 1979). At the time of the reports she was 25 years old, happily married, and the mother of 3. Her story, and those of the other similarly afflicted individuals, illustrates the pervasive effects of a very specific aberrant pattern of concrete experience. None of us thinks twice about having been born with a direct connection between our mouths and our stomachs. The experience of hunger and its satiation by the ingestion of food—the direct connection between oral activity and the sense of comfort which occurs as the result of our own muscular activity in the form of sucking, chewing, and swallowing—is so routine and obvious as to be ignorable. Not so for Monica.

Immediately after her birth, it was necessary to establish both a gastric and an esophageal fistula. The former was the orifice through which she was to be fed, and the latter served to drain her pharynx and larynx of saliva and other secretions, that would pass down a normal esophagus into the stomach. While, thanks to the esophageal fistula, she was able to have some experience with the mouthing and swallowing of food, the connection we take for granted between hunger, eating, and a feeling of satiation, was not established until after the functioning portions of her esophagus were joined together with a segment of colon. This happened when she was roughly 22 months old. Until then her nutritional needs were met by the direct injection of the nutriment into her stomach. She had no capacity to participate in the regulation of either the rate of intake or the amount she received. If her stomach were filled and the person "feeding" her continued to inject nutriment, she simply experienced the visceral discomfort of a distended stomach. When she was of an age at which babies begin to discriminate whether they like or dislike a particular food (i.e., when, for babies with an intact esophagus, feeding time becomes the occasion for a social interchange between infant and mother), for her it simply did not matter. Anyone who has ever fed an infant or toddler knows about infantile regulatory prerogatives in the feeding situation. We take them for granted until they run counter to what we, as authoritative adults, feel is fit and proper for the little one to consume and how he or she goes about consuming it. These very early "differences of opinion" between parentally defined expectations and the manifestations of autonomous infantile functioning becomes the basis for a variety of social interchanges. As parents, and as observers of parents, we have all witnessed both friendly loving exchanges and "power struggles" between adult and child. I choose the dramatic term *power struggle* to underscore that it is in the feeding situation that the infant first expresses something which can be interpreted as an "intentionality" different from that of his or her caretaker. Spitting out food, closing the mouth, turning the head away, are all forms of communication which imply the beginnings of intentionality on the baby's part. What are the consequences of all these average and expectable experiences being abrogated?[4] In addition to the story of Monica with which I will continue, we have seven other cases which were followed by Dr. Scott Dowling (1977).

---

[4]Experiences which we so take for granted in the average expectable caretaker–infant dyad, that we ordinarily have no curiosity about the remarkable fact that they occur.

Monica's initial hospitalization lasted only fifteen days. She then went to live in her maternal grandparents' home with her parents and older sibling. I quote from Dr. Engel's remarks at the 1979 panel.

> During these first six months of her life, she was cared for and nurtured by a responsible grandmother, although all of the feeding was done by the mother, who was away at work much of the time. Because of conflict between Monica's father and the grandparents, Monica's mother was forced to leave the grandparents' house with her children when Monica was six months old. The mother was pregnant at the time and rapidly became depressed in the context of social isolation, separation from her own mother, and the burden of a "defective child." Monica herself became fretful, irritable, had prolonged crying spells. With the mother's failure to respond to this crying, she developed an anaclitic depression characterized by severe withdrawal, weight loss, and marked developmental arrest. [Note that weight loss occurred even though Monica had no control over the amount of nutriment she received.] A one-month hospitalization at the age of one year, during which she was cared for by a responsive and affectionate nurse led to a temporary remission, but the depression reappeared with the birth of Debbie, a younger sibling, one month after discharge from the hospital. At the age of fifteen months, Monica was rehospitalized. During this hospitalization, she established strong affective bonds with Dr. Franz Reichsman and a nurse. Her response in the form of gradual weight gain and renewed maturation and development was impressive, and at 22 months mouth–stomach continuity was surgically established by means of a colonic anastomosis of esophagus to stomach. She was discharged shortly before her second birthday, successfully eating by mouth for the first time [p. 109].

All human behavioral research is complicated by the fact that it is impossible to establish a controlled situation in which only one variable is operative. Engel listed the following six interferences which he identified as impacting Monica's first two years of life. These are, over and above the idiosyncratic variables which characterize any growing up infant's interactions with the world:

1. Deprivation of oral feeding experience until 22 months;

2. Questionable bonding with mother for whom the fistula inter-
   fered with the development of normal mother–infant symbiosis;
3. Disruption of the bond with the grandmother at 6 months;
4. Mother's depression and progressive alienation from Monica,
   beginning at 6 months;
5. Prolonged hospital stays;
6. Excessive utilization of biological emergency systems, flight-
   fight, and conservation-withdrawal [pp. 109–110].

It is important not to overinterpret the impact of such an
aberration as that from which Monica and the seven other youngsters suffered. All but the first of the enumerated interferences
could have happened in the course of the infancy of a child with
an intact esophagus. In addition, there were some very positive
aspects to Monica's early life. During her first 6 months she was
the beneficiary of a very nurturing grandmother. Although it was
not in association with her gastric feeding or any ability to experience satiation, she was given food by mouth. In addition she was
able, notably because of the efforts of Dr. Reichsman, to form
strong attachments to two figures at the hospital. Engel also underscores that she was a "generally attractive" little girl, with an
irresistible smile, which enabled her to elicit support from others
as she grew up. Throughout her life Monica "conveyed a sense
of helplessness which, in association with her personal attrac-
tiveness, evoked very positive responses from people. . . . This
mode of interaction with others is now being evidenced with her
own children who accomplish tasks for her in response to minimal signals" (Panel, 1979, p. 116).

She was generally delayed in development. At 3 years of age
she could not yet walk. Her use of large muscles was always poorly
coordinated. By contrast fine motor functioning was not impaired. Monica's IQ leveled off at 100, somewhat less than that
of her siblings. The psychologist who tested her found her to be
shallow and with little interest in the environment. Throughout
her life she continued to be a passive–submissive person who got
along well because she could attract others to care for her. She
married an appropriately caring man, and at the time her case
was discussed she had three children of her own. A striking observation, made when she was 25, speaks to the persistent influence

of very early experience. It also underscores the probability that a child under 2 can both identify with a specific aspect of parenting behavior and turn this, for her a passive experience, into an active pattern of behavior. When Monica fed her babies she would lay them across her lap in precisely the same supine position she was placed in when, as an infant, she was fed through the gastrostomy tube. It is also the position which she spontaneously used when, at age 4, she was filmed feeding a doll. The contrast with how Monica's mother and siblings feed their children was characterized as startling. They cradled their infants in their arms, whereas Monica held the baby flat on her lap and offered it little support. Other aspects of Monica's functioning as an adult may be only partially, or not at all, related to the specific experiences associated with the management of esophageal atresia. This pattern of infant feeding by one who is described as a generally "good" mother, seems, unequivocally, to be a direct derivative.

Dowling (1977), who had been acquainted with Monica when he was a medical student, followed seven youngsters, born with esophageal atresia for varying periods, some into their teen years. Common to all them were the following:

1. Developmental steps were late in appearance, slow in progression, and lacked the quality of forcefulness or insistence seen in most other children.
2. There was little evidence of pleasure in new motor accomplishments or in new forms of interaction with persons or objects.
3. There was minimal persistence on the part of the child in pursuing a new activity until it was mastered.
4. Modulation and accommodation of an activity or form of affective expression to new circumstances was lacking.
5. Newly acquired skills were not maintained in the face of such vicissitudes as variations in maternal care or minor physical illness.
6. There was a profound failure to progress in terms of gross motor development. This was in striking contrast to the relatively normal progress in terms of visual and fine motor skills.

Dowling noted, in particular, the similarities of these findings to the observations of Provence and Lipton (1962, pp. 109–110)

in children who, having been institutionalized as infants, had suffered from very early environmental deprivation. There was, however, one striking difference. When the institutionalized children,
between 18 and 24 months old, were placed in foster care they
showed a dramatic early improvement. They appeared less bland
and seemed to take active roles in initiating contacts with adults.
As time went on, however, it became apparent that the institutionalized children, like the youngsters Joyce and Joey whom I also
described in the chapter on environmental deprivation, were totally undiscriminating in the contacts they made. One couldn't
call them attachments because they showed no discrimination
between an individual with whom they had repeated contacts in
the past, and total strangers. Their relations were consistently
superficial if, indeed, one could characterize how they behaved
as evidence of an interpersonal relation. The youngsters with
esophageal atresia, by contrast, showed from very early on, a distinct preference by their parents. Over the years they developed
specific, strong attachments to members of their family, something the child who had suffered early maternal neglect never did.

This very striking difference in the two groups of children's
capacities to establish states of object relatedness, even though
they shared so many other traits in common, underscores how
specific the effects of environmental contributions can be. While
they very frequently occur together, the environmental vicissitudes which result in poor gross muscular development, passivity,
lack of interest in the world around them, and lack of energy and
initiative, are different from those which are necessary for making
loving attachments.

How subtle both the environment's and the organismic contributions to patterns of concrete experience may be is illustrated
by Stern's (1971) study of the visual interactions of a mother with
her fraternal twin sons. There were clear differences in how she
responded to them. She was ambivalent both about her husband
and about the fact of having had twins. Her ambivalence, however, appeared to have split, with positive feelings resting with
Mark whom she identified with herself, and negative feelings directed more toward Fred, the twin "more like father." Stern
chose to study visual interactions because, "During the first several months visual motor behavior (eye movement, eye closing

and head turning) is the only motor system (besides sucking) over which the infant has substantial voluntary control." When the boys were $3^1/_2$ months old, Stern began making frame-by-frame analyses of motion pictures of their mother's visual interactions with each child. There were clear differences. Twelve months later there were differences in the two boys' personalities and behavior which appeared to be related to the earlier observed differences in mother's visual interactions with them.

When they began to observe the two dyads (Mother and Mark, and Mother and Fred) Stern and his colleagues had the impression that she was "controlling, overstimulating, and insensitive" in that she imposed on the infant the level of social contact she wanted when she wanted it. She showed little regard for the infant's state of responsiveness. It was also the case that this impression pertained mainly to her relation to Fred (the unfavored twin). From the films it was possible to establish that there were clear differences in the way mother interacted with the two infants. There followed differences in the way the two dyads evolved. As early as $3^1/_2$ months when mother approached Fred he would turn away. When she withdrew he would turn toward her. The pattern proved to be both statistically highly reliable and very different from her interaction with Mark, the favored twin. He seemed to have the capacity to "control" the level of visual contact he had with mother, whereas Fred's behavior appeared to be determined by hers. At 12 and 15 months Fred was found to be a more fearful and dependent child. He greeted people with face aversion. His anxiety in the presence of strangers was more intense and lasted longer than his twin's. Mark appeared to be freer to wander off and he could become more engrossed in independent play.

While what Stern established, in the course of analyzing his films, seems unassailable, there are many obvious problems with the interpretation of his findings. We cannot, for example, be certain as to why mother acted as though she preferred Mark. Babies certainly differ in temperament and there is no a priori reason to assign the basis for their differences, as Stern does in this case, to early mother–infant interaction as opposed to organismic factors which the infant brings to the very early interchange. Infants born blind, for example, do not respond as do sighted infants to visual stimuli. Their failure to do so is often experienced, even by women who are already experienced and successful as mothers, as a rejection. Because mother, in turn, withdraws from her infant, a vicious cycle ensues. As a consequence, approximately 25 percent of the congenitally blind, ultimately present with a syndrome very similar to, if not identical with, infantile autism. Some mothers seem to rise above the frustration of their blind infants' lack of responsiveness. By dint of extraordinary efforts they manage to bypass the visual mode and to enter into a reciprocating relation with their babies through the mediums of coenesthetic stimulation and sound. Psychologically well-functioning, congenitally blind individuals, who have the capacity to establish mutually gratifying affective relations and to be productive individuals, are the result.

David, the Bubble Boy (Freedman, Montgomery, Wilson, Bealmar, and South, 1976), afforded us the opportunity to observe the psychological development of a child, without neurological or sensorial deficit, who had to be denied many of the sensory experiences which, like a well-functioning esophagus, we take for granted in life. An older brother had died of Combined Immune Deficiency disease. When it was established, during the mother's pregnancy, that this child was also to be a boy, arrangements were made to transfer him directly into a germ-free environment. It was his fate to spend his entire life, some 12 years, under such isolated conditions. I was able to participate in his care during his first five years. David was not the first infant to be consigned to such a living circumstance. Simons, Kohl, Genscher, and Dietrich (1973) described the mental development at age $2^1/_2$ of two youngsters who had lived under similar conditions. Both were found to suffer from significant learning disorders. Their retardation was regarded as evidence of permanent impairment of intellectual functioning. It was the authors' opinion that their patients' retardation and evidence of an autisticlike syndrome were the result of their prolonged stay in the isolator. Since David was not retarded and certainly showed no evidence of autism, we have to assume that the extraordinary circumstances under which he lived in and of themselves do not make arrested or deviant psychological development inevitable. I will describe how David lived during the period I observed him, as well as some details of his cognitive and affective development.

This otherwise healthy male infant was delivered by Caesarian section and immediately transferred to a transparent plastic tent. This provided a virtually germ-free environment. Over the years he was moved to a succession of larger "isolators" which effectively kept him from contact with pathogens. Gloves built into their walls allowed access to him. He could be picked up, handled, and played with. However, all these activities were carried out under the constraints imposed by the unyielding plastic barrier between him and his caretakers. This precluded his experiencing some forms of sensory stimulation which are inevitable elements in the lives of youngsters who are reared under less atypical circumstances. He never, for example, felt the warmth or texture of another person's skin, or smelled another person's breath or body. The process of molding his body to that of a caretaker was limited in the extreme, and the opportunity to use his arms in order to embrace another person was unavailable to him. Neither could he engage in mutual ventral–ventral clinging. Bowlby (1969) has asserted that these latter activities are critical experiences for early psychological development.

David's relation to caretaking figures was also atypical. After his first few months he spent roughly half his life at home, where a second germ-free environment was constructed. He was transported back and forth in a van especially equipped for the purpose. During the early phase of his hospitalization, he did not have a single, relatively constant, caretaker. As would be the case for a more typical hospital patient, a succession of nurses and attendants were involved in his daily ministrations. In addition, there were the members of the medical staff who came and went. Included in the group were some individuals with whom he had frequent contact throughout his life—his mother when he was at home, and some members of the medical team—as well as a large number (especially nurses and attendants) who were more transient but who, at any given time, were active participants in his care. In addition, he was subjected to repeated painful interventions. Blood drawing and other procedures, relevant to the monitoring of his immunologic status, were carried out regularly. Also, his status as a "celebrity" resulted in much passing attention from visiting professionals as well as the media. From *his* standpoint, groups of people would "descend" on his room and stand around, talking and looking at him. Often they ignored him personally. Having finished their business, they would leave as abruptly as they had arrived. Similarly, newspeople would arrive, turn on their bright lights, do their interviews with the staff, pay some perfunctory attention to him, take their fill of pictures, turn their lights off, and depart. Despite these episodes of intense attention, the conditions of his existence—the imperative that he remain within the confines of his isolator—made it inevitable that at times he would be left for extended periods to his own devices. He always received excellent hygienic care, but compared to the average expectable experience of comparably aged infants, the quality of the mothering and of other social experiences available to him was highly variable and atypical.

In yet other respects his experience as an infant was unique. He was never encumbered by more than very light clothes or by bedding. He never experienced the transitory malaise of colds or other minor infections. At least before he achieved toddler status, he had a much freer existence and much more opportunity to exercise his muscles and explore his limited environment than could be available to an infant reared in more conventional circumstances. From the very beginning of his extrauterine existence he had also been exposed to a rich variety of visual and auditory stimuli. Against this background, I will review some aspects of this child's developmental history and compare his progress to generally accepted norms for his age.

In the areas of motor development and locomotion, which are regularly delayed in the more typically environmentally deprived as well as in many congenitally blind children, he achieved the following: at less than 4 months he was able to get up on his hands and knees and raise his abdomen from the surface. He could also sit with slight support. In the literature, the youngest age at which these achievements are reported is $6^1/_2$ months (McGraw, 1945). He would also squirm to and retrieve objects when he was prone. At 4 months (a month younger than the norm) he was able to coordinate hand and eye. By 6 months he could crawl on all fours and get over obstacles without difficulty, which is ordinarily a 10-month achievement. At 6 months he could also recover objects that he had dropped, and he was already using both hands in coordination. In addition to handling and transferring objects from hand to hand, he was able to handle two objects independently. These are 8- to 9-month achievements according to standard developmental norms (Griffiths, 1954). Two months later, at 8 months, he crawled skillfully (a 12–15 month achievement), sat himself up and sat for protracted periods without support (norm, 10 months), stood without support (norm 13–14 months), and could both squat and stoop (norm 17 months). He also walked alone when he was 8 months. By 11 months he walked freely and was able to turn around and seat himself in a little chair. The ability to turn around and sit down in a chair is usually considered an 18-month achievement.

In the areas of social and affective development, his progress during this early period was neither as consistent nor as impressive as his motor development. At 4 months he appeared alert and he was usually responsive. He reacted to being bounced about by smiling and he also smiled when visitors came into the room. Consistent with his age, there was at that time no evidence of a selective smile which would differentiate between familiar people and strangers. At 6 months he made babbling noises in relation to his activities, an age-appropriate activity. He did not, however, direct vocalizations even to familiar observers when they spoke to him. To do so would also have been age-appropriate. Whether he was on his hands and knees, sitting or standing, rhythmic rocking came to occupy increasing amounts of his waking time during the period up to his ninth month. Although he was responsive to the overtures of others, during this period he made no effort by sound or gesture to initiate an interaction with another person.

When he was 8 months old our speech pathologist estimated his language development to be at a 4-month level. At 12 months, if he babbled (a 6-month achievement), he did so infrequently. Occasionally he squealed as he went about his play activities. He did not, at 12 months, ever try to attract attention by shouting (an 8-month achievement) or make the phraselike babbles which Griffiths lists as a 9-month achievement. Throughout this period, he manifested a wide range of affective behavior. He reacted with evidence of pleasure when he was held and tossed about, became visibly angry when he was frustrated, and protested appropriately when he was subjected to the various procedures carried out by the medical team. However, we were impressed that he rarely, if ever, initiated contact with others by either voice or gesture, and repetitive rhythmical behavior persisted. Although he played with the wide variety of toys available to him, he evinced no interest in involving others in his activities. Typically, his play activities were also accompanied by rocking.

His disregard of his environment, the delay in prelanguage development, and the persisting involvement in rhythmical self-stimulatory behavior when he was 8 to 9 months old led us to reassess the quality of the care he was receiving. When one considers our findings and what appear to have been the result of our interventions, it is important to keep in mind that his was an isolated case. Conceivably, much of what was observed during his first 44 months could have been the result of maturational processes alone. The possibility that genetic differences may have accounted for the differences between our findings and those of Simon et al. also cannot be excluded. In this regard it is important to keep in mind that our subject was the child of a stable, middle-class, professional family, whereas the German youngsters were the offspring of unstable parents of limited intellectual abilities and with a history of significant psychiatric problems. It should also be noted that even if we assumed that our efforts accounted for the developments now to be described, we had no way of defining with certainty what role any one of the specific interventions we undertook played in his overall progress.

At the outset we were impressed that despite, or perhaps because of, the highly varying environment in which he lived and the very large number of persons to whom he was exposed, he had significantly less opportunity to establish affective ties with any one individual than would have been the case under more typical conditions of child rearing. When he was in the hospital he was subjected to the routines of a busy service. Whether he was played with or not depended on the work load at any given time. Socializing in the course of such routine activities as cleaning and feeding, depended on the interest and other obligations of the assigned caretaker. Often there was little. It is noteworthy, for example, that even at 24 months he did not regularly participate in his own feeding. The reason given for this was that it would be too difficult to clean up after him. It seemed to us that the isolating effect of his environment as well as the often perfunctory manner in which caretaking activities were carried out might be relevant to the relative retardation of language and social development.

In the light of these considerations, a campaign of intensified stimulation was instituted both in relation to caretaking activities and independently of them. A systematic program of prespeech stimulation was instituted. In order to increase his awareness of coordinated sight and sound, a television set was placed near his isolator. A specific caretaking person was assigned to him during his periods of hospitalization. When he was at home, systematic efforts were devoted to playing with him both during the discharge of caretaking activities and independently of them. Whether because of these efforts or coincidentally, within a few weeks, there was a considerable increase in the amounts of his prespeech vocalizing in the form of babbling, as well as evidence of greater word comprehension. For many months, however, his speech development continued to lag roughly four months behind the norms of his age. At 22 months he understood and followed directions to the extent of being able to help the nurses with such tasks as the transfer of materials into the isolator and the tidying of the isolator. He would also repeat the names of familiar objects and identify the objects themselves appropriately. Occasionally he spontaneously used single nouns such as *momma*, the names of the nurses and various toys. Spontaneous speech, as in the form of initiating requests, was still only rarely in evidence.

Two months later, at 24 months, he was a happy, outgoing, mischievous little boy. He would initiate a request (e.g., say "light on"), when he wanted just that. The speech therapist estimated his ability to communicate to be at least at age level. She noted, however, that his vocabulary could not be tested against standard 2-year norms. (How many toddlers, after all, have occasion to use words like "isolator" and "transfer"?) Rhythmic self-stimulating behavior was still detectable in the form of some muted rocking when he was manipulating and studying objects. However, he played actively, displayed a wide range of affects, and a capacity for maintaining interest in activities as well as involvement with others which was well within the range of the average and expectable for 2-year-olds. At this time, he expressed himself in forms and contexts which left the observer with little doubt but that he experienced and expressed understandable and appropriate affect.

Subsequent development continued at the same pace. When he was 28 months old, both his oral receptive and oral expressive abilities were judged by our speech therapist to fall within the $2^1/2$- to 3-year-old range. At this time he was able to complete all the 30-month elements of the Bayley Scale which, given his living circumstances, could either be administered or approximated.

From the standpoint of his affective development, too, he continued to progress along lines which fell within the normal range for youngsters being reared under more usual circumstances. Problems emerged which were typical of 2- to 3-year olds, and revolved around the effort to establish sphincter control and his wish to continue to take a bottle. Thus, he seemed to be well on his way to bowel and bladder continence when, during the 26- to 30-month period, it was decided that he should be weaned. When he was only being encouraged to drink from a cup with his meals, he became irritable, but seemed willing to settle for bottles at naptime and bedtime. When he was denied these as well, however, his behavior regressed in a variety of ways. Although he had been fairly well trained to use a "potty," he again became incontinent of feces. He deliberately spilled his milk when it was poured into a cup. A member of the research team, who had instituted the practice of seeing him every evening, observed that thumb sucking and rocking increased dramatically. He became distressed when she was ready to leave and insisted on being rocked. He also would awaken during the night and cry for his nipple and for "mommie." It is of interest that up to this time he had never called for his mother. The following episode, which occurred during this period, indicates something of the quality of his feelings and preoccupations. One evening, after the nurse who had been feeding him set aside his dish at his request, she asked him who would feed him the rest. He replied "Aunt Patty" (the member of the team referred to above). When the nurse then asked him what else he did with Aunt Patty, he replied "Pooh pooh in my pants." When ultimately his bottle was returned to him he was very possessive of it and at first continued to be irritable. Within a few days, however, he returned to his earlier status. Full continence was established by 33 months. He continued, however, to take a bottle at naptime and bedtime for some months.

During this period there was no evidence of genital interest in the form of masturbatory activity. Subsequently he manifested both interest and pleasure in his penis. This was evidenced by such expressions of pleasure as "tickle my tee tee" when he handled it. We were impressed, however, that this only happened after his third birthday.

Finally, yet another aspect of David's development merits comment. By the time of his second birthday he was spending approximately half his time in the hospital. The rest of his time was spent some forty miles away in his parental home. He was transported from one place to the other in a vehicle from which he could watch the surrounding countryside. In addition, both when he was in the hospital and when he was at home, he was exposed to a wide variety of visual stimuli. These included the comings and goings of individuals who visited him and the flow of traffic on the street in front of his room. He was, at least on the level of his perceptual experience, in a position to contrast the confining character of his own situation with the freedom to come and go which was characteristic of others. Nevertheless, and despite the very clear evidence of his intellectual competence, it was only about the time of his third birthday that he expressed interest in leaving the isolator, and its new addition, a much larger laminar flow room, to which he had ready access. This was all the more striking because he had observed the preparation of this new room, and in the process had watched various members of the team entering and leaving it. At approximately 30 months he did invite a visiting child to open the door and come into the room. He did not, however, articulate the reverse possibility, of himself going out, until his 35th month when he expressed the contingency, "When I get out of here. . . ." It is of interest that once it occurred to him he used this conditional form repeatedly and in a variety of sentence contexts. Over a period of several days he was heard to say, "When I get out of here I will come with you into the kitchen . . . I will get into the car . . . I play the piano."

Although he was certainly physically capable of removing himself from the bubble, up to his fifth year, when I last saw him, he had given no indication of the intention to translate the verbally expressed contingency into action. Indeed, even its explicit expression dropped out after several weeks. For many months thereafter he seemed, from the evidence of his overt behavior, to accept his confinement in the bubble without question or conflict. The two events which I will now describe, however, indicate otherwise. They seemed to provide clear evidence of the operation of the mechanisms of displacement and denial.

1. One of the participants in the study, who had made it a practice to visit David every day and who had tried to explain to him the importance of maintaining the integrity of the isolator, had been out of the country for an extended period. David had been prepared for his absence and was looking forward to his return. When he returned he spoke to David on the phone and told him it would still be some days before they could meet. David appeared distressed but made no comment. Within the hour, however, he deliberately punctured the floor on the isolator in at least half a dozen places.

2. David, aged 50 months, was at home playing with his mother when his older sister, accompanied by some friends, burst into the room. She asked excitedly to be allowed to go with one of their mothers "to buy hamburgers." As they left the room, David jumped up shouting, "I want to go too." Within seconds, however, he stopped very abruptly, stepped back, and said softly, "No I don't."

COMMENT

At first glance it would appear that there could be no two more different observers of children than Darwin and Watson. Darwin, who had already spent six years on the *Beagle*, and was already thinking through what became our theory of evolution, was both an observer and a synthesizer. Having observed and recorded phenomena, whether in the plant world, the animal world, or in his own children, he attempted to derive general principles which would make sense out of what he had seen. Watson, on the other hand, started with a sharply defined hypothesis concerning the way things "are," and proceeded as though his hypothesis were established fact. Darwin concluded that little boys had an instinct for throwing things and he considered this as much an inborn phenomenon as is the snapping jaws of a newborn crocodile. Watson considered the newborn to be like an amorphous mass of metal which had to be molded and pounded into shape. You might be born with the potential to be afraid but you had to be trained to know what to be afraid of. Both were limited by what we, as psychoanalysts, would today call their countertransference. Both believed, in his own way, that he as an observer could function dispassionately, that in the making of his observations his own personal history and biases were irrelevant. Both were wrong. Our observations themselves and our interpretations of them are invariably affected by the filter of personal biases and prejudices through which we observe.

The stories of Tracy, who unlike most congenitally blind children grew up well; of the difference in reactions of pigtail and bonnet monkey infants to separation; of the ability of Monica and other children with esophageal atresia to make loving attachments even though in many other respects they were very similar to environmentally deprived children; of the stable differences in experience which apparently resulted in major differences in the characters of Stern's twins; and of David, who at age 5 was a bright attractive youngster despite literally never having been touched by human hands, all underscore the difficulty of defining what elements of early experience are essential for optimum psychological development. I choose the word *optimum* rather than *healthy* or some other value laden term to emphasize that the assessment of mental health always involves a relativistic judgment, one based on the prejudices of the evaluator. It appears to be the case that, if psychological development is to proceed, if such psychic structures as self or ego are to coalesce, there must be some form of very early experience in the coenesthetic mode. We know what form this experience usually takes in the cultures with which we are familiar. What might happen in a culture with radically different values from ours? In the next session we will consider child rearing on the Israeli Kibbutz as it was during the formative years, prior to the establishing of the State of Israel.

CHAPTER 8

The Preoedipal Period: The Earlier Phases

When the first child was born in the kibbutz "nobody knew what to do with him. Our women didn't know how to look after babies." But eventually "we saw it couldn't go on like this. By the time there were four children in the settlement we decided something must be done. How were the women both to work and look after their children? Should each mother look after her own family and do nothing else?" [Bettelheim, 1969, pp. 19–20, quoting a pioneer kibbutznik].

If one does not take the boundaries between the phases too literally, if one allows for the possibility that the later phases will gradually superimpose themselves over their predecessors, it is convenient to subdivide the preoedipal period into three phases. The earliest phase has been called by some the *undifferentiated* phase while others use the term *primary narcissism.* I prefer the former term because narcissism implies self-love or self-centeredness and I don't believe the infant in this phase has a self to be in love with. Another term which I find attractive is the *monadic* phase which reflects my prejudice that, during the first few months, as the infant becomes aware, awareness is limited to his or her own here and now sensory experience. Sensory experience, to the extent that "sensory" is a meaningful word during this period, is in the *coenesthetic mode* (Spitz, 1945a,b). Beginning

147

sometime after the first few months, the infant enters into what is, in my scheme of things, the authentic phase of *primary narcissism. Diacritic experience* now becomes available. The baby shows every evidence of being aware that things come and go but, as Piaget has shown, does not have the ability to ascribe separate existences to them. A baby, at this time, may become frustrated and angry. It is, however, a visceral frustration; the feelings are not directed at a particular object to which he or she has ascribed a separate existence. The third, or dyadic phase, emerges as the baby becomes aware of the existence of another (i.e., an agent "out there") who plays a role in his or her being gratified. We believe this phase begins at roughly 7 months with the appearance of separation and stranger anxiety. At least it begins then in the average expectable world of good-enough mothering. For me this is also the time of secondary narcissism. In effect, the baby expects, one might say feels entitled, to have its needs gratified by the agencies he or she perceives to be "out there." The angst is no longer mere frustration; it has a direction, there is a potential frustrating "something" out there, as well as a source of gratification. As the infant becomes a toddler, the discovery is made that the world is not, after all, his or her oyster. A price must be paid for gratification; there are limits imposed on the child's tendency to do "what comes naturally." The narcissistic position with which he or she entered into dyadic relations gradually gets overlaid with what Glover (1935) called the phase of obsessional primacy (see chapter 9). In some of the material which I will review, the individual's history is followed well beyond infancy and toddlerhood. This is particularly the case with regard to the children of the Israeli kibbutzes. I justify this as extrapolations concerning the outcome of particular techniques of handling the preoedipal period.

The process of getting oneself born is often used as the epitome of a stressful experience and the prototype for the later ability to experience anxiety. Aside from the fact that there is, to my knowledge, no evidence that children delivered by Caesarian section are any less able to be anxious than the rest of us, there is reason to wonder whether, for the baby who is being born, the "birth experience" is an experience at all. Most of the cerebral structures to which we ascribe the capacity for mental functioning are not available at birth. Furthermore, Lagercrantz and Slotkin (1986) have pointed out that the splanchnic nerves, the portion of the autonomic nervous system which is the route from the brain and, therefore, the "psyche," to the visceral organs and endocrine glands, are not yet functional at the time of birth. The catecholamine[1] surge which accompanies the birthing process, and which results in the manifestations of stress the baby shows, is the result of lack of oxygen. This alteration in blood chemistry activates both the adrenal gland, which produces adrenaline, and patches of catecholamine secreting cells which are located along the baby's aorta. It is their combined secretions of catecholamines which constitute the organism's response to the stressful situation. During the months after birth, both the cerebral regulatory systems and the autonomic nervous system mature, the specialized cells along the aorta disappear, and the regulation of stress responses becomes a function of the central nervous system. Ultimately "responses" become "psychological experiences"; that is, for any given individual, the evocation of the response comes to reflect his or her evolving psychic structures, and therefore idiosyncratic experience. For the infant en route out of the uterus, however, it would appear that while the physiological stress is unequivocal, the imputation to the child of psychological stress is most probably gratuitous—an instance of adultomorphizing. What we, as observers, interpret as psychologically traumatic, may well be a nonexperience for the infant. Indeed, Lagencrantz and Slotkin believe that from a strictly physiological standpoint, it may actually be beneficial to the infant to be born via the vagina. The surge of catecholamines "clear the lungs and changes their physiological characteristics to promote normal breathing, mobilizes readily usable fuel to nourish cells, ensures that a rich supply of blood goes to the heart and brain, and may even promote attachment between mother and child" (p. 100). If this scenario is accurate, one can conclude that the beginnings of psychology must await at least the following: (1) Relevant aspects of the nervous system must have achieved levels of maturation adequate for

---

[1]Catecholamines are a family of chemical compounds which include the hormones–neurotransmitters adrenaline, noradrenaline, and dopamine. These substances are involved in the body's response to stress. Hence such colloquial phrases as, "His adrenaline is pumped up."

it to assume regulatory functions with regard to the rest of the organism. (2) The splanchnic nerves must have become sufficiently functional to transmit central nervous system "messages" to the viscera as well as back to the brain. (3) The peripheral sensorimotor system must also have matured sufficiently to carry its "messages." Since for each individual these maturational events occur in a unique and distinctive ambience, the nature of each individual's psychology will also be unique and different—this latter is the developmental factor.

The terms *bonding* and *attachment* refer to two mechanisms through which the earliest internalizations of the environment probably occur. That both happen is beyond question; not so clear, however, is: (1) What the critical elements are in the complex interaction of mother and infant which must be present if the interaction is to happen. (2) How these earliest experiences set in motion the processes which eventuate in the formation of psychic structures. The plight of the very early environmental deprivates, and the striking differences between them and those who were "deprived" after some period of good-enough mothering, is evidence enough of the critical importance of the earliest mother–infant relation. In view of our discussion of David, the bubble boy, as well as the results of the kibbutz experience which we will discuss shortly, it is not possible, however, to say precisely what elements in the prototypical mother–infant experience are critical. The experience turns out to be more complex than it appears to be when we watch a loving mother hold her newborn baby. Sylvia Brody (1981) reviewed the history of the development of the concepts of bonding and attachment. The summary which follows depends heavily on that review. It included critical assessments of the work of Klaus and Kennell, who introduced the concept of bonding, as well as that of Bowlby (1940, 1958) who was concerned with attachment behaviors. It is important to remember that both these concepts evolved out of observations made in very similar, highly selected populations. Klaus and Kennell (1976) did their work in a public hospital, and Bowlby's studies were based on his efforts to understand the origins of delinquency in impoverished populations. Both came to conclusions which made the mother–infant dyad the critical element which determines the infant's future destiny.

Klaus and Kennell (1976) used the term *bonding* to characterize what they felt should happen between mother and infant in the early postnatal period.

> They had observed that failure to thrive and maternal neglect or abuse were often associated with prematurity, birth defect or neonatal illness. As these conditions traditionally have required separation of the new born from the mother, they reasoned that the misfortunes that befell the infants resulted from a failure of maternal attachment right after the infant's birth. In contrast, it appeared that a positive maternal bond developed more naturally and more regularly in infants born at home or when mothers had rooming in privileges in the hospital. Therefore, they considered that close sensory contact with the mother's body as soon as possible after delivery might promote the affectional bond necessary for the mother's satisfaction as well as her motivation to care for the infant, and for optimal development of the infant. They called the process *maternal–infant* bonding and defined it as a unique and enduring relation between mother and infant, set in motion by the mother's touching, fondling, holding, cuddling, nursing, and making eye contact with the baby—behaviors comparable to the maternal responses to signaling behaviors of infants described by Bowlby [Brody, 1981, p. 3].

From a series of observations reported by Klaus and Kennell, as well as others, Brody felt there was "evidence that a brief period of skin-to-skin contact between mother and infant within an hour or one-and-a-half hours after delivery has at least some short-term effects on their relation." She cautioned, however, that before one could assess the significance of these results one would have at least to consider the following possibly confounding factors:

> (1) To what extent experimental mothers are self-selected, not merely in agreeing to participate, but in the prior decision to deliver their infants by natural methods and to breast-feed; (2) Whether silver nitrate was put in the infants' eyes before the EC [extended contact]—Klaus and Kennell recommend that it not be done but have not specified it as a condition in their studies; (3) In the cases showing negative results, what factors can have interfered with positive outcomes; (4) The continuity and quality of maternal contacts over longer periods of time; (5) and various

social factors, including the quality of the mother's marriage [pp. 5–6].

The immediate benefits of extended contact appear to be definite. However, Brody points out that without these kinds of data, one cannot do more than speculate about its long-term implications. She also mentions that she has "reason to believe that Klaus and Kennell regret that they may have unintentionally conveyed the idea . . . that what happens in the first hours or days of life during EC may be decisive for later development" (p. 12).

John Bowlby, who had become interested in the high incidence of delinquency among the children of the poor in Britain, seems to have been among the first to call attention to the relevance of the ambience in which infants and children grow up. He wrote (1940):

> Perhaps another reason for the neglect of a study of environment has been the gradual recognition that individuals to a great extent choose their environment and so are often the authors rather than the victims of circumstance. Now, however true this may be for adults and even adolescents, it is far less true for infants and it is with the environment in infancy that I am principally concerned. It seems to me to be as important for analysts to make a scientific study of early environment as it is for the nurseryman to make a scientific study of soil and atmosphere. Psychoanalysts, like the nurseryman, should study intensively and at first hand (1) the nature of the organism, (2) the properties of the soil and (3) the interaction of the two (p. 154).[2]

The situation and problems Bowlby was describing in the slums of pre-World War II London are precisely the same as those we are seeing in the American slums and ghettos of the 1990s. Over the next many years Bowlby presented evidence that the roots of later delinquent behavior lay in the failure of the infant to make an appropriate attachment to his or her mother during

---

[2]Today, this statement seems so obvious as to amount to a platitude. In 1940, however, analysts were still almost entirely dependent on the retrospective inferences they drew from their adult patients' memories. Even Melanie Klein, who "observed" infants, did so through an adultomorphizing filter which imputed adult cognitive functions to newborns. I put "observe" in quotes because there is no evidence that she made controlled systematic observations.

the earliest years. From his analysis he came to the conclusion that attachment, and, therefore, the possibility of adaptive psychological development, required appropriate environmental response to at least five "instinctual" needs. Again I quote:

My main thesis is that the positive dynamic is expressed through a number of instinctual responses, all of which are primary in the sense used in this paper and, in the first place, relatively independent of one another. Those which I am postulating are *sucking, clinging, following, crying, and smiling,* but there may well be many more. In the course of the first year of life, it is suggested, these component instinctual responses become integrated into attachment behavior. How this process of integration is related to the parallel process in the cognitive sphere is difficult to know. It seems not unlikely, however, that there are significant connections between the two and that a disturbance in the one will create repercussions in the other [Bowlby, 1958, pp. 365–366; emphasis added].

He cites the work of Harlow, whom we have already discussed, in support of this conclusion. It is impossible to overestimate the importance of Bowlby's work. To the extent that our modern understanding of and approach to the study and management of the "children of the ghetto" has changed for the better in the past fifty years, his influence has been a major factor.

From the standpoint of his psychoanalytic critics there are problems with Bowlby's work which have to do primarily with the extent to which he assumes that his "instinctual behaviors" are innate and their very specific gratification essential. In effect he seems to disregard the roles of psychic structure formations and their idiosyncratic effect on particular individuals' motivations and behavior. Time has demonstrated that some of his specific assumptions were incorrect. Of his five postulated absolutely essential primary behaviors, at least three have been put to the test, in natural experiments, and found not to be essential. For the child with esophageal atresia sucking, if it is made available, is a sporadic "sometime" thing. When it happens, it has no relation to the rest of the infant's physiologic experience. Yet these children, unlike the delinquent children, who must have had adequate sucking experience to survive, form intense attachments.

David, the bubble boy, was incapable of clinging. The circumstances of his existence precluded his putting his arms around, or of achieving skin contact with, another person. Yet, as we saw, he became a bright, friendly, affable child. Tracy, the congenitally blind child, could not follow. Yet, when she was last seen at roughly age 3, she was developing well. As much is true of other congenitally blind individuals who, like Stevie Wonder, are neither autistic nor delinquent.

What is it, then, which much happen in the "experience"[3] of the infant, for attachment to develop? This much we know, the verb "to attach" is transitive; it requires an object. It is evident that to have a psychological object requires some awareness of an other. "Experience," in some form, with "presence and absence," with a "coming and going,"[4] would appear to be essential for the objectification of another to whom one can become attached. The other then becomes a representation in the infant's emerging mind. At the same time processes of identification are also occurring. Structures are being created in the infant's mind which include not only the anticipations of physiological need gratification, but also the specific context in which the process of gratification occurred. These, in turn, coalesce with other structures to eventuate in what becomes the essence of the individual: a self or an ego differentiates. When Monica fed her infants, she held them in the same position in which she had been held when she was an infant. It is difficult to imagine how a woman in her twenties could have reached back into her most primitive and preverbal experience and converted a passive experience from her infancy into an active pattern of behavior. On the face of it, it seems highly unlikely. Yet it appears to have happened—an internalization which became an element of her self, a way of feeding her baby which she experienced as natural and normal, in other words, ego syntonic. A series of studies by Wyrwicka (1981)

---

[3]"Experience" is in quotes to underscore the possibility that much of what we are talking about happens before the infant is capable of awareness. Indeed, it is my opinion that the capacity for awareness grows out of the "experience" the infant is having during the process of becoming attached.

[4]I use quotes to underscore that these, at least to begin with, are, in all probability, not psychological experiences. Rather, they are changes in the infant's physiological state which are induced by the environment.

suggest the mechanism by which this might happen. Taking advantage of the ability to stimulate directly the pleasure centers of the brain, she conditioned adult female cats to prefer such uncatlike foods as bananas, cereals, and vegetables. Later, when these cats and their newborn kittens were fed together, the latter developed and sustained the same food preferences as their mothers had been conditioned to choose. One can only conclude that a process of internalization and "psychic structure" formation had occurred in these never to be verbal animals!

MATURATION AND DEVELOPMENT ON AN ISRAELI KIBBUTZ

Rapaport (1958) suggested that the cumulative experience of roughly forty years (now nearly one hundred) of child rearing on Israeli kibbutzim has, in effect, been the equivalent of yet another natural experiment. He suggested to Bettelheim, who was working with delinquent children in Chicago, that a study of child rearing practices on the kibbutz, and their outcomes, might help clarify the source of some of the problems he was seeing. In Bettelheim's (1969) words, "Among the pressing problems still unsolved in American child rearing are those of the slum child, of the restless dissatisfaction of youth in general, and of particular disturbances among them, like drug addiction or juvenile delinquency. Since the Israeli kibbutzim seem to be free of such afflictions, that alone seemed a potent reason to ask if their educational methods could be applied to our problems" (p. 4).[5]

A related problem, one which remains with us today, is how to assess the importance of the biologically defined mother–child dyad. In the West we have accepted that it is this relation that provides the ideal conditions for growing up. Indeed in the 1960s, when Bettelheim studied the kibbutzim, the prevailing opinion was that the outcome of separating mother and child would be disastrous for the latter. But the rearing of children in groups and apart from their nuclear families, was a hallmark of the kibbutz

---

[5]These were essentially the same problems as confronted Bowlby in England thirty years earlier and which confront us now in America thirty years later.

movement. As the introductory quotation from Bettelheim indicates, the practice was not intended to be "experimental." There was no intention to invent a new way to rear children. For the early kibbutzniks their method of child rearing was born of what they regarded as necessity. It is also the case that in their details the patterns of child rearing practices have by no means been static. Policies were, and presumably still are, continually reviewed and changed to conform with what is conceived to be the best interests of the children. At the time Bettelheim wrote (1969) sixty years had passed since the founding of the first kibbutz. He was therefore able to observe the outcome of at least two generations of kibbutz rearing and to interview some of the older people who had pioneered the movement. It is to a consideration of kibbutz child rearing practices and their outcome, as reflected in several generations of kibbutz reared Israelis that we will now turn.

The kibbutz movement had its origins during the 1890s in the segregated Jewish communities of Central and Eastern Europe. Like Zionism it was an expression of the aspiration to establish a national rather than a religious identity for Jews. Those who chose to join kibbutzim believed that going back to the soil was an essential step in the creation of nationhood. Thus, all kibbutzim were, to begin with, agricultural communities.[6] The first permanent settlement was established at Deganyah on the shores of the Sea of Galilee in 1907 (Ben-Sasson, 1976). By the time of World War II there were many well-established communal agricultural settlements in what is now Israel. In numbers the kibbutzim have never accounted for more than 3 to 4 percent of the Israeli population. Rapaport lived on a kibbutz for approximately two years after he fled from his native Hungary. He was, therefore, an adult observer rather than a product of the kibbutz child rearing system. His report is based on that experience. In his words:

> [The kibbutz movement] arose from the Zionist–Socialist youth movement of Eastern Europe, the main tenets of which were: (a) Zionist ideology; (b) socialist ideology; and (c) the principle of realization, i.e., the commitment to translate ideology into action.

---

[6]Economic forces have since resulted in changes. Many kibbutzes now own factories and employ workers. This would have been an anathema to the founders.

In keeping with the Zionist tenet, the Movement steeped itself in the history of Jewry, in its contemporary cultural, social and political situation, in the contemporary conditions of Palestine, and in the reviving Hebrew language. In keeping with the Socialist tenet, the Movement adopted a socialist ideology and explored its ethical, humanistic, social, economic and political implications, striving to create within itself human relationships based on reason, justice, cooperation, and equality. In keeping with the principle of realization, the members of the Movement prepared to go to Palestine, to become people of the soil—in contrast to their East European parents who were intellectuals or merchants or artisans or laborers in industries threatened with extinction by advancing industrialization—and to create on that soil a Hebrew community based on reason, justice, equality and cooperation [p. 588].

A central tenet of the kibbutz philosophy was the complete equality of the sexes. There was no question but that women and men would work together in all aspects of the communal life. While the fundamental aspiration of the movement was to create a brighter future for these migrants from the ghettos of Eastern Europe, they appear not to have given much thought to the role of reproduction as essential to any future. As the introductory quotation from Bettleheim indicates, having a baby was experienced as an intrusion. It distracted a woman from her assigned job. A method had to be found which would both insure the optimum rearing of the children and not divert their mothers from regularly assigned work. A system had to be put in place in order to resolve this problem. The description of kibbutz rearing, which follows, is from Rapaport (pp. 592–593). It is important to keep in mind that he is not writing about a specific community. All kibbutzim were, by design, small, self-contained, and self-governing agricultural communities. They ranged in size from a few hundred to no more than two thousand people. Philosophically they were both fiercely democratic and socialistic. The actual carrying out of their convictions, however, varied from community to community. Rapaport's description, therefore, must be regarded as an overall characterization, rather than an accurate description of a specific community. He writes:

1. Collective upbringing begins when the child and the mother return from the hospital to the kibbutz. The infant spends his

first year in the "infants' house," in which there may be up to
15 infants, who, under optimal conditions, are cared for by a
metapelet[7] and her two aides, all trained for their work. For six
weeks the mother does not work; after that she gradually returns
to her regular work, though she continues to feed the child on
"work time" until he is weaned (six to eight months), whether
the feeding is from the breast or from the bottle. The feeding
mothers are usually together at the six feeding times of the 4-
hour schedule. For the first six months the infant does *not* leave
the infants' house, but is visited there by the parents and siblings for an hour in the evening. After six months he is taken
to the parents' room for the evening visits. Otherwise, the care
of the child is entirely entrusted to the metapelet.

2. In general, after the first year the children move to the "toddlers' house," where a *new metapelet* looks after a group of four
to six toddlers, taking care of their needs, training in eating
and toilet training. The visits with the parents now become two
hours long in the evening, and include the whole Sabbath, but
remain a time of play, walks, and entertainment. Between the
second and third years a nursery teacher enters the toddlers'
group; like the *metapelets*, she looks after their physical needs,
but is primarily concerned with their social and intellectual development.

3. At four years of age the children enter kindergarten, and generally move to a new house; the group is enlarged to 16–18, with
a new teacher and *metapelet*. This larger group, though it will
change its form of life, will stay together until it enters high
school at 12. Free and supervised play, excursions to the farm,
arts, group readings, visits with the parents on evenings and
holidays, are the children's daily routine; and their care, discipline, and the fostering of group spirit and intellectual development are the responsibility of the *metapelet* and teacher.

4. A year or two in kindergarten is followed by a "transitional"
year, i.e., preparation for grammar school, and with it an hour's
work daily in taking care of their house, school, garden and a
few fowl. In the grammar school, teaching is by the project
method, and the children have their say in it. The relation to
the teacher is informal and passing to the next grade is automatic.

---

[7]*Metapelet* is the Hebrew term for the workers with infants and small children. Despite
the insistence on full equality in responsibilities and job assignment on the kibbutz, the
metapelets seem always to be female.

5. With the twelfth year comes the high school, a male teacher and educator, and membership in the youth movement. The group is enlarged to 25 members and includes children from other kibbutzim and from cities. At this point the childen begin to work $1^1/_2$ to 3 hours a day on the big farm. The curriculum is more like that of a European than of an American high school. Besides the teachers, the educator and the group itself play a major role in planning and in the maintenance of discipline [pp. 592–593].

Since child rearing practices, more or less conforming to the foregoing, had been followed for roughly forty years when Rapaport wrote, and seem to have continued since, we have the necessary elements for what amounts to a prospective outcome study. In addition, since there was at precisely the same time the kibbutzim were being established, a massive emigration of people from the same segregated Eastern European communities to the West, we have a control group of individuals whose ancestors shared the same Eastern European ghetto experience as well as the same "gene pool."

Characterologic traits which the second and third generation kibbutzniks share with descendants of the remainder of the late nineteenth, early twentieth century Jewish Diaspora from Eastern Europe can be regarded as maturational (i.e., genetic in origin). To the extent that kibbutz reared individuals are different and distinctive, we can consider the difference to be developmental in their origin (i.e., resulting from the interaction of the maturationally defined potentialities of the individual and the specific environmental influences to which he or she was exposed).

According to both Bettelheim and Rapaport, for example, typical toddler behaviors which tend to trouble adults (e.g., enuresis, thumb sucking, and temper tantrums) are seen, at about the same frequency as they are in the United States. The presence or absence of these, for the adult troubling behaviors, one must conclude reflect differences in the maturational progress of a group of youngsters who are chronologically of roughly the same age. Just as in the United States, their effects on long-term development will reflect how the child rearing environment deals with them. Like the changes which occur at the time of puberty, they are maturationally driven. The determining influence of the environment can, however, be seen in other areas. I cite some examples from the many Bettelheim includes.

In the children's houses there is no segregation according to sex. Boys and girls dress and undress, shower and toilet themselves together without regard to their sexes. Despite, or perhaps because of the intimacy of their living conditions, there is little sexual interest between individuals either while growing up, or when they are grown up. The comment is made that it is difficult to be romantic about someone who not only bathed and showered with you, but also sat on the next commode to you until you were well into adolescence.[8] There is also, according to Bettelheim, no manifest homosexuality. Psychological testing, he reports, also reveals little evidence of latent homosexuality.

Bettelheim was particularly interested in the determinants of delinquency. The following paragraphs report the results of one of his inquiries into this problem.

> I therefore made it a point to ask about delinquency, without naming any particular kind. What then appeared was the following: In regard to car stealing, which they mentioned spontaneously, and which is a major form of delinquency in America, they told me that "this has become quite a problem here." When I asked how frequently it happens, the answer was "All the time." I asked, "In this kibbutz here?" and again the answer was "yes." I asked how recently a car had been stolen, and it appeared that this had happened more than a year ago. Why, then, did they talk as if it happens all the time? "Because it also happened a few months ago in a neighboring kibbutz." Thus the stated urgency and frequency of a phenomenon had clearly to do with the intensity of alarm felt by educators, and not with the facts.
>
> When I asked for a detailed description of the last incident of car theft, it turned out to involve a group of adolescent boys who had used a kibbutz truck after hours. They drove to the nearest city (fifteen miles) to see a movie, after which they put the truck back in place. The truck, of course, was kibbutz property, and since the boys were children of the kibbutz, they viewed it as their property

---

[8]Bettelheim, however, suspects this is an oversimplification. He feels there are powerful inhibitory forces at work.

too, a fact that nobody questioned. What constituted the delinquency was their staying out after hours. Under these circumstances, their use of the car, in the eyes of the educators, made it stealing [pp. 329–330].

In a summarizing paragraph Bettelheim writes:

Despite some exceptions, a kibbutz child's emotional involvement with his parents—and along with it his attachment, both positive and negative—is much less intense than that of an average middle-class American child. The emotional deficit, if it is such, is compensated by an incredibly strong attachment to his peer group, and by the much more diluted, but nevertheless very real emotional ties to the kibbutz as such and all its members. These are incomparably stronger than are an American child's ties to his cousins, his playmates, to other relatives and friends of the family, or to his community. (The only comparison might be an American's attachment to his religion, if it were focal to his life, as it is, for example, among the Hutterites or the Amish) [p. 109].

As adults, the children of the kibbutz turn up in disproportionate numbers in leadership positions in the state of Israel. Their role in the military is particularly noteworthy. Although at the time of the Six Day War, they made up only about 3 percent of the Israeli population, they accounted for at least 25 percent of the casualties suffered by the Israeli army. It is said that in terms of their ability to make intense personal relations like those we value, they do less well than individuals who have been reared according to our traditions. Their devotion and affective attachments remain focused on the kibbutz in which they grew up and on the state of Israel.

All of the above to the contrary notwithstanding, it is not the purpose of this review to advocate the virtues of kibbutz life. To reiterate, it is presented as a "natural experiment." The people who created the kibbutz movement came from a known, well-defined population. A very high percentage, perhaps the majority, of American Jews come from the same Eastern European "gene pool." The characterologic differences we see between the two groups must, therefore, be attributed to the differences in their respective patterns of rearing. It would, of course, be a mistake to attempt to explain all the differences on the basis of infancy and toddlerhood. On the other hand, what happens later is certainly in the nature of a continuation of the earlier experience.

During its earliest preoedipal years the brain of the child is neither a tabula rasa, as some philosophers used to think, nor is it the repository, in however rudimentary a form, of drives, intentions, and goals. Rather, it is a structure in the process of maturing along lines laid down by the individual's genetic endowment. Because, for any given individual, maturation occurs in an idiosyncratic ambience, the ultimate characteristics of brain and mind will reflect the externally derived influences which impinge on it (i.e., development). In this chapter I have reviewed four facets of the early maturational and development processes. I begin by presenting evidence that, from a psychological standpoint, birth is a nonevent for the child as it is being born. I then consider the phenomenon of bonding, and conclude that very early mother–infant contact does facilitate the establishment of a bond. Without continuing good-enough mothering, however, the beneficial effects are evanescent. As an example of very early environmental influence, I describe a study by Wyrwicka, who stimulated directly the "pleasure center" in the brains of adult female cats while feeding them vegetables. The animals changed their eating diets and became vegetarians. When these cats had kittens, who ate along side of them, they assumed the eating habits of their mothers—an instance of very early internalization. Finally, I discuss the child rearing practices in Israeli kibbutzim. These violate the conventional wisdom of the West, yet they result in individuals who are well adapted to the world in which they live.

CHAPTER 9

The Preoedipal Period: Phase of Obsessional Primacy

> Obsessional neurosis is unquestionably the most interesting and repaying subject of analytic research. But as a problem it has not yet been mastered. It must be confessed that, if we endeavour to penetrate more deeply into its nature, we still have to rely upon doubtful assumptions and unconfirmed suppositions [Freud, 1925, p. 113].

Times change, fashions change. Despite Freud's opinion of seventy years ago, the study of obsessions has, in fact, not proven a very rewarding area for psychoanalytic research. Indeed the recent psychoanalytic literature is notably sparse even in referring to the subject. For example, neither *obsession* nor its companion term *compulsion* is listed in the index or in the table of contents of Tyson and Tyson's *Psychoanalytic Theories of Development* (1990). It is as though the failure of the various psychotherapeutic approaches, including psychoanalysis, to "cure" severe obsessional states has led to a sense of futility.

In the meantime, psychopharmacologists have synthesized a number of drugs which seem, at least temporarily, to ameliorate the worst of obsessional symptoms. With regard to explaining why obsessional symptoms occur, as opposed to what to do about them, the pharmacologists cite evidence of metabolic alterations in such regions of the brain as the cingulate gyrus, the caudate

163

nuclei, and the orbitofrontal cerebral cortex (all known to be associated with the experiencing and regulation of the expression of affect). These, in turn, are generally accepted, but never proven, to be secondary to gene-determined, inherited vulnerabilities. In any event, it appears that by increasing the availability of the neurotransmitter serotonin, the severity of the symptoms in obsessive–compulsive disease (OCD) can be alleviated. A class of drugs known as selective serotonin reuptake inhibitors (SSRIs) has been developed. There is good evidence that these agents may, indeed, be helpful in some individuals with severe obsessional symptoms. I don't believe, however, that many people are convinced that they are curative. In this regard, a recent, somewhat oxymoronic, comment in a letter to the editor of the *Archives of General Psychiatry* is eloquent. Pigott and Murphy (1991), who were responding to a critique of an earlier paper by them, wrote "In Reply—Since OCD is generally characterized by only partial remission with effective treatment, we agree with Tamini and Mavisakalan that the choice of initial and subsequent pharmacotherapy represents a particularly important issue ... " (p. 858; emphasis added). That such a statement should have been published unchallenged in one of the most prestigious of psychiatric journals seems to me to be indicative of the limitations of the exclusively pharmacologic, nonpsychodynamic approach to the problem of obsessiveness.[1] At the same time, it is not possible to dismiss the possibility of either the presence of changes in the structure of the brain, or of the usefulness of medication in the management of severe obsessional states. Why these changes occur and why drugs are effective, however, is another matter. In this chapter I will make a case for the relevance of the psychodynamic underpinnings of obsessiveness.

The following vignette, from a case reported by Munich (1986), is illustrative of the problem of relating severe obsessional symptoms as in OCD to the characterological traits we refer to as obsessional. The patient sought treatment because of a variety of difficulties such as diffuse anxiety and depression, low self-esteem, and work inhibition. He was also recently separated from his wife.

---

[1]We usually use *obsessional* as an adjective as in *obsessional neurosis* or *obsessional character*. In what follows I will be using the noun form *obsessiveness* or *obsession* to refer to a parameter of adaptation.

Munich considered him to be an "obsessional character." The patient denied ever having experienced obsessional symptoms prior to his entering into analysis. On four occasions, however, during a five-year long analysis, he developed the compulsion to return to his apartment, after he had left for work, in order to make sure the gas was turned off. On the first occasion, early in the analysis, the symptom lasted for a month. During the middle phase it recurred and continued for two years. Finally, there were two brief recurrences as he approached termination. In each instance the occurrence of the symptom could be related to the anxiety provoking nature of the ongoing work. The patient insisted that he had never experienced anything like this before. He added, ironically, that he had not expected to be made worse by analysis. I raise two questions. First, how are we to account for the emergence of symptoms of OCD in a man who up to the time of his analysis, had no history of such problems? Second, what are the underlying shared characteristics which, as Sandler and Hazari (1960) point out, make it possible for us to use the term *obsessive* alternatively as a laudatory characterization or as a form of disparagement?

I begin with a review of the etiologic speculations of psychoanalysts in the past. Anna Freud (1966) summarized what was, at that time, the views of most analysts. She discussed the "widely held precondition" that the obsessional individual must regress libidinally from the phallic to the anal–sadistic level, while his ego and superego "retain their moral and aesthetic standards." She also proposed that a constitutional preference for the use of such defense mechanisms as reaction formation, intellectualization, and isolation characterizes obsessional individuals. This, in my opinion, somewhat convoluted hypothesis was predicated on the assumption that obsessional phenomena[2] are always pathological, and always manifestations of intrapsychic conflict,[3] an assumption which, in my opinion, does not accord with the observations of everyday life. Miss Freud, and virtually all other psychoanalysts

---

[2] The word *symptom* refers specifically to subjective discomfort while *phenomenon* refers to what is observed by self or others: phenomena may or may not be associated with subjective discomfort.

[3] Elsewhere (Freedman, 1971) I have discussed a number of clinical and theoretical objections to this hypothesis.

who wrote on the subject, agreed that there is a connection between the vulnerability to develop an "obsessional neurosis" and experiences inherent in the individual's passage through toddlerhood. Because both the symptoms with which obsessional patients presented and their early memories were so frequently related to the travails of toilet training in particular and bowel function in general, the toddler period came to be referred to as the anal–erotic period.

Some analysts (Abraham, 1921; Landauer, 1939), however, felt that to focus on battles over bowel function and the pleasure experiences associated with the anal area was much too limiting. They recognized that the environmental demands on small people, as well as the toddler's own interests, are too numerous and wide ranging to be reduced to so simple a relation. Landauer, for example, observed that conflicts over table manners can be every bit as intense and bewildering for the toddler as those which have to do with sphincter continence. Typically, toddlers are not competent to understand why particular expectations or prohibitions are being imposed on them. It is the imperative to give up one's strivings (so to speak, one's inclination to do "what comes naturally") and comply with the adult's demands and prohibitions that is critical. In Abraham's terms the toddler must learn to make a virtue out of a necessity. He or she must behave "correctly," that is, do what is "right." But *right* is a very elusive and ambiguous term. The 1981 edition of the *Merriam Webster's Collegiate Dictionary*, for example, contains no fewer than 31 numbered definitions. Most often the toddler can only know whether he or she "got it right" after the fact, as a consequence of the effects of behavior. For the toddler, who is just beginning to find his way as a separate center of initiative, this means learning to behave "correctly" as defined by the strictures of parental authority. Often "correctness" is only known from the parent's response to the results of behavior. The youngster must, in this regard, always be playing catch-up.

In keeping with the less restrictive approach of Abraham and Landauer, Edward Glover (1935, p. 268) called the period, roughly between 18 months and $3^1/2$ years, the phase of obsessional primacy. In Figure 9.1 this phase is visualized, albeit significantly extended in time, in relation to both the saltatory

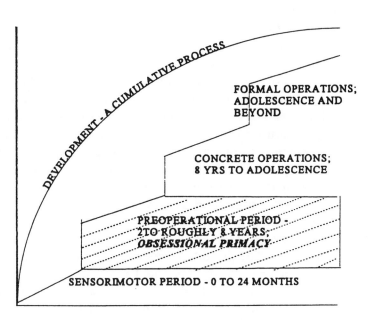

Figure 9.1. Development is a continuous cumulative process; maturation is saltatory. Here only Piaget's maturational sequence is shown. The cross-hatched area indicates the period during which obsessiveness develops.

course of cognitive maturation and the cumulative, "analog" process of development. Other aspects of maturation, such as the libidinal line and those identified by Erikson (1950) and McDevitt and Mahler (1989) are, of course, also in progress. Each is affecting the cumulative process of development. Glover, who makes no reference to Piaget, distinguished between the "highly differentiated end state which is the obsessional neurosis, and this primary obsessional state." The latter, he felt, is a facet of everyone's toddlerhood. He emphasized the cognitive limitations of the child during this period. He proposed that the toddler must, of necessity, experience the parent's behavior as either "for me" or "against me." When, for example, a frightened parent abruptly yanks a child out of the path of an oncoming car, the child is neither able to comprehend the danger he or she was in, nor to appreciate that the parent's angry appearing behavior was in fact an expression of love and concern. Glover's age range for this primary state is, I believe, too narrow. There is much evidence that the phase of obsessional primacy extends through what Piaget called the preoperational period of cognitive development and beyond.

Erikson used the term *muscular-anal* to refer to the same developmental period Glover designated as obsessional primacy. The word *development* should be emphasized because the youngster has now matured into toddlerhood. The pace of the emergence of newly functioning brain structures appears, at this time, to take second place to the interaction of the "already installed" equipment with the environment. Developmental changes primarily reflect the internalized influence of the environment on brain structure and function, as opposed to the gene-determined changes which we refer to as maturational. Mahler and McDevitt characterized this same period as the time the individual achieves a sense of object constancy. They feel that during this period (from 18 to 36 months) the child has achieved a primarily positive attachment to the maternal representation. With this achievement the "good" and "bad" aspects of the mothering one are fused into a single representation.[4] The maternal image has become intrapsychically available to the child (see chapter 2 on the development of the smile). Erikson felt that the nature of the interaction between the spontaneous activity of the small child and the surrounding universe is critical. In a generally supportive and affirming environment the child will emerge from toddlerhood with a sense of autonomy. If the child's experience is punitive and restrictive, a propensity to feelings of shame and self-doubt will result. At this age, autonomy on the one hand and shame and doubt on the other, can be viewed as the end points of a continuum of possible feelings about one's self. Erikson felt, and I agree, that the residua of these infantile feelings remain with one for life. I suggest, further, that the obsessional diathesis, the propensity to use modes of adaptation which we characterize as obsessional, derives from this phase of development.

---

[4]An illustration of the process of lessening of ambivalence: A 4-year-old boy was forbidden by his mother to get into a swimming pool with his much older cousins. He became furious, stomped his feet and said, "I'm not going to listen to your words any more." The words were hardly out of his mouth before he went over to her and kissed her.

However it is designated, it is the case that toddlerhood must happen to everyone who is to continue to mature and develop.[5] With its advent the child becomes more or less independently mobile and develops the rudiments of the ability to use language. I emphasize rudiments because, as we saw in discussing Piaget, the words an adult and a child may exchange with one another, like their perceptions of various aspects of the world around them, most often do not have the same meaning for the two. I present the accompanying cartoons, by O'Brian (1964), to convey something of the nature of the state of communicative dissonance which must inevitably exist between them. Examples of these dissonances abound in folklore, jokes, and the amusing anecdotes people tell about their children. But their effects are not always cute and amusing. The anecdote from Mrs. Fraiberg's patient which I recounted in the previous chapter, is a small example of the kind of baleful effect that can result from the miscommunication between parent and child. It is at this time too that the youngster also begins to be experienced by his or her caretakers as a separate center of initiative. In average expectable child rearing circumstances, this means that educational processes begin. The "free spirit" of the incipient toddler is henceforth hemmed in by a variety of demands and constraints. Parents feel bowel training is essential. They object to the breaking of precious belongings, messy eating, writing on the wallpaper, and countless other activities that seem perfectly normal and natural to the preoperational child. They also institute prohibitions like, "Don't go on the street, a car might hit you," which are perfectly obvious to an adult but don't make particular sense to a 3- or 4-year-old. The child is confronted with a bewildering array of expectations and prohibitions.[6] To these the little one must respond appropriately, or else! The impossibility of the toddler's knowing what is

---

[5]*Anal, anal-erotic, anal-muscular, negativistic, obsessional primacy, preoperational,* and *terrible twos* are some terms used to refer to this period.

[6]In his autobiographical study *Good bye To All That* Robert Graves (1929) writes "So my father sent me to King's College School, Wimbledon. I was just seven years old. My father took me away after a couple of terms because he heard me using naughty words, and because I didn't understand the lessons. I had started Latin but nobody explained what 'Latin' means; its declensions and conjugations were pure incantations to me. For that matter, so were the strings of naughty words. And I felt oppressed by the huge hall, the enormous boys . . . and compulsory Rugby football, of which *nobody told me the rules*" (p. 21). We now know, from Piaget's studies, that at 7 he *could not have comprehended the rules* even if he had been told of them.

"No dessert until you've eaten all your mashed potatoes."

"Be brave. It's not going to hurt."

"Now see what you've done!"

"And stay in your room, young man!"

Drawing by William O'Brian. © 1964, 1992 The New Yorker Magazine, Inc. All Rights Reserved. Reprinted with permission.

Drawing by William O'Brian. © 1964, 1992 The New Yorker Magazine, Inc. All Rights Reserved. Reprinted with permission.

appropriate until "after the fact" is only part of the problem. In addition, it turns out that what is "appropriate" by adult standards, may be anything but from the standpoint of the small person's perceptions. It is in regard to all of this that the etymology of the word *obsession* is of particular interest and relevance.

According to the unabridged *Oxford English Dictionary* (1933), the word *obsession* derives from the Latin verb *obsidere*. In its original usage it meant to sit at or opposite to, to beset or besiege as in a military operation. Over time the obsessing agent became less precisely defined as to location, and the object of the obsession became less clear. By the midsixteenth century, the very specific meaning "siege," in a military sense, had been extended to include, and ultimately largely to be replaced by, the connotations of to haunt or to harass as by evil spirits. At the same time, to be obsessed also came to be applied to any experience of this type to which an individual as well as a community could be subject. In the midnineteenth century one could still be "beset by foreign, backstairs and domestic influences, by obsessions at home and abroad." The earliest entry which uses the word *obsession* to refer to the private, entirely internalized and idiosyncratic experience of one individual is dated 1893 (H. Crackantlarope, *Wreckage* 99) "The thought of death began to haunt him till it became a constant obsession." Only in the Supplement to the *Oxford Dictionary*, however, does the word, both by definition and illustrative example, come to take on the connotation of a process going on entirely within an individual. It is also at this time that the illustrative examples begin to come from the psychoanalytic literature.

There are obvious similarities between the experiences of the resident of a town, whose tranquil existence was abruptly disrupted by an obsessing Roman army, and that of the young person who enters toddlerhood blissfully unaware of what is to come. For both there is a compelling necessity to respond appropriately to the unanticipated intrusions. In neither case does the hapless victim know in advance what that "appropriate" response will turn out to be. That will only be determined by the events that follow one's actions (in the phenomenalistic world of the toddler, causality is determined by contiguity). Doubt and uncertainty are inevitable for the growing child, not to mention the adult, who is faced with both an uncertain world, and also the inability to know in advance what will be the effects of his or her behavior. If only one could be certain to *get it right*. But one can only be certain after the fact.

Here the plot thickens. With respect to the "obsessed" citizens of a besieged town, getting it right could be defined as doing what was effective in getting the siege lifted. In addition to their military efforts, they could turn to their gods for help. They could pray, make sacrifices and do other things which they had come to believe would induce their deities to affect the course of events. Sometimes the results were such that their efforts appeared to have succeeded. Actually one such instance is described in the Old Testament. Jerusalem was being besieged by an Assyrian army which had already conquered virtually all of Israel. But God answered the prayers of the inhabitants of Jerusalem and the Assyrians lifted the siege and left. I quote, "And it was, that night, that an angel of Yahweh went out and struck one hundred eighty-five thousand in the Assyrian camp, and they rose in the morning and here they were all dead corpses. And Sennachereb traveled and went and returned, and he lived in Nineveh" (2 Kings 19:35). It is generally assumed that there was an epidemic of some sort in the Assyrian camp. So far as the Israelites were concerned, however, they had done what was right for God and He rescued them. When, some years later, the Babylonians besieged and captured Jerusalem, it was apparent to the Israelites that they had not acted properly in the eyes of the Lord, and were being punished. The same God who loves and protects can also be extremely harsh and punitive. For the toddler, turning to higher authority poses yet another, even more vexing dilemma. Most typically, the "obsessing force" as well as the protecting and the punitive agencies are one and the same. At least they come packaged in the same skin. As both Spitz (1957) and Glover (1935) have pointed out, the selfsame parent may at one time be experienced as "all good" or "for me," and at another as "all bad," or "against me." The alien invader at the gate is also the loving protecting parent.

It is arguable that the same modes of cognitive and affective reaction which were shown by the ancient Israelites under siege and are manifested by toddlers during the phase of obsessional primacy, also characterize most of us in times of stress. Who

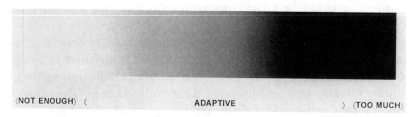

(NOT ENOUGH) 〈   ADAPTIVE   〉 (TOO MUCH)

Figure 9.2. Titer of Obsessiveness

amongst us has never knocked on wood? For us adults who sort of know that knocking on wood isn't really going to affect the course of events, the act amounts to a controlled "miniregression." It is the case that some level of obsessionality characterizes all of us—at least all of us who have successfully negotiated the "oral" or "sensorimotor" phase.[7] It is in this sense that I like to think of obsessionality as a parameter of adaptation. Much like blood pressure or respiratory rate, our individual titers of obsessiveness vary as a function of the demand being put on us by the environment. We would hope, for example, that a person running a hundred-yard dash would have a markedly elevated blood pressure during the race. We would be very concerned, on the other hand, if someone maintained that level of pressure while resting quietly at home. I suggest a similar situation with regard to one's titer of obsessiveness. We expect that someone embarking on a difficult or hazardous task is likely to be very careful in planning and preparation. He cannot afford to be as "laid-back" as he might be at other times.[8] Figure 9.2 illustrates this point. There is a wide adaptive range over which one's titer of obsessiveness can vary.

---

[7]Early environmental deprivates such as we have already discussed, who do not develop the ability to establish object ties, probably also do not establish the capacity for obsessiveness.

[8]A neurosurgeon, known for his meticulous work, was having an argument with a hospital administrator. The latter, in exasperation, finally said, "The trouble with you is that you are a goddam obsessional." To this the neurosurgeon replied, "You know you're right, but tell me, when you have to have your head opened up would you prefer it be done by an obsessional like me or by someone who is going to shit in the wound?"

OBSESSIVENESS AND RELIGION

Although he didn't cite the Old Testament in this connection, the many and striking similarities between obsessional states and religious practices did not escape Freud's notice. He wrote (1907):

> In view of these similarities and analogies, one might venture to regard the obsessional neurosis as a pathological counterpart of the formation of a religion, and to describe that neurosis as an individual religiosity and religion as a universal obsessional neurosis. The most essential similarity would reside in the underlying renunciation of the activation of instincts that are constitutionally present, and the chief differences would be in the nature of those instincts which in the neurosis are exclusively sexual in their origins while in the religion, they spring from egoistic sources [p. 126].

Six years later, in discussing primitive religions, Freud (1913) also wrote:

> Anyone approaching the problem of taboo from the angle of psycho-analysis, that is to say, of the investigation of the unconscious portion of the individual mind, will recognize, after a moment's reflection, that these phenomena are far from unfamiliar to him. He has come across people who have created for themselves individual taboo prohibitions of this very kind who obey them just as strictly as savages obey the communal taboos of their tribe or society. If he were not already accustomed to describing such people as "obsessional" patients, he would find "taboo sickness" a most appropriate name for their condition. Having learned so much, however, about this obsessional sickness from psycho-analytic examination—its clinical aetiology and the essence of its psychical mechanism—he can scarcely refrain from applying the knowledge he has thus acquired to the parallel sociological phenomenon.
>
> A warning must be uttered at this point. The similarity between taboo and obsessional sickness may be no more than a matter of externals; it may apply only to the *forms* in which they are manifested and not extend to their essential character. Nature delights in making use of the same forms in the various biological

connections: as it does, for instance, in the appearance of branch-like structures both in coral and in plants, and indeed in some forms of crystal and in certain chemical precipitates. It would obviously be hasty and unprofitable to infer the existence of any internal relationship from such points of agreement as these, which merely derive from the operation of the same mechanical causes [p. 26].

The phenomenon of scrupulosity, as well as its relation to obsessiveness, is well recognized in the Catholic Church. As one reads the following extracts from the *Catholic Encyclopedia*, it should be kept in mind that children reared in that faith begin to be taught the Catechism when they are somewhere between 5 and 7. It is assumed that at that age they can understand the difference between right and wrong. Keep in mind, too, Piaget's findings concerning the cognitive state of preoperational children of this age, including the quality of their moral judgment.

In the section on psychoneurotic disorders the following appears, "Obsessive concern with matters pertaining to the moral life together with a compulsive meticulousness in confession and in the avoidance of objectively sinful acts is called scrupulosity. *It is a pathological exaggeration of what in ordinary usage is considered healthy, normal, scrupulous, honest and meticulous attention to the details of one's occupational and professional tasks*" (p. 979; emphasis added).

In yet another entry, the phenomenon is addressed in a more general sense.

Scrupulosity: The scrupulous person's life journey has been aptly likened to that of a traveler whose pebble-filled shoes make every step painful and hesitant. Scruples render one incapable of making with finality the daily decisions of life. This psychic impotence, providing a steady source of anxiety and indecisiveness, is especially prevalent in ethical or pseudo-moral areas. It causes ordinary, everyday questions to be viewed as impenetrable and insoluble. Decisions require a disproportionate amount of time and energy, and are always accompanied by feelings of guilt and doubt. Never at peace, the mind compulsively reexamines and reevaluates every aspect of a matter about which scruples center. With increasing doubts and mounting fear the mind is so blinded and confused that volitional activity becomes difficult or impossible. The will is unable to act without immediately reacting against its previous decision. There is a more or less constant, unreasonable, and morbid fear of sin, error, and guilt. The mind demands mathematical certitude in moral matters, and when this is not forthcoming, there is a fear reaction that is both unreasonable and unholy [p. 1253].

In an earlier edition (1911) of the same work the author finds it necessary explicitly to reject the notion that scrupulosity may be a special state of grace: "The idea sometimes obtaining that scrupulosity is in itself a spiritual benefit of some sort is, of course, a great error" (p. 640).

It would be fatuous to assert that behavioral characteristics like those described under the rubric of scrupulosity are limited to people reared in the Catholic faith. Nonetheless they have been sufficiently noteworthy within the context of that religion to merit these entries in its most authoritative reference work. We have here two facts which, taken together, can be viewed as elements in yet another "natural experiment": A very large cohort of children, actually many millions, are required to learn a series of principles and guides to belief and behavior which, according to what we know today, *they have no competence to understand.* In the same population a condition arises, and is sufficiently prevalent so that it is given a very specific name, scrupulosity, and is identified as related to an excess of obsessiveness. The encyclopedists make the distinction, as have I, between "normal, scrupulous, honest and meticulous attention to the details of one's occupational and professional tasks" and a maladaptive excess of these traits. They also emphasize that scrupulosity is especially a problem in "matters pertaining to the moral life together with a compulsive meticulousness in confession and in the avoidance of objectively sinful acts." These are precisely the matters with which the catechism is concerned. I know of no evidence that indicates that severe, maladaptive obsessional syndromes occur more frequently among Catholics than among the non-Catholics of this world. What we do have, however, is documentation from an independent source which supports the hypothesis that obsessiveness is a parameter or a mode of adaptation which emerges during toddlerhood and develops during the preoperational years.

This, then, in broad outline, is a statement of the nature of the adaptive challenges with which everyone who passes through the phase of obsessional primacy must cope. For any given individual, the specific forms they take play major roles in defining the shaping experiences which, in turn, will determine how the person deals with the rest of life. Quite literally in order to survive, the toddler must comply with the dictates of the parenting ones. How rigorously, and in what idiosyncratic ways, constraints and demands are imposed, varies from parent to parent. Each toddler's experience is, therefore, unique. Also idiosyncratic are temperamental and behavioral properties of the child which contribute to determining how he or she will respond to the parent's interventions. As Darwin pointed out in 1853 boys are very different from girls. He had never heard of attention deficit disorder but he knew on the authority of his father as well as from personal experience that boys are three times as difficult to rear (see p. 119). The cognitive limitations which Piaget has identified are, however, universal. If the child is to survive and "prosper" in the world he or she is destined to inhabit, it will be necessary for that child to comply with many imperatives long before maturation and development have proceeded to a point at which cognitive understanding of their significance is possible. As children we all did things because our parents told us to, and as parents we have all insisted that our children do as we dictate because we tell them to. Neither the cognitive competence nor the affective development of the preoperational child permits things to be otherwise. If children are to be the beneficiaries of good-enough parenting, it is inevitable that they develop some level of obsessiveness. I apply no modifier to this word because I am not talking about an obsessional character or an obsessional neurosis. Rather, I am now referring to what I believe to be a parameter of adaptation, one which emerges at a particular point in the process of maturation and development and becomes as much a part of our adaptive equipment as blood pressure, pulse, respiratory rate, acid–base balance, and innumerable others.

ADULT SEQUELAE OF COGNITIVE DISSONANCE DURING TODDLERHOOD

The complexity of the lives of small people, taken together with the residual effects of experiences between toddlerhood and the emergence of adulthood, make it necessary to be cautious in dealing with our patients' memories. Differences in the perception of a given event as well as screen memories and retrospective falsifications are facts of human psychology. The historical accuracy of what we hear must, therefore, always be suspect. It is also the case that Freud's caveat (1913, p. 140) to the effect that the "similarity between taboo and obsessional sickness may be no more than a matter of externals," a matter of analogy rather than homology, continues to be relevant. There are, however, a few instances in which observations of the same individual during the phase of obsessional primacy and again in adulthood seem to lend support to the hypothesis that events during the child's phase of obsessional primacy are related to the idiosyncratic manifestations of obsessiveness in later life. Ritvo (1966) described a young man who, because of phobic symptoms, had been analyzed between ages $5^1/2$ and $8^1/2$. When he returned to analysis fifteen years later Ritvo observed that, "The same conflicts for which he sought a solution as a child in the phallic–oedipal phase by the formation of phobic symptoms he later tried to cope with by the obsessive doubts about the functioning of his mind" (p. 131).

The illustrative cases which follow are from my own practice.

Case Examples

Case 1:   At the time she consulted me CD was a 31-year-old married woman. She came to therapy complaining of periods of depression, recurrent migraine headaches, and severe bruxism. She described a loveless, frustrating marriage to a cold, austere man whom she both idealized and resented. Her principal goal in life, one which had continued to elude her after 7 years of marriage, was to achieve evidence of his affection and respect. Her inability to succeed in this goal despite her most vigorous efforts to please and placate him, was her major conscious preoccupation and source of frustration. She regarded her relation with this man as a continuation of the experience of her earlier years and she was aware that she was no more successful with him than she had been with her parents. When he expressed his indifference or even disdain for her, criticized her best efforts to please him, showed no interest in her sexually, she simply redoubled her efforts to get things "right." Her home was meticulous, her dinner parties unexceptionable, and her children models of proper deportment. At the same time she was never at ease in company. She both experienced herself and appeared to the observer as awkward, gawky, and naive. She was the child of an affluent, nominally Jewish family which valued intellectual pursuits. The patient remembered, from her adolescent years, painfully, long dinner table discussions from which she felt excluded. Even as an adult she was convinced that she was less intelligent than her siblings. This, despite the fact that only she among her siblings succeeded in graduating from an appropriately prestigious college. With respect to her husband, she felt something akin to awe.

I have chosen to present this case because of a letter the patient received from her mother during the course of her analysis. I believe the excerpts I include speak eloquently to the mix of cognitive and affective dilemmas this young woman had faced during her growing years, during the period of obsessional primacy. The adaptive style she developed then continued to characterize her both during and subsequent to the oedipal period. Analytic work uncovered an early childhood pattern of unrewarded efforts to please and feelings of frustrated rejection and helpless inexpressible anger, which seemed to complement the experience she was having with her husband. As a result, the patient was moved to inquire about her early life from her mother. The mother replied:

> Even if I were not beset by a million details, writing about your early childhood would be a painful assignment. I'm not sure, but I'd hazard the guess that every parent feels that if she only could do it over, she wouldn't louse it up so badly. In your case my hair shirt is much stiffer than in most because you were unlike the others whose reactions were more like ours and, therefore, easier to understand than yours and, further, there was not then the easy

approach to psychiatric help that there is now. . . . I don't believe we were sufficiently aware of the seriousness of your problems. We were much more concerned about Ann, who openly rebelled, than about you who was so easily cowed.

At the time you seemed a problem from long before you were you. As you know, I had a dreadful pregnancy. I started to miscarry while I was visiting my mother in March. Dr. B, a famous gynecologist, said at the time that he'd never seen miscarriage signs go so far and then stop. Then in June my mother died unexpectedly and I was terribly upset. In August, I developed something called a separated symphysis pubis, three months before you were due. This was a dreadfully painful condition for which nothing could be done until after your birth, when I lay for a month in a pelvic hammock. Then, as I'm sure you know, you were the second girl when we had wanted a boy each time, and the doctor told me that after such a pregnancy I should never have another child. You were not, therefore, received with the enthusiasm a boy would have been, and right there it can be said that, that's no way to start life.

Then right from the start you were not a friendly baby. The moment you saw a stranger you cried, and later when you were old enough to know the stranger wasn't going to bite you, you clung for dear life to our clothes. Unfortunately, even with children, you tend to give what you get, and if a child's reactions were irritating, you find yourself being irritable, instead of knowing enough to ask yourself, "What in the world makes her act this way?"

Both you and Ann were impossible to house-break due, of course, to my stupid rigidity about it. We had a wonderful Scotch nurse, Kathie. One day (you were about 4), I saw that your whole backside was bruised, and when I asked Kathie about it, she told me you had fallen down the cellarway. I pressed her, and she finally admitted she had spanked you for wetting your pants. I'm pleased to say that within twenty minutes she was out of the house. I think that was when we got Mary, who loved you the best. I don't remember why she left, but I think it was then that we had Miss Greene who was a very nice girl who I thought had not much effect on any of you, but Ann tells me that you cried inconsolably when she left to get married. . . .

I do remember being told by someone at Country Day that there was a marked difference in you after Don was born, that until then you had shown leadership qualities. . . . It seemed strange, your reaction to Don, because from outside appearances you chose Ann to fight with and seem jealous of, while your real enemy was Don. This came out later when you would get into fights-to-the-death with him, and the look of hate on your face was something I wish I hadn't seen. Then you began to withdraw. For no reason that we could find, you would take to your room and sulk and, as you know, you did that all your life with us. When I'd go to your room and try to get you to tell me what was wrong, you'd always say "nothing." I'd try to tell you that we could talk as adults, but I guess the door had been locked and I was too late. It was pretty frustrating, and I believe it was those moods which led us to getting you with Dr. Z. But by then it was really too late. Oddly enough, the only rebellion I can remember is that on Sundays when the rest of us were in dungarees, you would come to dinner in your red organdy dress and patent leather shoes. When we'd ask you where you were going, you'd say that this was the only day when you could dress up. I suppose that what you were saying was that you would like to go out and have a reason for dressing up, but we didn't recognize it then. You never tried to run away; you never did or said anything naughty; and I don't remember your ever voicing hate for anyone. In fact, you were always the one who tried to please, the attentive, thoughtful one, just as you are today. The flowers when someone was sick, the posters when we returned from a trip. We used to chuckle when you went somewhere—your hat on straight, just so, your little white gloves, prim, proper, like a little old lady you looked. So very unlike Ann, it was such a relief. I guess the whole picture is rather pathetic—your efforts to be accepted, and our idiotic inability to recognize them. This, however, is one of the few things I don't take the blame for!

The Country Day tragedy, which I believe that even until today you hold against us, was not our decision at all. Mrs. R had us come to school, told us that academically you were in a position to go ahead but that socially, emotionally, it was felt you ought to repeat. This was very much like a dentist telling you your tooth ought to come out. What did we know, who were we to tell Mrs. R and the rest of the gods there that they were wrong, and that for your self-esteem you should stay with your class, willy-nilly? I don't think you'd do it yourself today, if you were in the same position. As it turned out, it was a terrible thing to do to you, but how were we to know? As you remember, we *did* have the guts to take you out a year before you were to finish. At the River School,

I think you were happy, and this showed even within a month after you went there.

You ask how you were about voicing your opinions. The answer is—absolutely nil. You retreated. Always you retreated. You always seemed to feel that you were being personally attacked, that you were always made to seem wrong, rather than to stand up to your original assertion. And too, you always flatly refused to look up anything. When Pop would leave the dining table to look for something in the encyclopedia, you would lose interest and take it all as a personal insult. As a matter of fact, you had very little intellectual interest, and no curiosity. In short, I think you sort of gave up. Perhaps you resented the competition of the others, perhaps you felt that your strength lay in your helplessness. I don't know. But nothing we could do would get you enthusiastic about a subject. Then the theater came into your life, and I think that was particularly alluring because no one in the house knew the first thing about it.

Case 2:   I first met RL when she was 58 years old. She had been married for 37 years, was the mother of 6 and the grandmother of 6. I saw her twice a week over a period of roughly three years. Unlike AB, her origins were blue collar. She came to therapy complaining of being depressed and anxious. She described episodes of uncontrollable rage which left her feeling guilty and unworthy. She also suffered from hypertension and migraine as well as a variety of bowel and gynecological problems. Some twenty years earlier she had been hospitalized and received electroconvulsive treatment (ECT) and antidepressants for similar complaints.

She was born into a rigidly Roman Catholic home. Her mother, who was 17 at the time of her birth, had fled her own chaotic parental home, married a man 12 years her senior, and converted to his faith. The patient recalls her mother as an unrelenting disciplinarian. There was in her early life no question about what was right and what was wrong; her mother was the repository of all such information. As she matured, and found herself more and more at odds with mother, who, by this time, had returned to the fundamentalist faith in which she had been reared, the Church took on this role. She was married to a hardworking meticulous accountant who was also engaged in a search for perfection. Their relation to one another can be characterized as one of mutual frustration. Six children notwithstanding, they could never permit themselves to enjoy sex "with abandon." The dictum that sex was for procreational purposes only was a guiding principle. It was a duty not a pleasure. At the same time they were committed and devoted to one another.

During her growing years, and in her adulthood as well, the patient never questioned that there was a right and a wrong. She simply shifted from her mother as the ultimate arbiter to her religion. Not the least of the problems she experienced in adolescence derived from the discrepancies between what she had come to accept as eternal verities and her mother's increasingly embittered view both of her marriage and of the Church's dictates. She described how confusing and perplexing she found these "mixed messages" and her increasingly frenetic efforts to do everything "right" and get everything "right." When she failed, when things didn't turn out as she anticipated they should, despite her best efforts, she either became depressed or enraged. As an adult, she was confronted with Vatican II which, in effect, abrogated many of the rules for behavior which she had understood to be God given and, therefore, had followed slavishly. She was also confronted with the fact that her parish priest, a man whom she had regarded as her personal intermediary with God, was both an alcoholic and less than honorable in other ways.

Although she was an excellent student and a competent pianist, she was incapable of spontaneity. She played professionally but she could not improvise. She also refused to perform without a score in front of her because she was afraid she might make a mistake. The following episode speaks, I think, for itself. After one of our sessions she felt impelled to visit a nun who had taught her in high school. This very elderly lady greeted her saying, "Oh R, how nice it is to see you again. Tell me, are you still as scrupulous as you used to be?" About two years after her treatment began, her mother died. In the course of going through the latter's effects she found the two letters which follow. They were written during her eighth year. I present them unedited.

March 22nd 1939

Dear Mother

I love you with all my hert do you love me to I hope you do I am good in school I can read I can wright I know my Home Work I know my catechism I know my spelling in School I can draw good in School to. How are you today I hope you are not sick I will try to do my work good I know my singing to I bet when you was a little girl you Knew all of that to. I am very good I know you love me to my love

R–N–M

Sometime after she wrote this letter her four-year younger sister died, apparently unexpectedly. The following letter (undated) was also among her mother's effects:

Dear aunt Lille

I have vary bad News Vary bad little alice is dead she dide mondey morning We where all very sad and I am still sad I know you will be vary sad to plese pray for her you know how sweet she and you did not hardle see her inney O please aunt Lille please try to come down saterday and stay until Sunday because I am vary lonely to be hear all by my sofe but Mother and Daddy is not vary much with just them But with Alice Mother and daddy is mlenty to me then I'll never see her agin   R

I was able to be of help to both these patients by identifying, and working with a particular mode of transferential relation[9] they shared, one which I call an obsessional contract. In the following paragraphs I will discuss the origins of obsessional contracts, offer examples of them from literature and consider how their identification can be useful in therapy.

THE OBSESSIONAL CONTRACT

The proposition that two women, whose origins, cultural backgrounds, and childhood life styles were so different as those of Mrs. D and Mrs. L, could be responding to the same underlying

---

[9]Transference: "The displacement of patterns of feelings, thoughts and behavior, originally experienced in relation to significant figures during childhood onto a person involved in a current interpersonal relation . . ." (Moore and Fine, 1990).

"deep" psychodynamic forces, does not, at first glance, seem plausible. On the basis of the reasoning which follows I believe, nonetheless, that this was the case. Striking though they would have been to the observing adult, during the earliest oral (basic trust, symbiotic, sensorimotor) period of their lives, the dramatic differences in their respective physical ambiences were irrelevant. Each was the beneficiary of good-enough mothering. Their age-appropriate needs were met, and their ability to be aware did not include appreciation of the discrepancies in their environments. Unlike the environmentally deprived children we have discussed earlier, they were able to bond to parenting figures, to make attachments, and to develop a sense of basic trust. For each, the behavioral precursors of expectations[10] coalesced into complex representations. These, in turn, made possible the anticipation of a particular result from a given action. Like all other infants during this period of maturation, neither was yet able to differentiate an action or experience from the context in which it occurred. As we have learned from Piaget, awareness of the independent existence of objects "out there" was also in the process of being established.[11] With the emergence of the awareness that there are such separately existing objects, the possibility of the development of idiosyncratic patterns of attachments and interactions as opposed to reactions also emerges. While we are primarily concerned here with human object relations, it is important to keep in mind that during late infancy and early toddlerhood children also establish intense attachments to inanimate objects—what Winnicott referred to as transitional objects. It is roughly with the onset of toddlerhood that the youngster begins to be aware of the world of objects, a world which for

---

[10]We know that such precursors begin to emerge in the first few weeks of postpartum life when the infant turns his or her head to an object (mother's nipple or examiner's finger) which strokes the cheek. I refer to such integrated behaviors as precursors because we have no basis for assuming that they involve such higher representational functions as might be expressed in such a thought as, "Aha, I am hungry and here is this source of satiation to which I can now turn"—or some variant thereof.

[11]This account is of necessity abstract and speculative. The following anecdote is presented to help clarify the quality of the toddler's perception of other people. Seppy (aged 4) was frequently brought to visit his grandmother and ailing grandfather. The latter always sat in a particular armchair. When he visited after grandfather's death a female friend of the widow was sitting in the chair. Later his mother asked him whether he missed grandpa Ken. "Oh no," he replied, "They've got a new grandpa only she's a lady!"

the adults is so obvious as to be hardly worth noticing. During the preceding sensorimotor period the child can only experience relationships in functional terms, as gratifications and nongratifications, and only experience caretakers in terms of the functions they perform rather than as separate, unique individuals like him- or herself. Coincidental with this newly emerging awareness, the toddler is also in the process of becoming aware of the imperative to take into account the fact that parenting ones have expectations from him or her which differ from what the child might be inclined to do spontaneously. It becomes imperative to conform with the wishes and demands introduced by the caretaker.

Regrettably, it is not possible to hand the toddler a codified compendium of the rules which are now to be followed. As a toddler he or she must literally learn from doing, by the outcomes of behaviors. Moreover, as we have already discussed, the rationale behind what the child must do is beyond the toddler's comprehension. The child entering toddlerhood does not yet possess the ability to understand that the demands and expectations that are being imposed are based on reasons. Indeed in the phenomenologically bound world of the toddler, reason, cause, and effect are only beginning to be understood. It is the outcome, as defined by the response of the parents, which establishes for the child the principle that there is a "right" and a "wrong," a "good" and a "bad." In Erikson's terminology, the critical parameter at this time extends from a sense of autonomy to a pervasive feeling of shame and doubt; from "What I do is okay" to "What I do is dumb and shameful or bad." As the individual matures and develops, the limited capacities of the parents both as arbiters of "correctness" and as protectors may become apparent. It does not follow, however, that disillusionment with regard to the competence of parents will lead to the giving up of either the yearning for a sense of certitude and security, or the conviction that one must behave correctly if this is to be achieved. The dilemma for the child (and the adult as well) is how to determine what is correct. Surrogates are found for parents. One must be able to impute to them that they have the same level of functional competence as one had, during toddlerhood, taken for granted in one's parents. Thus, Mrs. D looked to her husband to provide these functions; Mrs. L turned to her religion. Both engaged in a form of transference relation which I have characterized as an obsessional contract. Their symptoms can be understood as resulting from their ongoing rage and frustration that their expectations and yearnings have not been fulfilled. Despite their best efforts to please and placate, neither could quite "get it right." The marks of love, esteem, and approbation they craved were never forthcoming.

Correctness, getting it right, is not an end in itself. Rather, for both the toddler and the adult it is his or her obligation under the obsessional contract. As adults we continue to make such contracts. We identify them in our adult patients in the form of transference reactions which say, in effect, "If I, the party of the first part, do what I am supposed to do, am good etc., etc. then the party of the second part (spouse, boss, teacher, therapist, God) will respond as I wish." Unfortunately, the party of the second part may not have signed off on, or may, indeed, be totally unaware of the existence of the contract. The making of such contracts is widely recognized in literature. The contract, to reiterate, is a transference phenomenon, if not identified as such in literature. I cite two examples. In the first, it is God and heaven which the protagonist assumes will ultimately provide her with that for which she yearns. In the second, it is his employer here on earth. Each person takes it for granted that (1) it is his or her obligation if he or she is to be rewarded, and (2) that appropriate behavior is ultimately defined by some higher authority (i.e., the "designated parent surrogate").

In *Uncle Vanya*, Chekov (1897) deals with such a contractual relation between one of his characters and God. She (Sonya) and her Uncle Vanya have been the long-suffering victims of her father's exploitation. He has just consented to return to the city from the family estate where he has been visiting. In return they will continue to support him there. The terms to which they have agreed, however, are such as to guarantee that they will spend the rest of their lives in penury. As the play ends Sonya says:

> Uncle Vanya, we have to go on living. We'll go on living day after day, a long procession of days and evenings, we'll submit patiently to whatever fate sends, we'll work selflessly, without respite, now and when we are old, and when our time is up we'll die as we

must, and then, on the other side of the grave, when we tell how we suffered and how we wept, and how bitter was our lot, God will have mercy on us, and you and I, dear uncle, will start a fine new life, a bright and glorious life, we will rejoice and look back calmly on what we suffer now and smile at it, and we shall rest. I believe, Uncle, I believe with all my heart and soul . . . We shall rest.

We shall rest. We will hear the angels singing, we will see the heavens streaming with diamonds, we will see all of earth's evil and all our suffering carried away in a tide of mercy that fills the whole earth, and our lives will be as gentle and peaceable and sweet as a caress. I have faith. I have faith. Poor Uncle Vanya, you're crying . . . you have no happiness in your life, but wait awhile, wait awhile, Uncle Vanya . . . We shall rest. We shall rest! We shall rest! [p. 156].

Remains of the Day (Ishiguro, 1989) is the account of the life of an English butler. During most of his career he served an English nobleman who was a Nazi sympathizer. Feeling that political matters should be left in the hands of his betters, he never permitted himself to question the judgment or behavior of his remote and aristocratic employer. Rather, he was a conscientious and resourceful servant and took great pride in his ability to manage a great house with a large staff. After his employer died in disgrace, the estate was sold to an American who took a very different view of servants. Among other things he enjoyed bantering with his butler, a practice which the latter found confusing and anxiety provoking. Yet this was evidently what was required. As the book ends he reflects: "It occurs to me, furthermore, that bantering is hardly an unreasonable duty for an employer to expect a professional to perform. I have already devoted much time to developing my bantering skills, but it is possible I have never previously approached the task with the commitment I might have done. Perhaps then, when I return to Darlington Hall tomorrow—Mr. Farraday will not himself be back for a further week—I will begin practicing with renewed effort. I should hope, then, that by the time of my employer's return, I shall be in a position to pleasantly surprise him" (p. 243). Similar contracts were made by both Mrs. D and Mrs. L.

Mrs. D, whose parents complained about the misdeeds of her siblings, concluded that if she could be kind, sweet, and generous enough, they would favor her. She did not know about the origins of the lifelong resentment her mother had for her. Nor could she understand that her frantic efforts to please and ingratiate evoked a bewildered and somewhat contemptuous reaction from them. When her best efforts left her still feeling unloved and unappreciated, she retreated into the condition her mother describes. She repeated the same pattern in her marriage. She began to improve when I pointed out that she was assuming that her husband wanted her to be dutiful and compliant, that she seemed to assume that he was monolithic and without doubts and uncertainties of his own. "What," I wondered, "would happen if you weren't so deferential and acquiescent?" Not long thereafter, when he was criticizing something about her housekeeping, she turned on him, told him to bug off, and added that if he didn't like what she had done he could damned well do it over himself. Much to her amazement, he backed down. He too was more than a little obsessional in his adaptive style. She discovered he craved to have someone to set limits for him as much as she did. I won't say that they lived happily ever after, but I will say that both her bruxism and migraine were markedly relieved. It should be clear that my intervention did not affect Mrs. D's propensity to make obsessional contracts. Quite the contrary, her symptomatic relief was based on her having entered into an idealizing transference relation with me. She was able to attribute benign and supportive parental properties to me. Since she was persuaded that I thought that standing up to her husband was a good idea, she went ahead and did so. That the result of what she did turned out to be beneficial for both of them is quite incidental. She was persuaded that I, her idealized therapist, felt she should do as she did.

Mrs. L, whose childhood letters I have already quoted, wrote a lengthy letter to her then very elderly mother shortly before the latter died. In it she states explicitly how much her perception of what is right and fit and proper is based on her transferential feelings. She reviewed her continuing frustrations and her bitter resentment over the unfair treatment of which she perceived herself to have been the victim. The following extract, written when she was in her sixtieth year, captures the flavor of the transference relation she had established with her therapist. It is not very different in quality from the poignant note she had written to her mother when she was 8 years old.

Thank God I was able to finally perceive that the fault was not in others but in myself and I knew I had to have help. Luckily I was able to find an excellent psychiatrist-psychoanalyst who led me or I should say guided me to look deep down inside myself, my past, root out and find all the hurt I felt inside, pull it out, talk about it, helped me to admit it and I not he began to see things in an adult way, not in the naive, childlike ways from which I had never really emerged. I did not change but a change in my attitude toward life and people did occur. Instead of staying mentally in one spot, and perhaps eventually becoming a bitter old woman, it provided the kick in the pants to push me forward.

CHAPTER 10

Developmental Interferences

> Of course whatever determinism survives in principle does not help us much when we have to deal with real systems that are not simple, like the stock market or life on earth. The intrusion of historical accident sets permanent limits on what we can hope to explain [Weinberg, 1992, p. 37].

INTRODUCTION

The phrase "developmental interference" is, in fact, an oxymoron. That is, given all we have discussed up to now, it should be clear that all development is by its very nature the consequence of interference. In the chapter on environmental deprivation we reviewed the results of insufficient interference from the environment during infancy. At least since the time of the twelfth century Holy Roman Emperor Frederick (see chapter 3, pp. 40–41), it has been reported repeatedly that gene-driven maturation, in the absence of age-appropriate input from the environment, is not compatible with survival, let alone psychological development. We should, then, be considering not interference per se, but (1) the nature of the environmental conditions to which a given maturing individual is being exposed, and (2) the point in the maturational process when the exposure occurs. We must also consider

how styles have changed with regard to the definition of beneficent versus harmful interferences. The Puritans and the Victori-
ans subscribed to the principle, "Spare the rod and spoil the
child." Today we would have them in jail as child abusers because
of practices they felt were in the best interest of the child. Similarly, the line between good hygienic care of an infant or young
child and sexual overstimulation is not an easy one to draw. It is
my opinion that hazy, preverbal "coenesthetic" memories dating
back to this period, when the differentiation of self from nonself
was in the process of being established in the context of the experiences of bodily ministrations, had much to do with what Freud
was hearing when he believed that all neuroses were based on
sexual trauma. By the same token, it was when he came to the
conclusion that much of what he heard was fantasy, in that it was
based on retrospective distortions of experience, that he came to
the conclusion that there were endogenous sources of motivation
and conflict, that not all psychological problems were the result
of externally imposed trauma. Sexual and physical abuse are only
two of a legion of potentially malignant vicissitudes which may
befall the developing child. A short list of other possibilities would
include serious protracted illness, parental loss, or social upheaval
such as those being experienced by children in Bosnia, Northern
Ireland and Rwanda today. To discuss all these, and the many
more that come readily to mind, would obviously be impossible.
The discussion which follows is based on yet another natural experiment, the "Battered infant syndrome."[1] We will be concerned
with the fate of infants who are battered from the earliest days of
their lives up to their third years. The data I will review indicate
that this very early experience both results in very specific later
personality characteristics and affects the quality of later object
relations as well. As a "natural experiment" it also has the special
advantage that it has been shown to recur from generation to
generation. When we see a battered infant, we are very likely to
be seeing in one or both of the baby's parents someone who was
also battered.

That very early environmental influences may have a pervasive and lasting effect on the growing individual has also been

---

[1]Much of the material in this chapter has already been published (Freedman, 1975).

postulated by Kernberg (1979). In his discussion of object relations he proposes that experiences during roughly the first three years result in the formation of substructures of the psychic apparatus that will gradually differentiate. It is evident that this hypothesis is congruent with much that has been implicit in psychoanalytic thinking from its very inception. In his postscript to the Dora case, for example, Freud (1905) characterizes transference as "new editions or facsimiles of the impulses and fantasies which are aroused and made conscious during the progress of the analysis . . . [which] have this peculiarity . . . that they replace some earlier person by the person of the physician" (p. 116). Nonetheless, it remains the case that interest in the genesis of object relations has only come into the mainstream of psychoanalytic investigation in recent years. In his brief historical review, Kernberg (1979) suggested that interest in this area had its origins in the development of the structural theory. He felt that the shift of emphasis from a topographic point of view, which tended to take character and adaptive style for granted while focusing on mechanisms of symptom formation, to one concerned with the genesis of character and personality as such, was a necessary precondition for the development of interest in object relations. It is not surprising, therefore, that much of the pioneering work in the field has been done either by analysts working with very young individuals in whom the incompleteness of the process of structure formation forced attention to the role of early relations, or by people particularly interested in psychotic and near psychotic individuals in whom the incompleteness or distortions of the ultimate psychic structure also focused attention on the problems of the genesis of object relations.

As is so frequently the case in psychoanalytic research, the validation of conclusions derived from these studies has been hampered by the considerable time lag which, given the duration of the human developmental period, must elapse between the presumed causal experiences and the observed end results. There are very few instances in which it has been possible to test either the predictions about future development which are derived from the observation of early development, or the inferences about early experience which are made on the basis of the study of older individuals. To my knowledge the best documented cases in which this can be said to have been somewhat done are those of Little Hans (Freud, 1909) and Frankie (Bornstein, 1949; Ritvo, 1966). The Wolf Man report (Gardner, 1971) and Niederland's (1959) and White's (1961) studies of Schreber's early life might also be considered in this connection were it not for the fact that nothing we know about either individual's childhood is the product of direct observation. Indeed, in none of the cited cases does the available observational data extend into the period of the first few months or even the first two or three years of life; that is, the period which most theorists today, like Kernberg, would regard as particularly critical in the determination of the nature of later object relations.

The phenomenon of infant battering[2] provides us with a patient population which, I believe, may make it possible to get around this limitation. We will consider, at least in a preliminary way, how the reported findings in this population compare with assumptions and conclusions of those workers who have been limited either to the direct observation of developing youngsters with inadequate follow-up studies, or to data obtained from psychoanalytic work with older individuals—situations in which there is no possibility for making direct developmental observations.

THE SYNDROME OF THE BATTERED INFANT

The syndrome of the battered infant and his parent is very frequently confused with the problems presented by (1) the child who, after a relatively benign infancy, is cruelly treated at a later age, and (2) that of the neglected (environmentally deprived) infant. Although instances do occur in which an abused infant has also been drastically understimulated during infancy, and brutal treatment either begins during childhood or, having begun in infancy, is continued into childhood, in fact each of these vicissitudes often occurs independently. In what follows I am concerned specifically with a population made up of youngsters aged 3 or

---

[2]The fact that infants are battered was first established by the *radiologist* Caffey in 1946.

less and their parents. These infants and toddlers are, in many respects, well cared for. The nature of the parental care, however, does have some distinctive features. Most dramatic among these is the propensity for the parent, from time to time, to subject the infant to such extreme degrees of physical abuse as to cause very major skeletal and visceral damage or even death.

In terms of numbers this is not an insignificant population. Kempe (1971), for example, reported that the diagnosis of battered infant was made 40 times a year at the University of Colorado Medical Center and cited a nearly identical figure (41 cases a year) from the Children's Hospital in Pittsburgh. While he felt that the true incidence was impossible to determine, he believed that it might be as high as six per 1000 live births. Twenty-five percent of all fractures occurring in infant and toddlers less than 2 years old, and 10 to 15 percent of all trauma seen in toddlers under 3 were believed by Kempe to be manifestations of the battered child syndrome.

The descriptions of a variety of authors who have dealt with this syndrome present some remarkably consistent findings. One, for example, concerning which there appears to be universal agreement, is the high degree of probability that the battering parent of today was himself or herself a battered child yesterday. The repetitious nature of the pattern of abuse has been directly documented over a span of three generations (Curtis, 1963; Steele and Pollock, 1968; Silver, Dublin, and Lourie, 1969). Steele and Pollock also present extremely suggestive evidence to the effect that the grandparents of the battered infants they were seeing experienced similar treatment at the hands of their parents (i.e., for a fourth generation). Because of this striking pattern of transmission it is possible to utilize the dyad "battering parent and battered child" as yet another natural experiment for the purpose of both testing hypotheses and extending our understanding of early processes of internalization, and the establishment of object relations. That is, we have the opportunity to observe simultaneously the end result of a particular style of rearing in the parent and the details of the experience as it is occurring in the infant.

THE PARENT WHO BATTERS

In his series of 400 battering parents, Kempe found that all social classes, races, creeds, religions, and levels of education and of income were represented roughly in proportion to their incidence in the general population of Denver. Approximately 5 percent of the battering parents were frankly psychotic in either the sense of being severely depressed or delusional or in having developed a specific "psychotic relation" to a scapegoated child. He characterized another 5 percent as "aggressive psychopaths," individuals who beat everyone, wives, children, friends, quite indiscriminately. These, Kempe remarks, are people who speak little and communicate through bashing people. Of the remaining 90 percent of battering parents—mothers and fathers—he can only say that they all seem to have serious problems in mothering.

Steele and Pollock (whose investigation of 60 families drawn from the same population is by far the most exhaustive psychiatric study I have found) say, "not all parents who are unemployed and in financial straits, poor housing, shattered marriages and alcoholic difficulties abuse their children; nor does being an upstanding, devout Christian with a high I.Q., stable marriage, fine home and plenty of money prevent attacks on infants . . . large segments of our culture, including many of the medical professions are still prone to believe that child abuse occurs among 'bad people' of low socioeconomic status. This is not true!" (p. 108). They attribute the reported high incidence of poverty, alcoholism, and broken homes as well as membership in certain racial groups among child beaters (Young, 1964; Greengard, 1964; Elmer and Gregg, 1967) to the fact that other authors had access only to cases drawn from public institutions. The Denver study drew on both private and public facilities.

Steele and Pollock feel that with few exceptions their patients had sufficiently severe emotional problems to be appropriate candidates for psychotherapy. They were, however, unable to find a single conventional psychiatric diagnosis which would characterize the whole group. Although obsessive compulsive character structures, unresolved sibling rivalry, and oedipal conflicts accompanied by obsessive guilt and pregenital fixation were potent accessories to the propensity to instigate abuse, none of these characteristics was universally found in their subjects. Indeed, they observed among them the same distribution of diagnoses that one would anticipate finding in any clinic population. They have attempted, therefore, to identify behavior patterns which are shared by these parents without regard to their relevance to the making of any generally recognized psychiatric diagnosis. Despite these parents' capacity at times to be overtly and intensely aggressive with respect to their infants, they do not, in Steele and Pollock's experience, "show evidence of an unusually strong basic aggressive drive." Rather, they find that "as a general rule there is significant inhibition of aggression in many areas of their lives" (p. 109).

They find it to be characteristic of the abusing parent that he will not possess an identity in Erikson's (1950) meaning of the term, namely, "the sense of being a unique separate individual with a consistency of personal character and ability to maintain solidarity with social groups" (Erikson, 1950, p. 162). Rather, he will be characterized by multiple separate and unamalgamated identifications. They state, "Our patient can feel like a confident parent and quickly change to being a helpless, ineffectual, inadequate child. They can be a kindly adult and shift suddenly to being a punitive adult. They know they are men and women but are not really sure of it. They have one firm concept of what they should be and another of what they actually are. Any sense of being reasonably good can be easily displaced by a conviction of badness" (p. 123). This characterization appears to apply despite the fact that the battering parents could not, as I have already mentioned, be assigned to any specific, generally accepted, psychiatric classification.

Typically, these parents expect and demand a great deal from their infants and children. Not only is the demand for performance great, but it is premature in the sense of being clearly beyond the ability of the infant to comprehend what is wanted of him and to respond appropriately. The children are dealt with as though they were much older than they really are. Observation, they say, "leads to a clear impression that the parent feels insecure and unsure of being loved, and looks to the child as a source of reassurance, comfort, and loving response. It is hardly an exaggeration to say the parent acts like a frightened, unloved child, looking to his own child as if he were an adult capable of providing comfort and love" (p. 109). Morris and Gould (1963) have characterized this phenomenon as a "role reversal."

Also characteristic is a curious 'sense of righteousness' about the parents of abused children. "Axiomatic to the child beater" is the principle "that infants and children exist primarily to satisfy parental needs, that children's and infant's needs are unimportant and that children who do not fulfill these requirements deserve punishment" (Steele and Pollock, 1968, p. 110). In contrast to the neglecting parent, the abusing parent has a considerable investment in the active life of his child. Punishment is meted out for failure to "shape up" and perform better. Steele and Pollock believe that this pattern of child rearing exists in abusing parents "quite independently of their other personality traits." They also suggest that rather than being an isolated, rare phenomenon, it is a variant, extreme in its intensity, of a pattern of child rearing pervasive in human civilization all over the world.

They distinguish between the functions of "mothering" and "motherliness." They define the former as the process of supplying the child with such practical mechanical services as feeding, holding, clothing, and cleaning, as well as protecting him from harm and providing motility. The latter term refers to "the more subtle ingredients of tenderness, awareness and consideration of the needs and desires of the infant." The capacity to abuse infants is, they find, associated with a deficiency in the capacity for motherliness. The infants they observed were almost uniformly well-fed, clean, and well clothed, in other words, they have experienced good mothering. The emotional attitudes of the mothering ones, however, were "fraught with constant tension and frequent disruption." It was frequently in the course of the carrying out of such mothering functions as feeding, cleaning, and comforting that abuse occurred.

Psychological testing has, in general, born out the clinical findings already reviewed. The parents' I.Q.s ranged from 73 to 130, with a majority of individuals in the average range. In cognitive style most seemed to be action oriented rather than given to dependence on thought and delay of impulse gratification. There were some, however, for whom this was not true. Strong oral dependent needs were found in every parent tested. Four-fifths of the group were found to have unresolved identity conflicts which were playing a major role in determining their behavior, and almost the same number showed significant depressive trends and feelings of worthlessness. Although feelings of suspiciousness and distrust and of being victimized were extremely common, only one individual could be classified as paranoid. Typically, a failure to establish a successful synthesis of identify fragments was observed. In addition to doubting their adequacy in their adult roles, some of the parents appeared to have retained, as an important aspect of their identity struggles, part identifications as little boys or girls.

Despite these findings, Dr. Richard Waite, the psychologist who tested their subjects, also concluded that "the test results indicate significant diversity in personality structure among these patients and in the complexity of defenses and ego-adaptive mechanisms available to them. They indicate that child-abusing behavior is not common to one or two diagnostic entities and this behavior can occur in people having relatively resilient egos" (p. 138).

THE ATTACK

Because the parents' memories tend to be hazy for the actual event, investigation of the circumstances under which battering occurs is difficult. In general, Steele and Pollock (1968) feel the following pattern is present: The parent approaches each child ministration episode with (1) a healthy desire to do something good for the infant; (2) a deep hidden yearning for the infant to respond in such a way as to fill the emptiness in the parent's life and bolster his or her self-esteem; and (3) a harsh, authoritative demand for the infants' correct response, which is supported by a sense of parental rightness.

When the infant's response is reasonably adequate no attack occurs. (Even so, they feel that the parent's attitudes are communicated to the infant and stimulate further aggression and accompanying strict superego development.) Should anything interfere with the parent's success or enhance his or her feelings of being unloved and inferior (e.g., persistent crying), authoritative feel-ings are likely to surge up and an attack to occur. They postulate that the parent undergoes the following pattern of dynamic shifts as a prelude to attacking the infant:

> [T]he events begin with the parent's identification of the infant for whom he is caring as a need gratifying object equivalent to a parent who will replace the lacks . . . [in his or her] . . . own being-parented experience. Since the parent's past tells him or her that those to whom one looked for love were also the ones who attacked him or her, the infant is also perceived as a critical parental fig-ure. . . . The perception of being criticized stirs up the parent's feelings of being inferior. It also increases the frustration of his or her need for love, and anger mounts. At this time there seems to be a strong sense of guilt, a feeling of helplessness and panic becomes overwhelming, and the haziness (mentioned above) is most marked. Suddenly a shift in identification occurs. The super-ego identification with the parent's own punitive parent takes over. The infant is perceived as the parent's own bad childhood self. The built up aggression is redirected outward and the infant is hit with full superego approval [Steele and Pollock, 1968, p. 131].

DISCUSSION

Briefly to summarize, the propensity of parents to batter infants is a sharply circumscribed transmissible entity which appears to have its origins in the events of the first few months of postpartum life. Because it has been shown to recur in as many as four succes-sive generations of the same family, it is safe to assume that the experience one witnesses in the battered child today are represen-tative of the early life of the parent who does the battering. Al-though the syndrome most frequently appears in association with an obsessional character structure, it has no necessary relation with that or any other identifiable clinical entity. The battering parent does tend to be socially isolated and lacking in a solid sense of identity. On the other hand, he or she is possessed of many strong resilient ego functions and is rarely psychotic.

No identifiable ethnic, religious, social, cultural, or economic factors have been shown to be associated with the propensity to batter. Typically, battering parents, although frustrated in their efforts to obtain evidence of their love, are unusually strongly attached, dutiful, and deferential to their own parents. At the same time they are themselves involved and concerned parents. They are inclined, however, to regard children as existing primarily for their, the parents', satisfaction. Lacking in basic trust, they see in their infant's response to their ministrations the measure of their own worth, both as parents and as individuals.

The actual attacks appear to occur at times when the infant's response is such as to leave the parent anxious and frustrated. While the immediate events are only hazily remembered, it seems clear that a shift occurs in the parent's feelings which allow him or her to batter the literally helpless infant while maintaining a sense of righteous indignation.

Persistence of the feelings of righteousness after the event suggests that the attack on the infant cannot be regarded simply as a manifestation of the hazy, disassociated state during which the battering apparently occurs. It is also noteworthy that these parents' aggressive behavior is always object directed rather than diffuse. It would seem that all three characteristics of the attack, the hazy state Steele and Pollock describe, the persisting sense of righteousness, and the specific object directedness of the attack, imply the presence in these individuals of a self system which exists separately from and parallel to the system which ordinarily characterizes them. They suggest, in other words, the existence of introjects, that is, life-long residua of past environmental stimuli, which modulate how the parent is perceiving both self and child.

Of the many questions to which a consideration of these data gives rise, perhaps the most obvious are how to account for the attachment of the battered child to the battering parent and how to explain his identification with and emulation of that parent in later life? Certainly the fact that the battered child's attachment is actually enhanced by the cruelty he or she has experienced runs counter to our propensity to explain the development of attachment and love in terms of need gratification. As evidence against the tension reduction hypothesis, however, it by no means stands alone. Other evidence in both the animal behavior and the psychoanalytic literature indicates that frustration of visceral needs and even cruel treatment (at least treatment which is cruel by average expectable adult human definition) may actually enhance the attachment of developing infants to their caretakers. Scott (1962) reports that puppies who are kept half-starved form much more intense attachments than do animals who are overfed. He also cites studies in which puppies were, on a randomizing schedule, treated either cruelly or with kindness. Those animals who were treated cruelly showed no difference in their reactions to their caretakers which could distinguish them from those who were always treated with kindness. Yet a third group of animals who were being treated with consistent cruelty avoided the caretaker. However, once the experiment was over, these last also showed no differences in their responses to the same individual from those shown by the members of the first two groups.

A. Freud and Burlingham (1942) have made analogous observations in humans. They state, "Children will cling to mothers who are continually cross and sometimes cruel to them. The attachment of the small child to his mother seems to a large degree independent of her personal qualities" (p. 47).

As far as they go, these observations appear to support Bowlby (see chapter 8, this volume, pp. 152–154) in his argument that the formation of infant to mother attachment cannot be accounted for on the basis of the gratification of an "oral" or any other simply defined visceral drive. On the other hand, it is also the case that they do not answer the very cogent criticism that Bowlby focuses on the manifest phenomenon "infant/mother attachment" to the exclusion of consideration of the intrapsychic representations to which the individual is responding (A. Freud, 1960; Schur, 1960; Spitz, 1960). The fact that behavioral evidence of attachment to the abusing caretaker is seen in both puppies and human infants says nothing about the nature of the introjected residua of what the observer regards as cruel treatment. It only underscores that the phenomenon of attachment is not simply explained as a product of love and tenderness or as the product of what we ordinarily define as oral needs. As in the case of Dora, we can only learn about the introjects through the study of later behavior and especially of later transferences.

It would, of course, be possible to argue that since the battered infant also experiences good mothering, its attachment can be explained on the basis of introjects derived from that aspect of its experience. Such an explanation could even be extended to account for the increased intensity of attachment seen in the battered individual. One could postulate some such mechanism as an increasingly desperate clinging to the "good mother" in an effort to protect one's self from the "bad." Such a hypothesis founders, however, in the face of the fact that the battered child grows up to be a battering parent. Clearly the introjects which form within the infant, and which govern his or her identifications as well as attachment behavior, include representations of what the outside observer would define as a cruel and punishing parent.

In the effort to account for this extraordinary situation it may be important to bear in mind that we have no empirical data to support the assumption that what we, as observers, judge as either cruel and damaging or as loving behavior is experienced by the young infant as we estimate it.[3] Neither do we have any basis for assuming that the neonate experiences what happens to his or her body as happening to him or her. Quite to the contrary, we have every good reason to assume that the capacity to differentiate between kindness and cruelty as well as the ability to be aware that the body being assaulted or tenderly cared for is his or her own is not part of the infant's a priori equipment. In earlier chapters we have reviewed the abundant evidence that the differentiation of self, the establishment of a body image and of ego boundaries, as well as the definition of the conditions under which attachment is made, are all products of experience.

Particularly impressive in the light of the above is the early age at which observers have witnessed primordial introjects being formed. Steele and Pollock have seen babies respond accurately to rather unreasonable parental demands within the first six months, and by age one or 2 show exquisitely sensitive responses to parental needs. In their opinion such very early identification with an insufficiently caring mother is the basis of the diminished

---

[3]In chapter 8 I have made a similar point about the experience of being born.

motherliness which characterizes both male and female child abusers.

There is other empirical evidence which indicates the possibility of such very early introjective processes. In chapter 6 we have reviewed evidence that the establishment of gender identity occurs in the first 18 months. We have also seen in chapter 4 how, when she became a mother, Monica, who was born with esophageal atresia and was fed through a gastrostomy tube during her first 18 months, held her own babies in precisely the same position she had been held, during that very early period of her life. We also know from Piaget's work (see chapter 5) that the differentiation of self from external material objects is not complete until the child is between 18 and 24 months. It is only at roughly this age that the toddler recognizes his or her reflection in a mirror for what it is, a reflection of him or her self. (Amsterdam, 1972; Gallup, 1979; P. Kernberg, 1983). Implausible though it may seem, the paradox appears to obtain that the infant has not only formed introjects but also made specific, circumscribed, behavioral identifications well before he or she has established a differentiation of self and object. Otherwise stated, the emergence of a sense of self occurs in an individual who already has unique characteristics which are products of the infantile organism's interaction with the environment. These are as unique and idiosyncratic constitutional characteristics of the individual as are those characteristics which reflect his or her genetic endowment.

Kernberg (1966), on the basis of his clinical work with adults, also postulated the operation of very early introjects. He used the term *self-object image* to refer to the persisting and intractable characteristics of his patients. He postulated that they were manifestations of introjects which had been established during this same early period. Like the battering parents, the individuals were characterized by selective and episodic loss of impulse control. Typically they also have good ego functioning and show good impulse control in all but one area. In that area, however, there will occur "alternative activation of contradictory manifestations of such an impressive nature that one comes to feel that there is a compartmentalization of the entire psychic life of the patient" (p. 236). Episodes of promiscuous sexual behavior, lying, and so on occur in an individual who in all other areas of life has good impulse control and who may at other times be rigorous in just those areas in which the 'acting out' occurs. One of Kernberg's analysands, for example, would alternate between periods of inordinate rage with him and feelings of extreme tenderness and appreciation. While in one affective state he had only a very dim awareness of ever having experienced the contrary affect; each state existed as a walled off entity. When he was angry with the analyst, it was not possible for him to tolerate or even conceive of the possibility that there existed within him simultaneously the potentiality for loving feelings. Because in their daily lives individuals, like this man, may show nothing to indicate lack of impulse control or indeed, any form of emotional instability, Kernberg does not feel it is adequate to dismiss this kind of reaction as a manifestation of ego weakness in the usual sense of the term. He suggests that in such individuals the "specific well-structured, completely irreconcilable affect states exist side by side." He proposes that in the context of pleasurable and gratifying coenesthetic experience with his or her mother, the infant builds up a good self-object image. But this is only one of the "self-object images" created in the infant. Kernberg goes on to propose that separately from this 'good' self-object image, another, 'bad' self-object image is also built up. This is based on frustrating and painful experiences. He believes that because these two images are built up under very different affective circumstances, they remain separate from one another. The good selfobject image gradually becomes the nucleus of ego while the bad selfobject experience is experienced as originating outside the self. It is by invoking some such mechanism that one can account for behaviors of which the protagonist says something like, "I can't imagine what made me do it."

Although there is much in Kernberg's formulation which appears applicable to the battering parent, there are important points of discrepancy. In the first place, the data already presented require that one distinguish between the processes which result in the formation of attachment and those which determine the specific introjects by which the terms of the attachment are epitomized. Second, it is not the case that the battering parent has come to regard his impulse to batter as existing outside himself. Despite the concern he may have for his child and his often gentle and kindly behavior, he also experiences that "curious sense of righteousness" both when and after he batters. The evidence states that the impulse to batter is experienced as much as a part of the self as is the impulse to be kind and loving.

Steele and Pollock (1968), in their formulation, propose that there exists "a marked imbalance between the two introjects with that of the frustrating mother being much more powerful than that of the empathic caring mother" (p. 117). Later, at the time of the resolution of the oedipal conflict, these separate identifications with good and bad mothers are reinforced and overdetermined by the identifications which become stabilized.

In connection with the establishment of early introjects they also make a distinction which seems to me to be of the greatest importance. Taking into account the paradox that critical identifications are made before the infant has differentiated self from object and is capable of establishing object relations, they suggest that the mechanism "identification with the aggressor" is preceded by a more primitive identifying process, one they characterize as "identification with aggression." It is on this basis that violent behavior, whether passively experienced or actively expressed, becomes ego syntonic. During the later (second and third years) development of object relations, as a result of more specific identifications with the aggressive parent, the already introjected ego syntonic capacity for aggression becomes channeled. For the child who has been battered in infancy this leads to narrowly defined, superego approved channels for expressing aggression. It is, for example, "right to destroy bad things or batter intransigent disobedient frustrating infants." At the same time separate regulatory functions such as a "sense of compassion for the innocent and helpless" also develop. The same parent whose capacity to abuse figures so prominently in this chapter, is also the source of love, tenderness, and consideration.

In chapter 6 we also reviewed Stern's (1971) kinesic analysis of the consistent differences in interaction between a mother and each of her 3-month-old fraternal twins. His observations suggest a possible mechanism by which such early functional identifications might be established. The mother, it will be recalled, regarded one of these youngsters as more like herself, the other she identified with her husband. By making a frame-by-frame analysis of serial motion pictures, Stern was able to show clear differences in the pattern of her visual contacts with each. When they were $3^1/2$ months old, the "scapegoated" infant showed marked inability to terminate visual contact with his mother. At the age of 17 months he was fearful and refused to make eye contact with strangers. Characteristically he would avert his face. He was also much more reluctant to leave his mother's side and become involved in play than his twin. There is no evidence that mother's behavior was premeditated. The differences in the way she handled her infants were not conscious.

It appears to be the case that the lasting modifications of the central nervous system, which are the physiological counterparts of the earliest introjects, may best be conceptualized in terms of functions rather than objects.[4] Depending on their effects on his or her physiological equilibrium, the infant can be thought of as "experiencing" the caretaking efforts of the mothering one as affects. These, an adult might characterize as "goodness" or "badness," "satiation" or "frustration," and so on. For the infant, however, they are only changes in physiological state. Only with the passage of time and the evolution of the capacity to differentiate objects do these functional introjects come to be related to a self and associated with specific object relations. They can then be utilized in the process of making identifications with specific objects. In the average expectable situation there is a consistency between the early introjected functions and those later introjected and identified with objects, which results in a fairly coherent and consistent self system. In the absence of such a consistent and coherent self system, the individual is vulnerable to the phenomenon of "splitting." That is, because two (or more) parallel systems exist, the individual may experience him- or herself in very different ways. Each would be complete in itself and without the regulating influence of opposing modulating affects. At any given instant one would, for example, be either all good or all bad. Stated in this way, I think one can see the possibility of a general principle which may be useful in the study of a variety

---

[4]Schafer (1968) seems to take a similar position. He writes: "I propose the first objects, those which exist before boundary setting processes are either observable or inferable, are experienced without localization in psychological space" (p. 75).

of states in which the evidence of the existence of parallel walled-off self systems exist.

In chapter 6 we have discussed Stoller's (1968, 1988) work on gender identity. It would appear from his description that the transsexual must be a case in point. The self characterization of the transsexual as a female imprisoned in a male body (or vice versa) certainly implies such a walled-off situation. This formulation is supported further, I think, by the fact that the transsexual individual can function indefinitely as a male or female as the case may be. While living as a male, for example, the genetically male transsexual does not, like the feminized homosexual, behave in a particularly feminine manner. He is also potent in heterosexual relations and displays none of the fear and repulsion for the feminine body which characterizes many homosexuals. Yet he is equally capable of passing as a woman and carrying out feminine roles and functions. Again it is as though two separate self systems exist side by side.

Another group of patients who, I think, might fruitfully be considered from this standpoint are those suffering from episodic disorders (Monroe, 1970). Some years ago Adatto and I (Freedman and Adatto, 1968) reported a youngster who had several seizures while in his analyst's office. In each instance, as well as on one occasion when he had an episode at home, it was possible to show that he was confronted with two mutually incompatible impulses under circumstances which precluded any acceptable resolution of his dilemma. Under these conditions he simply developed brief absences during which he lost the train of thought which preceded the episode. It seems to me that his rather clearly defensive retreat into unconsciousness may be only a step away from the use of the mechanism of splitting. The automatisms of psychomotor seizures, so-called uncontrollable impulses, and the phenomenon of multiple personality all might conceivably be considered from this standpoint. In none of these situations is one dealing with a psychotic individual by usual definitions. Yet, in each, there is evidence of a splitting such that two or more self systems exist within the same individual. Unlike the psychotic individual who claims to be Napoleon while sweeping the ward floor, in these instances the split is along lines which require either the suppression of the system not in use or, as in the case of the transsexual, a recognition of the incongruity which exists between the feeling systems. Yet the incompatible systems do exist side by side, even as they do in the psychotic individual, although there is no evidence of psychosis.

Throughout this chapter I have been at pains to find "implication neutral" terms to characterize the interactions between the infantile organism and the environment. I try to avoid the ubiquitous propensity to adultomorphize. On the basis of their physiologically determined reactions we are inclined to ascribe to the neonate and small infant intentions and motivations of which they are incapable. We must remember that behaviors which look intentional to the adult observer are not necessarily actuated by a "self" analogous to that which we take for granted in older people. Freud (1914) recognized this problem. He wrote, "I am bound to point out that a unity comparable to the ego cannot exist in the individual from the start, the ego has to be developed" (pp. 76–77).[5]

The syndrome of infant battering illustrates both such a parental propensity to adultomorphize and the very early age at which input from the environment can influence the ultimate character of the still to be differentiated individual. Environmental influences during the very earliest weeks and months of infancy can have circumscribed but lasting effects on the ultimate nature of the yet to be differentiated ego (or, in the present context, sense of self or "I"), as well as on the quality of object relations which are yet to form. Because of its dramatic nature, infant battering has been studied intensively. We have no reason, however, to assume it is the only very early environmental input which can affect the infant's later psychological development.

Recognition of the importance of such very early influences adds yet another dimension to the assessment we must make when we evaluate our older patients. To those etiologic considerations which we can think of as gene determined, and those which we can comfortably attribute to the efforts at adaptation of a differentiated "self" to the world he or she is experiencing, we

---

[5]In German Freud used the phrase *das Ich*, the "I" in English, for what his English translators elected to call "ego."

must add the residua of events in the environment which have affected the very process of self (or "ego" or "I") formation. Information about this epoch in our older patients' lives is not easy to obtain. It is in this regard that the syndrome of infant battering is probably unique. As psychotherapists, we can echo Weinberg, "The intrusion of historical accident sets permanent limits on what we can hope to explain."

Summing Up

Bowlby (1990b), in his recent biography of Darwin, refers to a conversation in which Darwin was asked what he thought were the most influential years of life. He replied, "Without doubt the first three." He went on to explain that, "it is a virgin brain adapted to receive impressions although unable to formulate or memorize these. They nonetheless remain and can affect the whole future life of the child recipient" (p. 430). Darwin made this comment sometime in the 1870s. At the time knowledge of the nervous system was even scantier than it was two decades later when Freud abandoned neurobiology. He "knew," as did Freud, that the brain is involved in all mental activities. Just what the relation is, how the spheres of mentation and brain function are related, was for both, and still is for us, an unanswered question. We are still unable to specify the precise physiological event in the precise neural structure which is the brain's correlate for a particular thought or feeling. We have, however, come to know a great deal about the neurophysiology of the processes of both thinking and feeling. We have also affirmed Darwin's assertion that the first three years are the most critical—if only because all that follows depends on what has been laid down during that period. The processes of brain maturation and development, however, are ongoing. The periods we designate as infancy and toddlerhood merge ineluctably into the later phases of childhood. I have, therefore, arbitrarily extended the age range under discussion to include what Piaget called the preoperational period (i.e., the first 7 or 8 years of post-partum life).

213

Epigenesis, as it is manifested in the twin reciprocating processes of gene-determined maturation and environmentally induced development, is the guiding principle for the understanding of the events of the early years of life. Maturational changes result in the emergence, sometimes very abrupt emergence, of new potentialities. How these potentialities will be expressed, however, is a developmental issue. The environmentally deprived infant fails to thrive; expectations from infants and small children that they are not yet able to comprehend carry another price—the plight of battered infants is a case in point.

It is clear today that the brain is a malleable organ. Its anatomic structure is affected by the environmental stimuli to which it is exposed. In this regard we also have come to understand the critical importance of timing. Readiness, the availability of a matrix competent to absorb and utilize new experiences, is as critical for psychological development as is the opportunity to have experience. Readiness, in turn, is a function not only of maturation but also of the individual's prior experience with the environment. On the one hand, the growing individual can only assimilate and make accommodations to environmental stimuli for which his or her brain is maturationally ready. On the other hand, assimilable experience must be available if the individual is to continue to develop. To the extent that the environment is idiosyncratic for any individual, its effects will be idiosyncratic.

For each individual the result is unique psychological characteristics for which there is at present little hope of finding corresponding neurophysiologic markers. It is in this sense too that the concept of developmental interference is an oxymoron. Without environmental influences, development cannot happen. We must differentiate between child rearing practices of which we disapprove and those which are consistent with our judgment of what are fit and proper. Both are interfering with how the infant-child would have matured and developed under other circumstances.

The Synapse

To appreciate the challenge Freud faced when he attempted to establish a neurological foundation for psychology, it is useful to consider the level of understanding of the anatomy of the nervous system in the late nineteenth century. According to Boring (1929), it was not until 1873 that Golgi demonstrated, with his newly discovered stain, the extended ramifications of nerve cell processes. Golgi assumed, however, that he was observing, in the brain, a weblike network of axon fibers, punctuated periodically by cell bodies. The hypothesis that each nerve cell is a separate entity was first raised by Cajal in 1889. This new way of viewing the microscopic structure of the brain was named the neuron theory by Waldeyer in 1891. Freud's (1895) use of the term *contact barrier* in the Project indicates that he was a proponent of this theory. The term *synapse* was introduced by the English physiologist Sherrington in 1906, some eleven years later. By then Freud had committed himself to a psychology with no direct relation to the nervous system. In the 1890s, however, the contact barrier was central to his effort to establish a system of psychology based on the form and function of the nervous system. The contrast between Freud's diagrammatic representation of a contact barrier (Figure A.1) and Lorente de No's (1939) presentation of what, using the Golgi stain, is in fact visible under the microscope (Figure A.2) is illuminating.

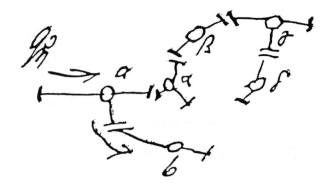

Figure A.1. "Contact Barriers" as envisioned by Freud (1895, p. 324).

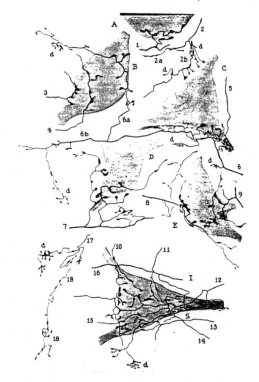

Figure A.2. The relation of presynaptic terminal to the postsynaptic cells (Lorente de No, 1939). Synapses on motoneurons (A to E) and on a large interneuron (I) of the spinal cord of a 15–16 day cat; 1 to 18 presynaptic fibrils. d, synaptic knobs in contact with dendrites. Silver-chromate method of Golgi (from Lorente de No, 1939, Figure 3).

Rather than the one-to-one relation he envisioned between two neurons at the contact barrier, the relation varies from roughly one thousand to one hundred thousand terminal branches from presynaptic neurons impinging on each postsynaptic cell. The presynaptic terminals are so numerous that Lorente de No referred to them as forming a synaptic scale analogous to the scales on a fish. In addition, the presynaptic terminals impinging on any given postsynaptic neuron come from many different sites in the nervous system. In order to activate the postsynaptic cell, messages from these many sites must impinge on a finite, contiguous area of the cell body. If a sufficiently large area is not impinged upon within a few thousandths of a second, the postsynaptic cell will fail to discharge. In effect, each synapse is a switch which, once tripped, will initiate the possibility of activating many other cells. Whether the latter will indeed discharge will depend upon whether there is timely activity from yet other cells. It is not possible to think of a mental process as reflecting the action of a single synapse or a chain of synapses. A much more likely scenario would involve waves of activity. The aphorism has been attributed to S. Kety that we may know a great deal about thinking and feeling but we are a long long way from knowing anything about the physiology of a specific thought and its affective accompaniment. It is obvious, however, that these more complex arrangements make the relevance of the neural substrate to the understanding of mental activity much more immediate and pressing than it seemed to be until well into the twentieth century. It is no longer possible to say, as Boring did in 1929, "At first glance the histological work seems to have but little bearing on psychology" (p. 66).

D. W. Winnicott

In addition to his work as both an adult and child psychoanalyst, Donald W. Winnicott conducted a pediatric clinic for some forty years. His familiarity with the practical concerns of mothers and babies had a major influence on his thinking as an analyst. He also treated disturbed adults. From this rich experience he developed some concepts which have enriched our understanding of both the emergence, and ultimate nature of object relations. Terms he introduced have become common parlance among both child and adult psychoanalysts, as well as dynamically oriented psychotherapists. The following definitions of those mentioned in the text are modified from the entry on Winnicott in *Psychoanalytic Terms and Concepts* (Moore and Fine, 1990).

Holding Environment. Winnicott introduced the term *holding environment* to characterize the environment established by a good-enough mother (see below), which provides the infant with sufficient stability and security to permit a necessary sense of omnipotence. He believed that this "primordial" experience is necessary if the infant is to be able to tolerate the inevitable vicissitudes and frustrations which are to come. Both Winnicott (1965) and Modell (1968) have also used the term to refer the nonspecific and supportive qualities of all psychotherapeutic situations.

Transitional Object. The transitional object is the infant's first "not-me" possession. The child uses an inanimate object (often a soft toy or a blanket) at times of separation from his or her primary love object (most typically the mother), as when going to sleep. The transitional object has come into popular culture in the form of the cartoon character, Linus, who always carries his blanket with him. Frequently transitional objects, whether the original or some later substitute, are not relinquished until well after toddlerhood.

Good-enough mothering. The term *good-enough mothering* refers to the provision of a holding environment characterized by an optimal amount of constancy and comfort for the wholly dependent infant. There is no defined prescription for good-enough mothering. Winnicott stresses that this is a spontaneous phenomenon. Over time the mother's ability to respond and to adapt automatically to the child decreases. Her increasing inability to respond, together with the child's progressing psychomotor maturation and development, serves to separate child from mother. In Erikson's terms basic trust is overlaid by an increasing sense of autonomy. It is important to distinguish autonomy in this sense from the indifference of environmentally deprived children to others. The latter are not being autonomous in the sense of "moving away" from a loved object, for whom there is an internalized representation. On the contrary, they never have had a love object in whom they reposed basic trust and from whom they can move away.

True self and *false self.* These terms describe what can be viewed as the opposite poles of a continuum. Winnicott defined the true self as the child's inherited potential. The quality of mothering, however, will determine how the potential evolves. Otherwise stated, inherited potential, absent good-enough mothering, will result in aberrations of development. Mothering, whether good enough or not, however, impacts the development of the sense of self. Hence this polarity is "normal." The terms refer to how the individual responds in experiences with others. To the extent that the individual is able to be spontaneous in his or her interactions, the true self can be said to be operative. To the extent that behavior is reactive, that is, generated by concern with how others may judge one's behavior, it is generated by the false self.

Additional Recommended Readings

CHAPTER 1

Freedman, D. A. (1980), Maturational and developmental issues in the first year. In: *The Course of Life,* Vol. 1, *Infancy,* ed. S. Greenspan & G. Pollock. Madison, CT: International Universities Press, 1989, pp. 193–319.

Tyson, P., & Tyson, R. L. (1990), The history of the developmental perspective. In: *The Psychoanalytic Theories of Development: An Integration.* New Haven, CT: Yale University Press, pp. 7–20, 21–37.

CHAPTER 2

Kernberg, P. (1983), Reflections in a mirror: Mother-child interactions, self-awareness, self-recognition. In: *Frontiers of Infant Psychiatry,* ed. J. Call, E. Galenson, & R. Tyson. New York: Basic Books, pp. 101–110.

Shapiro, T., & Stern, D. (1989), Psychoanalytic perspectives on first years of life: Establishment of object. In: *The Course of Life,* Vol. 1, *Infancy,* ed. S. Greenspan & G. Pollock. Madison, CT: International Universities Press, pp. 271–292.

This reading list was prepared for the curriculum committee of the Houston-Galveston Psychoanalytic Institute, Dr. Mary Scharold, chair, by Dr. Stephen Tew.

Silverman, M. A. (1989), The first year after birth. In: *The Course of Life*, Vol. 1, *Infany*, ed. S. Greenspan & G. Pollock. Madison, CT: International Universities Press, pp. 321–358.

CHAPTER 3

Freedman, D. A., & Brown, S. (1968), On the role of coensthetic stimulation in development of psychic structure. *Psychoanal. Quart.*, 37:418–438.
Spitz, R. A. (1945), Hospitalism: An inquiry into genesis of psychic conditions in early childhood. *The Psychoanalytic Study of the Child*, 1:53–74. New York: International Universities Press.
——— (1946), A follow-up report. *The Psychoanalytic Study of the Child*, 2:113–117. New York: International Universities Press.
——— Wolf, K. A. (1946), Anaclitic depression. *The Psychoanalytic Study of the Child*, 2:13–342. New York: International Universities Press.

CHAPTER 4

Beres, D., & Joseph, E. (1970), The concept of mental representation in psychoanalysis. *Internat. J. Psycho-Anal.*, 51:1–9.
Loewald, H. W. (1978), Instinct theory, object relations, and psychic-structure formation. *J. Amer. Psychoanal. Assn.*, 26:493–506.
Sandler, J., & Rosenblatt, B. (1962), The concept of the representational world. *The Psychoanalytic Study of the Child*, 17:128–145. New York: International Universities Press.
Tyson, P., & Tyson, R. L. (1990), The development of the ego. In: *The Psychoanalytic Theories of Development: An Integration*. New Haven, CT: Yale University Press, pp. 195–309.

CHAPTER 5

Sandler, A-M. (1975), Comments on the significance of Piaget's work for psychoanalysis. *Internat. Rev. Psycho-Anal.*, 2:365–377.
Tyson, P., & Tyson, R. L. (1990), A psychoanalytic perspective of cognitive development. In: *The Psychoanalytic Theories of Development: An Integration*. New Haven, CT: Yale University Press, pp. 163–173.

——— ——— (1990), The stages of cognitive development. In: *The Psychoanalytic Theories of Development: An Integration.* New Haven, CT: Yale University Press, pp. 174–191.

CHAPTER 6

Tyson, P., & Tyson, R. L. (1990), Gender development: A theoretical overview. New Haven, CT: Yale University Press, pp. 249–257.

——— ——— (1990), Gender development: Girls. In: *The Psychoanalytic Theories of Development: An Integration.* New Haven, CT: Yale University Press, pp. 258–276.

——— ——— (1990), Gender development: Boys. In: *The Psychoanalytic Theories of Development: An Integration.* New Haven, CT: Yale University Press, pp. 277–292.

CHAPTER 7

Brazelton, T. B., & Als, H. (1979), Four early stages in the development of mother-infant interaction. *The Psychoanalytic Study of the Child,* 34:349–369. New Haven, CT: Yale University Press.

Stern, D. N. (1985), Perspectives and approaches to infancy. In: *Perspectives and Approaches to Infancy.* New York: Basic Books, pp. 13–34.

Yarrow, L. (1979), Historical perspectives and future directions in infant development. In: *Handbook of Infant Development,* ed. J. Osofsky. New York: J. Wiley, pp. 897–917.

CHAPTER 8

Mahler, M. S., & McDevitt, J. (1989), The separation-individuation process and identity formation. In: *The Course of Life,* Vol. 2, *Early Childhood,* ed. S. Greenspan & G. Pollock. Madison, CT: International Universities Press, pp. 19–35.

——— Pine, F., & Bergman, A. (1975), Glossary of concepts. In: *The Psychological Birth of the Human Infant.* New York: Basic Books, pp. 189–293.

McDevitt, J., & Mahler, M. S. (1989), Object constancy, individuality, and internalization. In: *Course of Life*, Vol. 2, *Early Childhood*, ed. S. Greenspan & G. Pollock. Madison, CT: International Universities Press, pp. 37–60.

Settlage, C. (1989), Psychoanalytic theory and understanding of psychic development during second and third years. In: *The Course of Life*, Vol. 2, *Early Childhood*, ed. S. Greenspan & G. Pollock. Madison, CT: International Universities Press, pp. 365–386.

CHAPTER 9

Abelin, E. L. (1978), The role of the father in the separation-individuation process. In: *Separation-Individuation: Essays in Honor of Margaret S. Mahler*, ed. J. McDevitt & C. Settlage. New York: International Universities Press, pp. 229–252.

Parens, H. (1989), Toward an epigenesis of aggression in early childhood. In: *The Course of Life*, Vol. 2, *Early Childhood*, ed. S. Greenspan & G. Pollock. Madison, CT: International Universities Press, pp. 129–162.

CHAPTER 10

Breier, A., Kelsoe, J. R., Kirwin, P. D., Beller, S. A., Wolkowitz, O. M., & Pickar, D. (1988), Early parental loss and development of adult pathology. *Arch. Gen. Psychiat.*, 45:987–993.

Fraiberg, S. H. (1975), Ghosts in the nursery: A psychoanalytic approach to problems of impaired mother-infant relations. *J. Amer. Acad. Child. Adol. Psychiat.*, 14:387–421.

——— (1982), Pathologic defenses in infancy. *Psychoanal. Quart.*, 51:612–635.

Steele, B. (1983), The effect of abuse and neglect on psychologic development. In: *Frontiers of Infant Psychiatry*, ed. J. E. Galenson & R. Tyson. New York: Basic Books, pp. 235–244.

References

Abraham, K. (1921–1925), Psychoanalytic studies on character formation. In: *Selected Papers on Psychoanalysis*. London: Hogarth Press, 1949, pp. 370–476.

—— (1921), Contributions to the theory of the anal character. In: *Selected Papers on Psychoanalysis*. London: Hogarth Press, 1949, pp. 370–392.

American Psychiatric Association (1980), *Diagnostic and Statistical Manual of Mental Disorders*, 3rd ed. (DSM-III). Washington, DC: American Psychiatric Press.

—— (1994), *Diagnostic and Statistical Manual of Mental Disorders*, 4th ed. (DSM-IV). Washington, DC: American Psychiatric Press.

Amsterdam, B. K. (1972), Mirror self-image reactions before age 2. *Developmental Psychobiol.*, 5:297–305.

Aries, P. (1960), *Centuries of Childhood*, tr. R. Baldick. New York: Vintage Books, 1962.

Arnold, D., Ed. (1983), *The New Oxford Companion to Music*, s.v. "Tschaikovsksy."

Barker, P. (1995), *The Eye in the Door*. New York: Plume.

Bayley, N. (1949), Consistency and variability in the growth of intelligence from birth to eighteen years. *J. Gen. Psychol.*, 75:165–196.

—— (1993), *Bayley Scales of Infant Development*, 2nd ed. San Antonio, TX: The Psychological Corporation.

Benes, F. M., Turtle, M., Khan, Y., & Farol, P. (1994), Myelination of a key relay zone occurs in the human brain during childhood, adolescence, and adulthood. *Arch. Gen. Psychiatry*, 51:477–484.

Ben-Sasson, H. H. (1976), *A History of the Jewish People*. Cambridge, MA: Harvard University Press.

Bettelheim, B. (1969), *The Children of the Dream*. London: Macmillan.

Bible,The, 2 Kings 19:35.

Blank, H. R. (1957), Psychoanalysis and blindness. *Psychoanal. Quart.,* 26:1–24.

———— (1958), Dreams of the blind. *Psychoanal. Quart.,* 27:158–174.

Boring, E. G. (1929), *A History of Experimental Psychology,* 1st ed. New York: Century.

Bornstein, B. (1949), The analysis of a phobic child: Some problems of theory and technique in child analysis. *The Psychoanalytic Study of the Child,* 3–4:181–222. New York: International Universities Press.

Bowlby, J. (1940), The influence of early environment in the development of neurosis and neurotic character. *Internat. J. Psycho-Anal.,* 21:154–178. New York: International Universities Press.

———— (1958), The nature of the child's tie to his mother. *Internat. J. Psycho-Anal.,* 39:350–373.

———— (1960), Grief and mourning in infancy and early childhood. *The Psychoanalytic Study of the Child,* 15:9–52. New York: International Universities Press.

———— (1969), *Attachment and Loss,* Vol. 1. New York: Basic Books.

———— (1990a), The role of attachment in personality development and psychopathology. In: *The Course of Life,* Vol. 1, ed. S. I. Greenspan & G. H. Pollock. New York: International Universities Press.

———— (1990b), *Charles Darwin, A New Life.* New York: W. W. Norton.

Breuer, J., & Freud, S. (1893–1895), Studies in Hysteria. *Standard Edition,* 2:1–305. London: Hogarth Press, 1955.

Brody, S. (1981), The concepts of attachment and bonding. In: *The Vulnerable Child,* ed. T. B. Cohen, M. H. Etezady, & B. L. Pacella. New York: International Universities Press, 1993.

Burlingham, D. (1961), Some notes on the development of the blind. *The Psychoanalytic Study of the Child,* 19:121–145. New York: International Universities Press.

Byne, W. (1994), The biological evidence challenged. *Sci. Amer.,* 270/5:50–55.

Caffey, J. (1946), Multiple fractures in long bones of infants suffering from chronic subdural hematoma. *Amer. J. Roentgenol.,* 56:163–173.

Catholic Encyclopedia (1912), *Scruples,* Vol. 13. New York: Robert Appleton, pp. 640–641.

Chekov, A. (1897), Uncle Vanya. In: *Uncle Vanya and Other Plays by Anton Chekov,* tr. B. Hulick. New York: Bantam Books, 1994.

Conel, J. L. (1919–1959), *The Post-Natal Development of the Human Cortex,* Vols. 1–7. Cambridge, MA: Harvard University Press.

Coss, R. G., & Globus, A. (1978), Spine stems on tectal interneurons in jewel fish are shortened by social stimulation. *Science,* 200:787–790.

Curtis, G. C. (1963), Violence breeds violence—perhaps? *Amer. J. Psychiat.,* 120:386–387.

Darwin, C. (1853), Letter to W. D. Fox. In: *The Life and Letters of Charles Darwin,* ed. F. Darwin. New York: Basic Books, 1959, pp. 352–353.

——— (1877), Biographical sketch of an infant. In: *The Darwin Reader,* ed. M. Bates & P. H. Humphrey. New York: Charles Scribner, 1956.

Davis, K. (1940), Extreme isolation of a child. *Amer. J. Sociol.,* 10:554–575.

——— (1946), Final note on a case of extreme isolation. *Amer. J. Sociol.,* 52:532–537.

DeCroly, O. (1970), *Etudes de Psychogenese.* Brussels: Lamertin.

Dowling, S. (1977), Seven infants with esophageal atresia: A developmental study. *The Psychoanalytic Study of the Child,* 32:215–256. New Haven, CT: Yale University Press.

Elmer, E., & Gregg, G. (1967), Developmental characteristics of abused children. *Pediatrics,* 40:596–602.

Encyclopedia Britannica (1951), s.v. "Helen Keller."

Erikson, E. H. (1950), *Childhood and Society.* New York: W. W. Norton.

——— (1959), Identity and the Life Cycle. In: Selected Papers. *Psychological Issues,* Mongr. I. New York: International Universities Press.

Escalona, S. K. (1965), Some determinants of individual differences. *Trans. NY Acad. Sci.,* 27:802–816.

Fairbairn, W. R. D. (1963), Synopsis of an object-relations theory of the personality. *Internat. J. Psycho-Anal.,* 44:224–225.

Flavell, J. H. (1963), *The Developmental Psychology of Jean Piaget.* New York: D. Van Nostrand.

Fraiberg, S. H. (1951), Enlightenment and confusion. *The Psychoanalytic Study of the Child,* 6:325–335. New York: International Universities Press.

——— Freedman, D. A. (1964), Studies in the ego development of the congenitally blind child. *The Psychoanalytic Study of the Child,* 19:113–169. New York: International Universities Press.

Freedman, D. A. (1971), Congenital and perinatal sensory deprivation: Some studies in early development. *Amer. J. Psychiat.,* 127:1529–1545.

——— (1971), On the genesis of obsessional phenomena. *Psychoanal. Rev.,* 58:367–384.

——— (1975), The battering parent and his child: A study in early object relations. *Internat. Rev. Psycho-Anal.,* 2:189–198.

———— Adatto, C. P. (1968), On the precipitation of seizures in an adolescent boy. *Psychosom. Med.*, 30:437–447.

———— Brown, S. L. (1968), On the role of coenaesthetic stimulation in the development of psychic structure. *Psychoanal. Quart.*, 37:418–438.

———— Fox-Kalenda, B. J., Margileth, D. A., & Miller, D. H. (1969), The use of sound as a guide to affective and cognitive behavior. *Child Develop.*, 40:1099–1105.

———— Montgomery, J. R., Wilson, R., Bealmar, P. M., & South, M. A. (1976), Further observations of the effects of reverse isolation from birth on cognitive and affective development. *J. Amer. Acad. of Child Psychiat.*, 15:593–603.

Freud, A. (1951), Observations on child development. In: *The Writings*, Vol. 4. New York: International Universities Press, 1968, pp. 143–182.

———— (1960), Discussion of Dr. John Bowlby's paper. *The Psychoanalytic Study of the Child*, 15:53–62. New York: International Universities Press.

———— (1966), Obsessional neurosis: A summary of psychoanalytic views as presented at the Congress. *Internat. J. Psycho-Anal.*, 47:116–122.

———— Burlingham, D. (1942), *Young Children in War-Time*. London: Allen & Unwin.

Freud, S. (1895), Project for a scientific psychology. *Standard Edition*, 1:281–397. London: Hogarth Press, 1966.

———— (1905), Fragment of an analysis of a case of hysteria. *Standard Edition*, 7:1–122. London: Hogarth Press, 1953.

———— (1907), Obsessive acts and religious practices. *Standard Edition*, 9:115–127. London: Hogarth Press, 1959.

———— (1908), Character and anal eroticism. *Standard Edition*, 9:167–175. London: Hogarth Press, 1959.

———— (1909), Analysis of a phobia in a five-year-old boy. *Standard Edition*, 10:1–147. London: Hogarth Press, 1955.

———— (1913), Totem and Taboo. *Standard Edition*, 13:1–161. London: Hogarth Press, 1955.

———— (1914), On narcissism: An introduction. *Standard Edition*, 14:67–102. London: Hogarth Press, 1957.

———— (1915), Instincts and their vicissitudes. *Standard Edition*, 14:109–140. London: Hogarth Press, 1957.

———— (1925), Inhibitions, symptoms, and anxiety. *Standard Edition*, 20:75–172. London: Hogarth Press, 1959.

Furth, H. (1969), *Piaget and Knowledge*. Englewood Cliffs, NJ: Prentice Hall.

Gallup, G. G. (1979), Self-awareness in primates. *Amer. Scientist*, 67:417–421.

Gardner, M. (1971), *The Wolfman*. New York: Basic Books.

Gay, P. (1988), *Freud, A Life for Our Times*. New York: W. W. Norton.

Gibson, E. J. (1970), The development of perception as an adaptive process. *Amer. Scientist*, 58:98–107.

Glover, E. (1935), A developmental study of the obsessional neuroses. In: *On the Early Development of Mind*. New York: International Universities Press, 1956, pp. 267–282.

Gorski, R. A. (1978), Sexual differentiation of the brain. *Hosp. Pract.*, Oct.:55–61.

Gouin-Decarie, T. (1965), *Intelligence and Affectivity in Early Childhood*, tr. E. P. Brandt & L. W. Brandt. New York: International Universities Press.

Graves, R. (1929), *Goodbye to All That*. London: Penguin Books, 1957.

Greengard, J. (1964), The battered child syndrome. *Med. Sci.*, 15:82–91.

Griffiths, R. (1954), *The Abilities of Babies*. London: University of London Press.

Groce, N. (1980), Everyone here spoke sign language. *Nat. Hist.*, 89/6:10–16.

Gruber, H. E., & Voneche, J. J. (1977), *The Essential Piaget*. New York: Basic Books.

Guntrip, H. (1961), *Personality Structure and Human Interaction*. New York: International Universities Press.

Gustaffson, S. (1948), Germ-free rearing of rats: General technique. *Acta Pathol. Microbiol. Scand. Suppl.*, 73:1–130.

Harlow, H. (1959), Love in infant monkeys. *Sci. Amer.*, 200:68–74.

Hartley, M. (1990), *Breaking the Silence*. New York: G. Putnam.

Hartmann, H. (1958), *Ego Psychology and the Problem of Adaptation*. New York: International Universities Press.

—— (1964), The mutual influences in the development of ego and id. In: *Essays on Ego Psychology*. New York: International Universities Press, pp. 115–182.

Harvey, W. (1651), Excercitationes de Geneatione Animalium. Quibus accedunt quaedam de partu, de membrainis ac humoribus uteri & de conceptione. London: Octavian, Pulley. *N.E. J. Med.*, 300:733, 1979.

Herdt, G. H. (1981), *Guardians of the Flute*. New York: McGraw-Hill.

Ishiguro, K. (1989), *Remains of the Day*. New York: Vintage International.

Itard, J. M. G. (1801), *The Wild Boy of Aveyron*, tr. G. & M. Humphreys. New York: Appleton-Century-Crofts, 1931.

Jones, E. (1953), *The Life and Work of Sigmund Freud*, Vol. 1. New York: Basic Books.

——— (1957), *The Life and Work of Sigmund Freud*, Vol. 3. New York: Basic Books.

Kanner, L. (1949), Autistic disturbance of affective contact. *Nerv. Child.*, 2:217–250.

Kaufman, I. C. (1975), Learning what comes naturally. *Ethos*, 3:129–142.

Keeler, W. (1958), Autistic patterns and defective communication in blind children with retrolental fibroplasia. In: *Psychopathology of Communication*, ed. P. Hoch & J. Zubin. New York: Grune & Stratton.

Kempe, C. H. (1971), Pediatric implications of the battered baby syndrome. *Arch. Dis. Childhood*, 46:28–37.

Kernberg, O. F. (1966), Structural derivatives of object relationships. *Internat. J. Psycho-Anal.*, 47:238–253.

——— (1979), Some implications of object relations theory for psychoanalytic technique. *J. Amer. Psychoanal. Assn.*, 27(Suppl.): 207–240.

Kernberg, P. (1983), Reflections in a mirror: Mother-child interactions, self-awareness, self-recognition. In: *Frontiers of Infant Psychiatry*, ed. J. Call, E. Galenson, & R. Tyson. New York: Basic Books.

Kessen, W. (1965), *The Child*. New York: J. Wiley.

Klauss, K. H., & Kennel, J. H. (1976), *Maternal–Infant Bonding*. St. Louis: C. V. Mosby.

Klein, M. (1931), *The Psychoanalysis of Children*. London: Hogarth Press, 1949.

——— (1975), *The Writings of Melanie Klein*, Vol. 1. London: Hogarth Press.

Kluver, H., & Bucy, P. C. (1939), Preliminary analysis of function of the temporal lobes of monkeys. *Arch. Neurol. & Psychiat.*, 42:979–1000.

Lagercrantz, H., & Slotkin, T. A. (1986), The "stress" of being born. *Sci. Amer.*, 254/14:100–107.

Landauer, K. (1939), Some remarks on the formation of the anal-erotic character. *Internat. J. Psycho-Anal.*, 20:418–425.

Lenneberg, E. H. (1967), *Biological Foundations of Language*. New York: J. Wiley.

LeVay, S., & Haner, D. A. (1994), Evidence for a biological influence in male homosexuality. *Sci. Amer.*, 270/5:44–49.

Lidz, R. W., & Lidz, T. (1977), Male menstruation: A ritual alternative to the oedipal transition. *Internat. J. Psycho-Anal.*, 58:17–31.

Lorente de No, R. (1939), Transmission of impulses through cranial motor nuclei. *J. Neurophysiol.*, 2:402–464.

Lorenz, K. (1971), *Studies in Animal Behavior*. Cambridge, MA: Harvard University Press, Vol. 2, pp. 135–140.

Mahler, M. S., Pine, F., & Bergman, A. (1975), *The Psychological Birth of the Human Infant.* New York: Basic Books.

Mason, M. K. (1942), Learning to speak after six and a half years of silence. *Speech Disord.*, 7:295–304.

Mason, W. A. (1968), Early social deprivation in the nonhuman primates: Implications for human behavior. In: *Environmental Influences,* ed. D. Glass. New York: Rockefeller University Press/Russell Sage Foundation.

McDevitt, J. B., & Mahler, M. S. (1989), Object constancy, individuality, and internalization. In: *The Course of Life,* Vol. 2, *Early Childhood,* ed. S. Greenspan & G. Pollock. Madison, CT: International Universities Press, pp. 37–60.

McGraw, M. (1945), *The Neuromuscular Maturation of the Infant.* New York: Columbia University Press.

Modell, A. (1968), *Object Love and Reality.* New York: International Universities Press.

Money, J. (1988), *Gay, Straight and In-Between.* New York: Oxford University Press.

Monroe, R. R. (1970), *Episodic Behavior Disorders: A Psychodynamic and Neurophysiologic Analysis.* Cambridge, MA: Harvard University Press.

Moore, B. E., & Fine, B. D. (1990), *Psychoanalytic Terms and Concepts.* New York: American Psychoanalytic Association.

Morris, M. G., & Gould, R. W. (1963), Role reversal: A concept in dealing with the neglected/battered child syndrome. In: *The Neglected Battered Child Syndrome.* New York: Child Welfare League of America.

Munich, R. L. (1986), Symptom formation in the analysis of an obsessional character. *The Psychoanalytic Study of the Child,* 41:515–536. New Haven, CT: Yale University Press.

Niederland, W. G. (1959), The "miracled-up" world of Schreber's childhood. *The Psychoanalytic Study of the Child,* 14:383–413. New York: International Universities Press.

O'Brian, W. (1964), The golden years. *The New Yorker Magazine,* Feb. 29, 1965, pp. 31–32.

New Catholic Encyclopedia (1967), s.v. "Scrupulosity." New York: McGraw-Hill, Vol. 11, p. 979; Vol. 12, pp. 1253–1255.

New Compact Oxford Unabridged Dictionary (1971), s.v. "Obsession."
——— Supplement (1982), s.v. "Obsession."

Panel (1979), Monica: A 25-year longitudinal study of the consequences of trauma in infancy. M. Viederman, reporter. *J. Amer. Psychoanal. Assn.,* 27:107–126.

Papez, J. W. (1937), A proposed mechanism of emotion. *Arch. Neurol. & Psychiat.*, 38:725–743.

Parmelee, A. H., Cutsforth, M. D., & Jackson, C. L. (1958), The mental development of children with blindness due to retrolental fibroplasia. *Amer. J. Dis. Children*, 96:641–648.

Piaget, J. (1932), *The Moral Judgement of the Child*, tr. M. Gabain. London: Kegan Paul.

———— (1954), *Construction of Reality in the Child*, tr. M. Cook. New York: Basic Books.

———— (1969), *The Child's Conception of Time*, tr. A. J. Pomerans. London: Routledge & Kegan Paul.

Pigott, T. H., & Murphy, D. L. (1991), In reply. *Arch. Gen. Psychiat.*, 48:858.

Provence, S., & Lipton, R. C. (1962), *Infants in Institutions.* New York: International Universities Press.

Rank, O. (1929), *The Trauma of Birth.* New York: Harcourt Brace.

Rapaport, D. (1958), Behavior research in collective settlements in Israel. *Amer. J. Orthopsychiatry*, 29:587–597.

Ravelli, G. P., Stein, Z. A., & Susser, M. (1976), Obesity in young men after famine exposure in utero and early infancy. *N.E. J. Med.*, 295:349–353.

Ritvo, S. (1966), Correlation of a childhood and adult neurosis, based on the adult analysis of a reported childhood case. *Internat. J. Psycho-Anal.*, 47:130–131.

Sandler, J., & Hazari, A. (1960), The obsessional: On the psychological classification of obsessional character traits and symptoms. *Brit. J. Med. Psychol.*, 33:113–122.

Schafer, R. (1968), *Aspects of Internalization.* New York: International Universities Press.

Schaffer, H. R., & Callender, W. M. (1959), Psychological effects of hospitalization in infancy. *Pediatrics*, 24:528–539.

Schanberg, S., & Kuhn, C. M. (1980), Maternal deprivation in animal model of psychosocial dwarfism. In: *Enzymes and Neurotransmitters in Mental Disease*, ed. E. Usdiin, T. L. Sourkes, & B. H. Youdim. New York: J. Wiley, pp. 373–393.

Schur, M. (1960), Discussion of Dr. John Bowly's paper. *The Psychoanalytic Study of the Child*, 15:63–84. New York: International Universities Press.

Scott, J. P. (1962), Critical periods in behavioral science. *Science*, 138:949–958.

Sherrington, C. (1906), *The Integrative Action of the Nervous System.* Oxford: Oxford University Press.

Silver, L. B., Dublin, C. C., & Lourie, R. S. (1969), Does violence breed violence? Contributions from a study of the child abuse syndrome. *Amer. J. Psychiat.*, 126:406–407.

Simons, C. L., Kohle, K., Genscher, U., & Dietrich, M. (1973), The impact of reverse isolation in childhood on early childhood development. *Psychother. & Psychosom.*, 22:300–309.

Spitz, R. A. (1945a), Hospitalism: An inquiry into the genesis of psychiatric conditions in early childhood. *The Psychoanalytic Study of the Child*, 1:53–74. New York: International Universities Press.

——— (1945b), Diacritic and coenesthetic organizations. *Psychoanal. Rev.*, 32:146–161.

——— (1957), *No and Yes.* New York: International Universities Press.

——— (1958), *A Genetic Field Theory of Ego Formation: Its Implications for Pathology.* New York: International Universities Press.

——— (1960), Discussion of Dr. Bowlby's paper. *The Psychoanalytic Study of the Child*, 15:84–94. New York: International Universities Press.

——— (1965), *The First Year of Life.* New York: International Universities Press.

Steele, B. F., & Pollock, C. B. (1968), A psychiatric study of parents who abuse infants and small children. In: *The Battered Child*, ed. R. E. Helfer & C. H. Kempe. Chicago: University of Chicago Press.

Stern, D. N. (1971), A microanalysis of the mother-infant interaction: Behavior regulated social contact between mother and her three-and-a-half-month-old infant. *J. Amer. Acad. Child Psychiat.*, 10:501–517.

Stoller, R. (1968), *Sex and Character.* New York: Science House.

——— (1988), *Presentations of Gender.* New Haven, CT: Yale University Press.

Sulloway, F. (1979), *Freud, Biologist of the Mind.* New York: Basic Books.

Tyson, P., & Tyson, R. L. (1990), *Psychoanalytic Theories of Development.* New Haven, CT: Yale University Press.

von Feuerbach, A. (1832), *Kasper Hauser.* Boston: Allen & Ticknor.

von Senden, M. (1932), *Space and Sight.* Glencoe, IL: Free Press, 1960.

Watson, J. B. (1928), *Psychological Care of Infant and Child.* New York: W. W. Norton.

Weinberg, S. (1992), *Dreams of a Final Theory.* New York: Pantheon Books.

White, R. B. (1961), The mother-conflict in Schreber's psychosis. *Internat. J. Psycho-Anal.*, 42:55–73.

Winnicott, D. (1965), *The Maturational Processes and the Facilitating Environment.* New York: International Universities Press.

Wyrwicka, W. (1981), *The Development of Food Preferences: Parental Influences and the Primary Effect.* Springfield, IL: C C Thomas.

Yakovlev, P. I., & LeCours, A. (1967), The myelogenetic cycles of re-
    gional maturation of the brain. In: *Regional Development of the
    Brain in Early Life*, ed. A. Minkowski. Oxford: Blackwell, pp. 3–70.
Young, L. (1964), *Wednesday's Children: A Study of Child Neglect and Abuse.*
    New York: McGraw-Hill.

Name Index

Subject Index